First published in Australia in 2011 by
Margaret River Press

P. O. Box 47
Witchcliffe
Western Australia 6286
www.margaretriverpress.com

Text copyright © Margaret River Press

Photographs © Sue-Lyn Aldrian-Moyle

All rights reserved. Without limiting the rights under copyright reserved above, no part of this publication may be reproduced, stored in or introduced into a retrieval system, or transmitted, in any form or by any means (electronic, mechanical, photocopying, recording or otherwise), without the prior written permission of both the copyright owners and the publisher of this book.

Cataloguing-in-Publication data is available from the National Library of Australia

ISBN: 978-0-9872180-0-1

Text by Sue-Lyn Aldrian-Moyle and Lisa Hanley
Photographs by Sue-Lyn Aldrian-Moyle
Designed by Tracey Gibbs
Edited by Jane Cornes
Typeset by Tracey Gibbs in Beaufort
Printed by Scott Print, Perth, Western Australia
Published by Margaret River Press, Western Australia

Cover photographs:
Butter-poached Pemberton marron,
Tony Howell, Cape Lodge
(Photo by Sue-Lyn Aldrian-Moyle)

Margaret River Surf
(Photo by Christopher Gurney)

CHEFS OF THE
Margaret River Region

SUE-LYN ALDRIAN-MOYLE AND LISA HANLEY

MARGARET RIVER
· PRESS ·

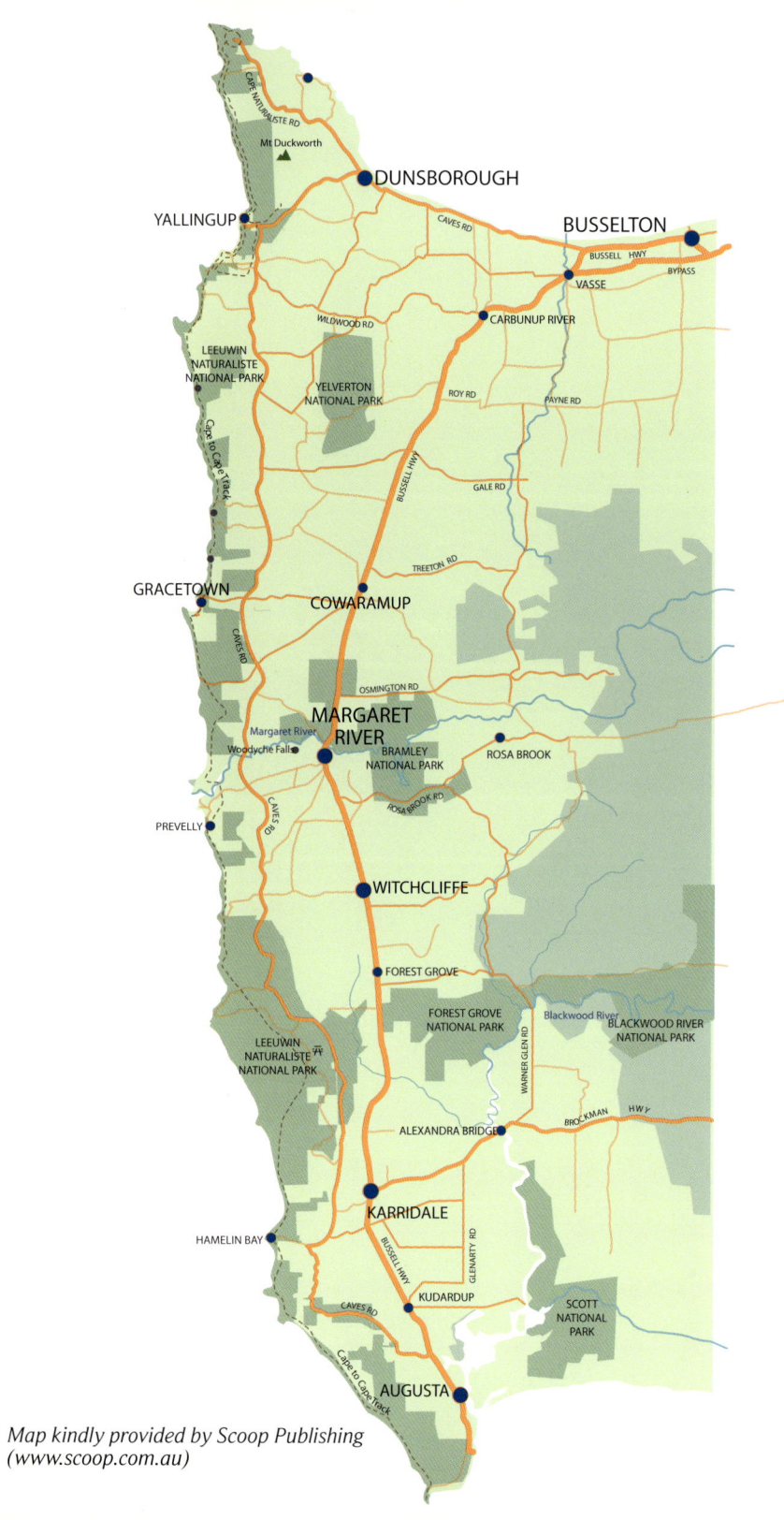

Map kindly provided by Scoop Publishing (www.scoop.com.au)

ACKNOWLEDGEMENTS

To the nineteen chefs featured in this book all of whom received no payment for their participation: we would like to thank you wholeheartedly for your generosity. You have welcomed us into your kitchens and let us peek into your lives, while openly giving your time and sharing your recipes. Thank you for being an absolute joy to work with. This book is possible only because of you. That Margaret River is the destination it is today is in no small way due to your considerable talents.

To the owners and managers of the restaurants featured in this book: thank you for allowing us to recreate these recipes and for giving us unrestricted access.

To the Garden Basket, Paul Iles from Blue Ginger, the Greengrocers, the Craven brothers, Brodie, Jarrad and Jason Turner at 34 Degrees Blue, McHenry's Farm Shop, Jimmy Gillmore the butcher and Cliff Owen the farmer: thank you for participating in the photoshoots and talking to us about your passions.

To our support team, Simon and Hamish Hanley and Andreas Aldrian-Moyle: a big thank you for your endless tolerance, patience and cooking skills. And to little Luka Aldrian-Moyle: your birth was the most special deadline of all.

Finally to our fantastic publisher Caroline Wood and associate publisher Robert Wood, who came up with this great idea and were instrumental in directing us and being our sounding board while we coordinated, collated, drafted and brainstormed: thank you so very much for allowing us the opportunity to put this book together with you.

Photo credits

Our thanks to Christopher Gurney and Jorg Imberger for supplying us with photographs for inclusion in the book as follows:

Christopher Gurney: cover, pages 2, 10 and 110

Jorg Imberger: pages 27, 38, 63, 111, 118, 119

TABLE OF CONTENTS

MAP OF THE REGION 4
ACKNOWLEDGEMENTS 5
AUTHOR'S NOTE 8
RECIPES AND PROFILES
ENTRÉES
    Bromell, Tony 15
    Watershed Premium Wines
    Beetroot strap with goat's curd,
    walnut dacquoise
    and coffee bean balsamic 16

    Drachenberg, Jake 21
    Clairault Wines
    Scallops, tea-smoked duck, bbq pork
    and masterstock 22

    Egan, Matt 29
    Cullen Wines
    Gluten-free twice-baked goat's cheese
    soufflé with cauliflower cream 30

    Howell, Tony 35
    Cape Lodge
    Butter-poached Pemberton marron 36

    Ilott, Andrea 41
    The Larder
    Blue Swimmer crab rice paper rolls 42

MAINS
    Angove, Dany 51
    Leeuwin Estate
    Salad of Pemberton marron,
    smoked salmon, avocado
    and orange poppy seed dressing 52

    Carr, Aaron 57
    Vasse Felix
    Roast barramundi, Puy lentils,
    charred baby leek, smoked bone
    marrow, potato fondant and jus gras 58

    Donohue, Claire 65
    Providore
    Crispy confit duck
    with organic spinach and beetroot salad,
    Persian feta and pomegranate glaze 66

    Harvey, Nigel 71
    Voyager Estate
    Margaret River venison with roasted
    pumpkin, papardelle, beetroot puree,
    sautéed spinach and chocolate-infused jus 72

    Houston, Rick 79
    Must Margaret River
    Slow-braised Burnside beef cheeks
    with handmade gnocchi 80

McLeay, Hamish	89	DESSERTS		
Bunkers Beach Cafe		Allen, Blair	123	
Lupin tempeh, coconut rice and satay sauce	90	The Studio Gallery and Bistro *Chocolate and vanilla bombe, praline, rose jelly, berries and fairy floss*	124	
Mifsud, Dennis	95			
Veda Catering		Babb, Michelle	131	
Maltese rabbit stew (stuffat tal-fenek)	96	Knee Deep Wines *Cookies and cream parfait with orange butterscotch sauce*	132	
Morvan, Francois	101			
Flutes at Brookland Valley		Janssen, Anthony	137	
Pan-fried duck breast and roasted whole quail with Purple Congo potato crush, wilted spinach and Shiraz jus	102	Gnarabar and White Elephant Beach Cafe *Eaton Mess*	138	
Reagan, Stephen	107	STOCKS AND OTHER RECIPES	142	
Newtown House		LOCAL SUPPLIERS	146	
Braised pork belly in soy, ginger, chilli and star anise with seared Canarvon scallops and steamed bok choy	108	PANTRY STOCK	149	
		GLOSSARY	150	
Winter, Ronnie and Simon	113	ABBREVIATIONS	151	
Chow Cuisine to Go		VENUE ADDRESSES	152	
Yellow Wagyu beef curry with hot 'n' sour salad	114	INDEX	154	
		ABOUT SUE-LYN	158	
		ABOUT LISA	159	

AUTHOR'S NOTE

Margaret River — a place that immediately conjures a vision of world-class wine, beautiful surroundings and an almost endless supply of quality dining rooms. While the South West Cape of Western Australia is relatively unknown, Margaret River is a globally recognised destination. All you have to do is mention the name and one is transported, perhaps to a deck overlooking vines on a beautiful, crisp spring day with a cold sauvignon blanc and a trio of just-cooked marron before you, or to a crackling open fire in the winter months as you enjoy one of the region's many award-winning cabernets with a slow-cooked braise of local Angus beef.

As the vines go through their seasonal changes, from bearing big, juicy bunches of ripe fruit to turning shades of vibrant burnt orange and red, so too does the dining experience in the region change. With some of the best produce in the world to play with, chefs lucky enough to live in such a beautiful part of the world work their magic.

To do justice to the food trail of this region would literally take weeks, or months, if you were lucky enough to have the time and money. There are so many treasures and beautiful fresh dishes to discover in this picturesque corner of Western Australia, where every sun-dappled, winding driveway seems to lead to a culinary experience just waiting to be found. A hearty breakfast in the warmth of the sun at the Bunkers Beach Cafe with nothing but the aqua blue of the Indian Ocean to clear your mind, is but one small piece of this dining journey.

Let this book begin to show you what is special and unique about the region. How about an autumn brunch cooked by Tony Howell at Cape Lodge, where just sitting in the dining room may be as close to being royalty as most of us will ever get? Or feeling the warmth of the sun through the umbrellas and making your way through an Art Series flight with delicious fare from Dany Angove's team at Leeuwin Estate? Other pleasures of the region include a long winter degustation lunch created by Nigel Harvey, enjoyed as you relax in the Dutch-style wingback chairs of the Voyager Estate dining room, or sipping a new release sauvignon blanc semillon with a Watershed Premium Wines taste plate on the deck overlooking the winery's vineyard, which, much like the lunch, seems to stretch on forever.

Most chefs featured in this publication have been the head of their kitchens for quite some time now, and have learned how to bring together the best of local produce, presenting us with food that perfectly enhances the award-winning wines of their own venue or those of neighbouring estates. Touring the Margaret River Region, you will soon find it's all about the long lunch, followed by dropping into one of many 'foodie' shops where you can pick up a range of locally-made produce for your own-made gourmet platter for dinner. Check out the list of local suppliers at the back of this book to discover some of these little gems, and be sure to pick up a bottle or two from somewhere along the way. Places like McHenry's Farm Shop and Hayshed Hill are good stop off points, stocking a great selection of both wine and produce.

Our aim in creating this book is to offer a tangible take-home memory that will inspire and help you transform your own kitchen table into a magical South West gastronomic experience. Perhaps you may choose to impress interstate or international guests who have not been lucky enough to visit the region. And perhaps after an evening of enjoying the food and accompanying wine in this book, they'll decide to visit the South West of Western Australia for themselves. And who knows? Perhaps while exploring the sandy, white beaches or surfing one of the pristine surf breaks, they'll meet one of the chefs celebrated in this book as they, too enjoy some off-duty time out.

Through the beautiful photography of renowned local photo-journalist Sue-Lyn Aldrian-Moyle, the breathtaking sights and localities of the region and its culinary excellence have been captured in all their beauty. As you will discover, Sue-Lyn's passion for photography is much like the recipes shared with you by our chefs; fresh, alive, vibrant and forever memorable.

I sincerely hope you enjoy this book and the chefs who grace its pages. May it help you on your way to an endless, evolving relationship with the Margaret River region and its fine selection of places to wine and dine.

Lisa Hanley

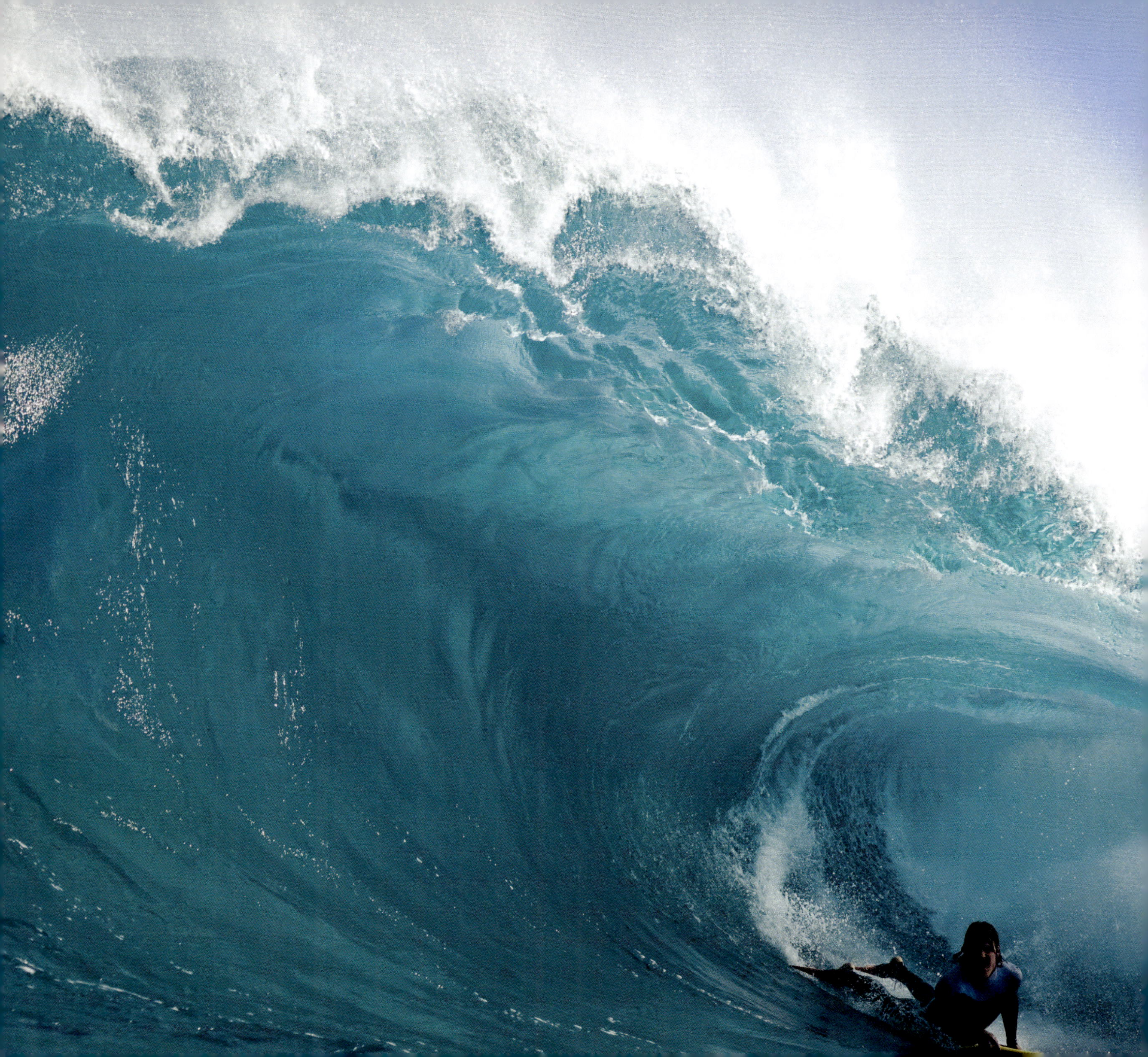

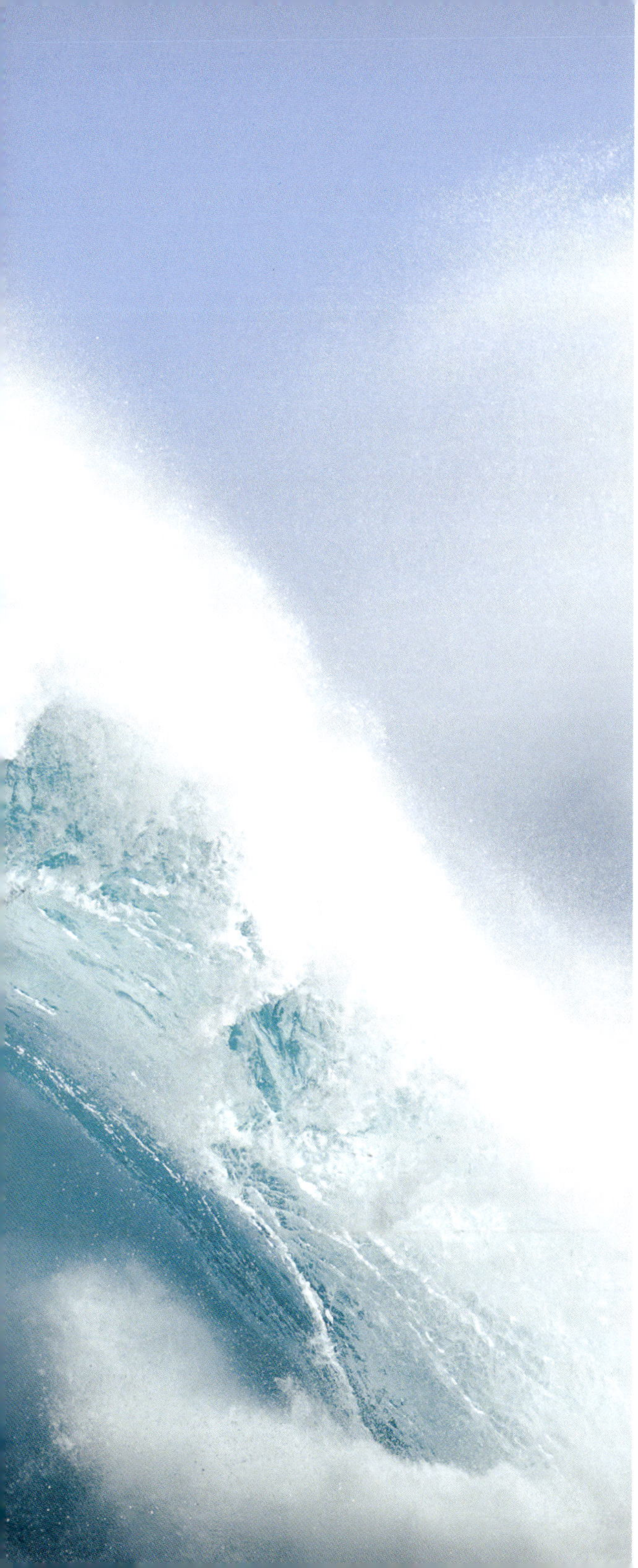

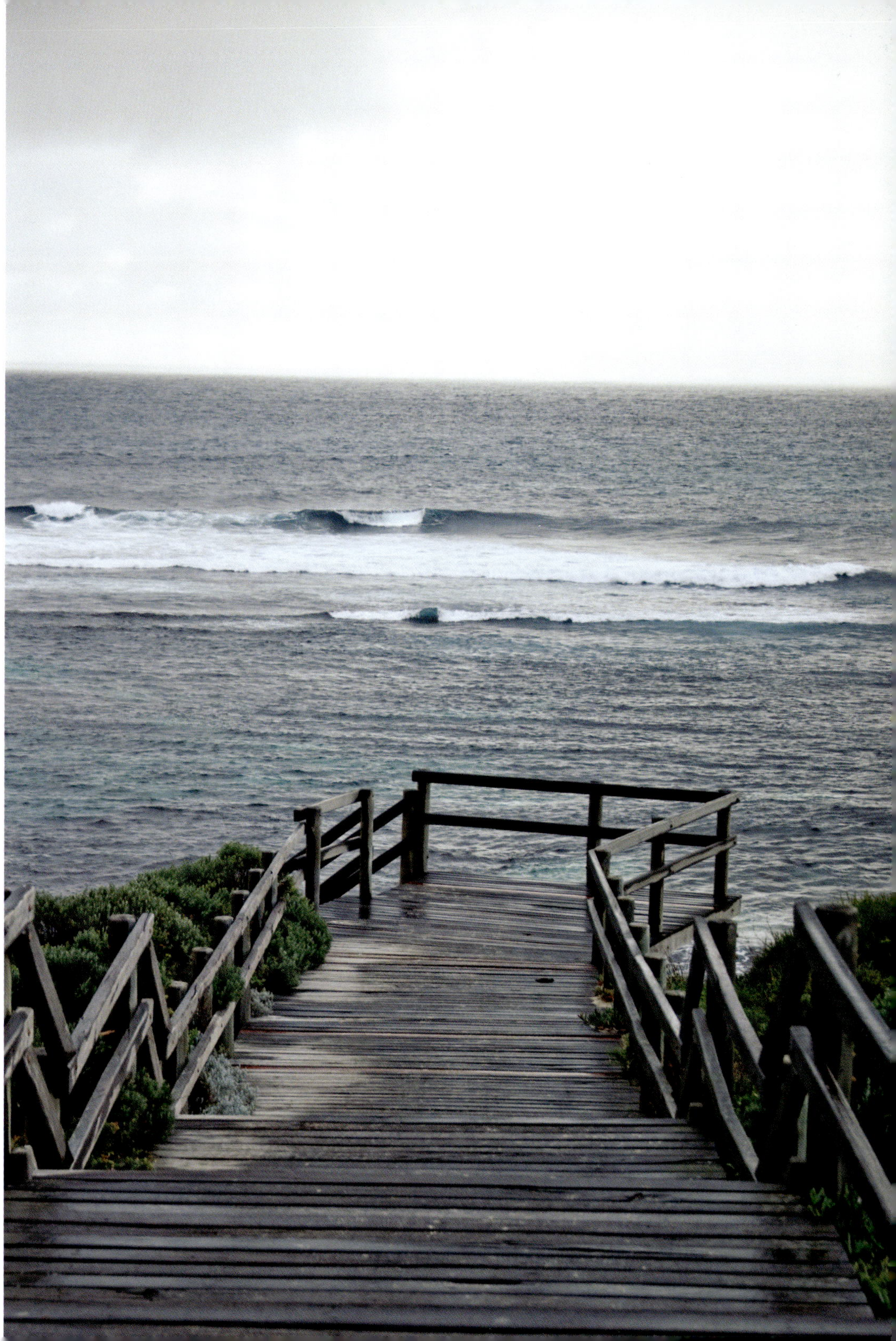

entrées

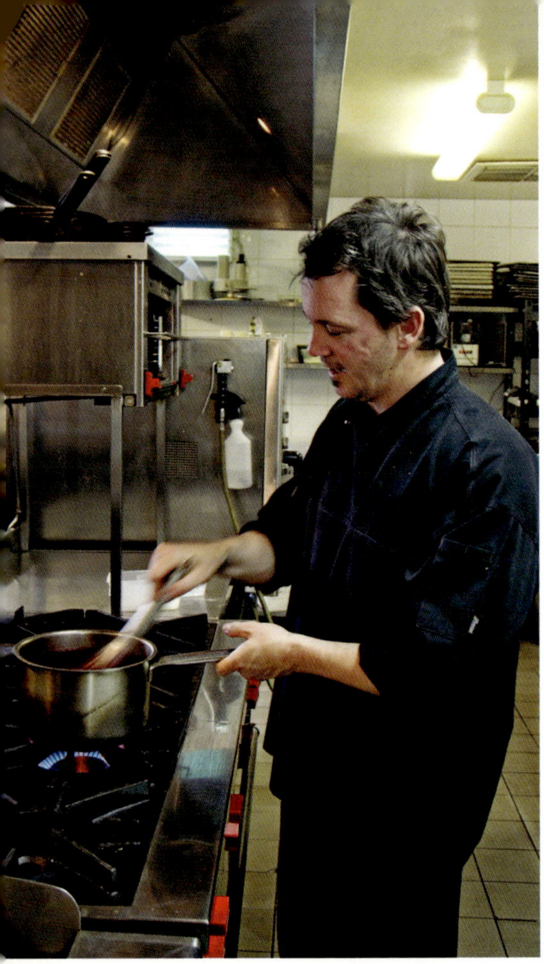
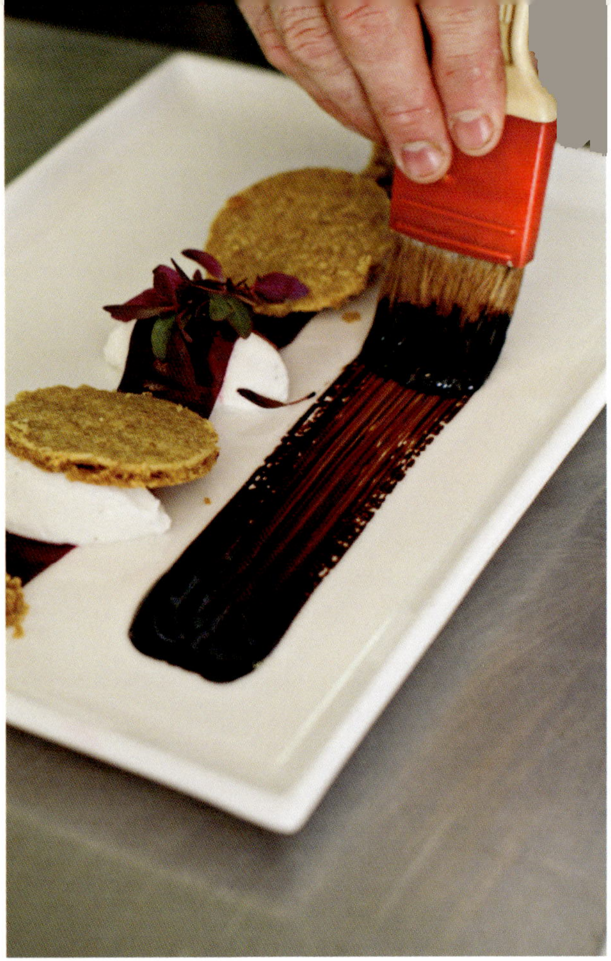
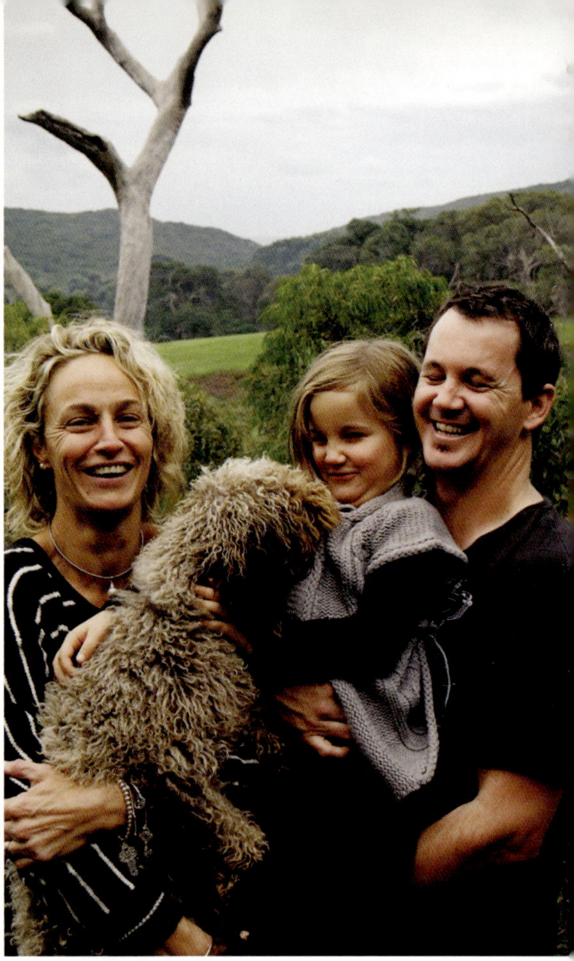
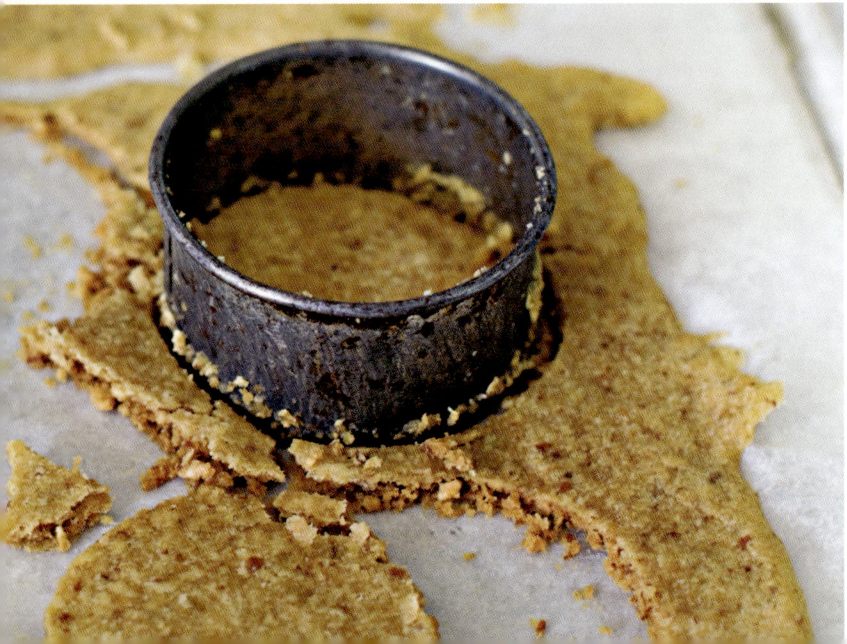
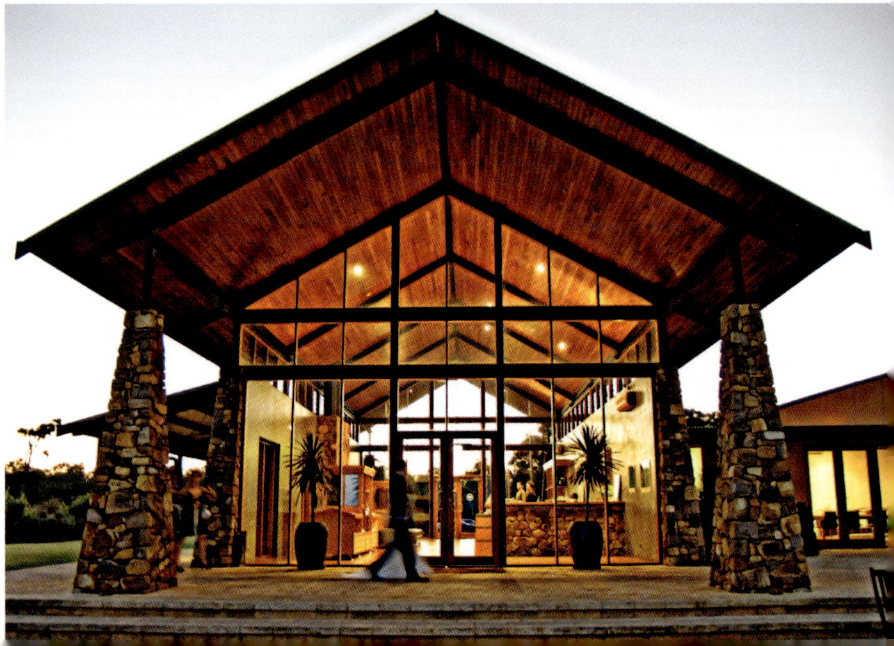

Tony Bromell

WATERSHED PREMIUM WINES, MARGARET RIVER

Tony's first day job was as a signwriter and screenprinter whilst he moonlighted casually as a kitchenhand at the Witch's Cauldron in Subiaco. Sensing that Tony was more interested in food than printing, his perceptive boss soon offered him an apprenticeship. After three and a half years at the Witch's Cauldron, Tony headed for the UK and cooked at Harvey Nichols in London's OXO Tower.

His travel experiences provided Tony with valuable lessons, skills and a knowledge of cooking that weren't a part of his life growing up. Travelling to Portugal, Morocco, France and Spain, Tony chased the surf ("particularly the big right-handers,") and enjoyed a spot of snowboarding in the Alps.

"It was there I developed my respect for French cuisine," he says. "Food in our household was fairly plain. Spaghetti bolognese was about as exotic as it got!"

Returning home, Tony worked in the Great Southern township of Denmark for 18 months, before landing himself a sous chef role under Nigel Harvey at Xanadu Wines. A subsequent move to Leeuwin Estate was followed by his current role at Watershed Premium Wines.

Tony and his kitchen team design Watershed's menu to make the most of fresh produce. "I don't change it strictly every three months because I'm more interested in how long specific produce is available, rather than whether it's spring or summer," Tony explains.

"For instance, some years we get peaches in early November and other years we don't see them until December. Our menu reflects this".

When not in the kitchen, Tony loves heading to Melbourne "for a game of footy, a drink at Siglo and perhaps another at Cumulus Inc before drifting down to Movida for tapas and finishing with duck at Longrain".

In his spare time, Tony still likes to surf. He's also restoring an old weatherboard settlement home, using the stained glass windows from Xanadu Wine's original cellar door. "They were first salvaged from a property in Fremantle by Xanadu's original owner Dr John Lagan," says Tony. With his restored home nearing completion, the chef says he's in Margaret River to stay. "My beautiful family, some great waves and an even greater lifestyle – these are the things that keep me here".

Beetroot strap with goat's curd, walnut dacquoise

AND COFFEE BEAN BALSAMIC

SERVES 6-8

You will need a sugar thermometer to make this recipe.

GOAT'S CURD
- 500 g goat's curd
- Salt
- Cracked black pepper

BEETROOT STRAP
- 470 ml beetroot juice, strained (from approximately 1.3 kg of beetroot)
- 60 g caster sugar
- 15 g pectin
- 5 g citric acid
- 50 ml water
- 335 g caster sugar, extra
- 100 g glucose

WALNUT DACQUOISE
- 1¼ cups walnut kernels
- ½ cup 00 flour
- 8 tbsp softened unsalted butter
- 2 egg whites
- 1 pinch salt

COFFEE BEAN BALSAMIC
- 1 L balsamic vinegar
- 50 coffee beans
- 50 g brown sugar

METHOD

GOAT'S CURD: PREPARE THE NIGHT BEFORE
Place goat's curd in stainless steel bowl and season well with salt and cracked black pepper. Line a strainer with muslin cloth. Add curd and refrigerate overnight to remove excess liquid.

BEETROOT STRAP
Line a shallow rectangular baking tray with silicone paper. Bring beetroot juice to boil in a saucepan. Mix together the 60 g of sugar and pectin and add to the boiling juice. Mix the citric acid and water together. When the juice comes back to the boil, add the remaining sugar and glucose. Cook over medium heat until the mixture reaches 107°C. Mix in the citric acid solution and pour immediately onto the baking tray. Taking a hold of the corners of the tray, slowly tip to either side so that the mixture flows evenly to both sides. Allow to cool at room temperature and refrigerate until set.

WALNUT DACQUOISE
Grease a shallow rectangular baking tray. Grind together walnuts and flour until they are a rough breadcrumb texture. Whip butter until pale and creamy. Fold flour and nut mixture into butter. Whip egg whites until just before soft peaks begin to form, then fold these into butter mixture. Spread out onto greased baking tray to a thickness of no more than 4 mm and chill for approximately 20 minutes. Remove from fridge and bake at 150°C for approximately 20-30 minutes or until firm to the touch. While still hot, cut into circular shapes, using a cookie cutter.

COFFEE BEAN BALSAMIC
Bring all ingredients to the boil and simmer until reduced by ⅓.

TO SERVE
Slice the set beetroot mixture into 25 mm strips. Using two tablespoons, form three quenelles of goat curd per plate. Lay a quenelle on either end of plate. Gently lift a piece of strap and lay over the two quenelles, forming a line down the plate. Place the third quenelle in the middle of the plate. Lay two dacquoise biscuits against outer quenelles and sprinkle with the crumbs leftover from dacquoise cuts. Brush plate with balsamic. Garnish with baby beetroot leaves.

Wine Match: Watershed Senses Sauvignon Blanc

Beetroot strap with goat's curd, walnut dacquoise

AND COFFEE BEAN BALSAMIC

TONY BROMELL
WATERSHED
PREMIUM WINES
RECIPE - SEE PAGE 16

Scallops, tea-smoked duck, bbq pork and masterstock

JAKE DRACHENBERG
CLAIRAULT WINES
RECIPE - SEE PAGE 22

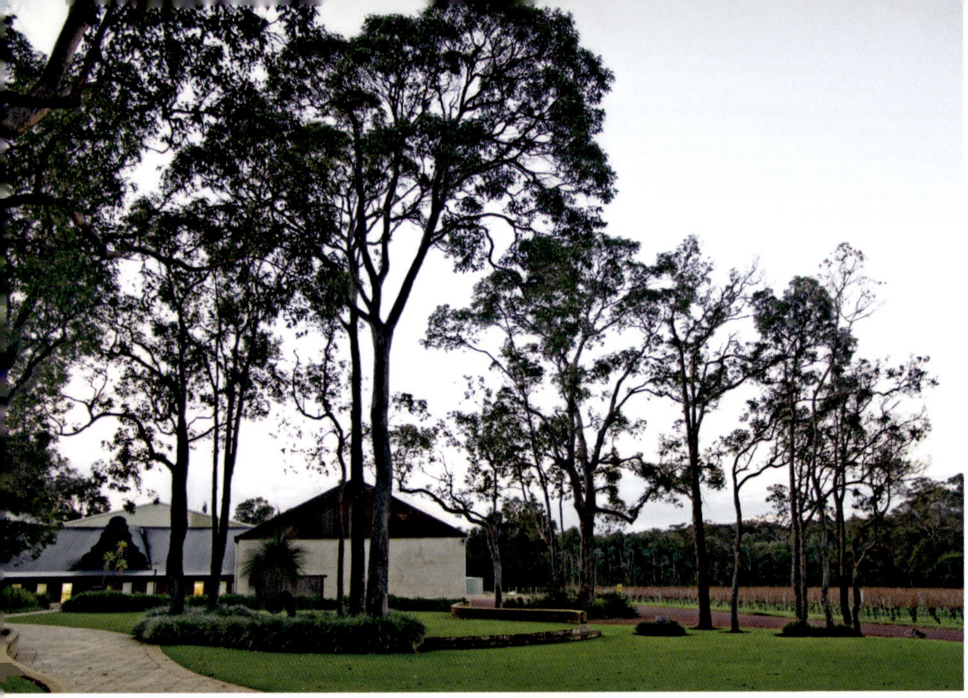

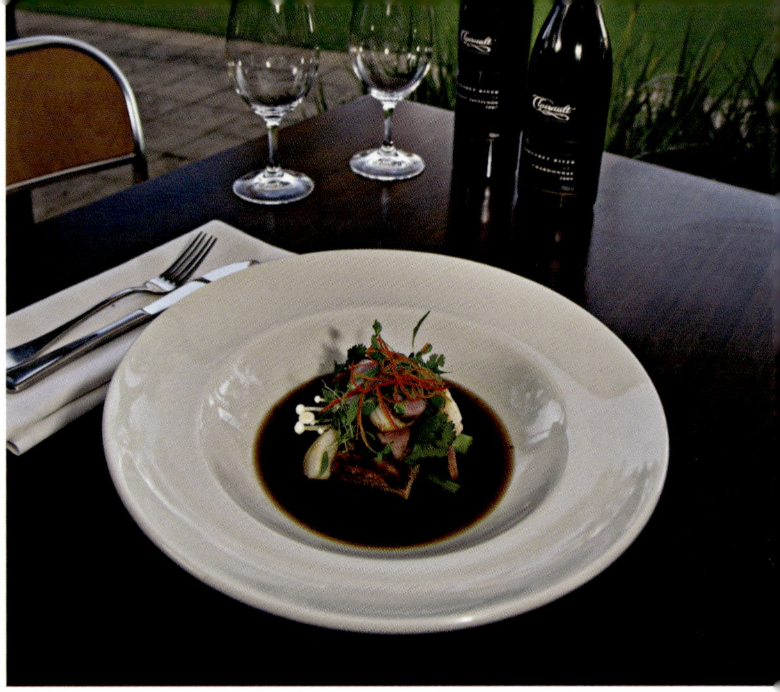

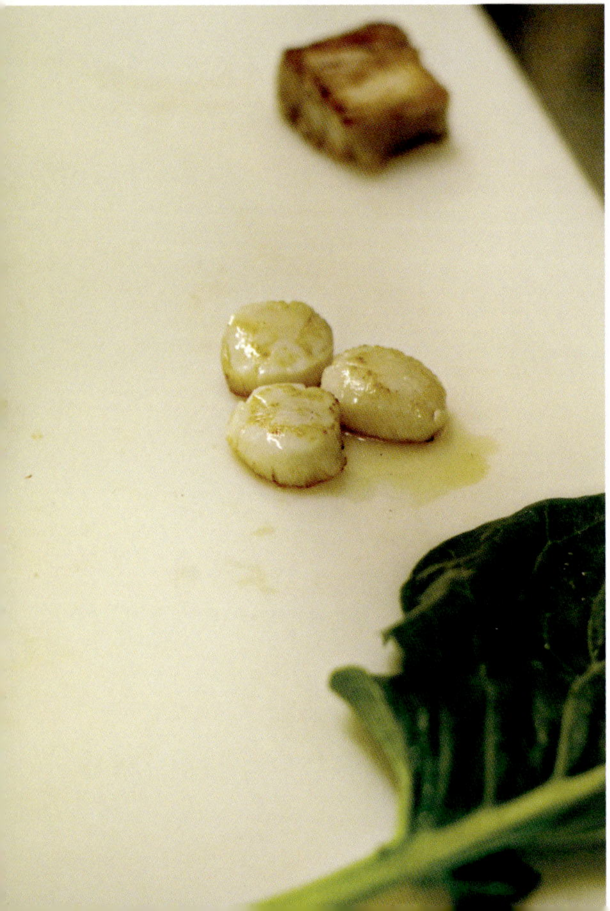

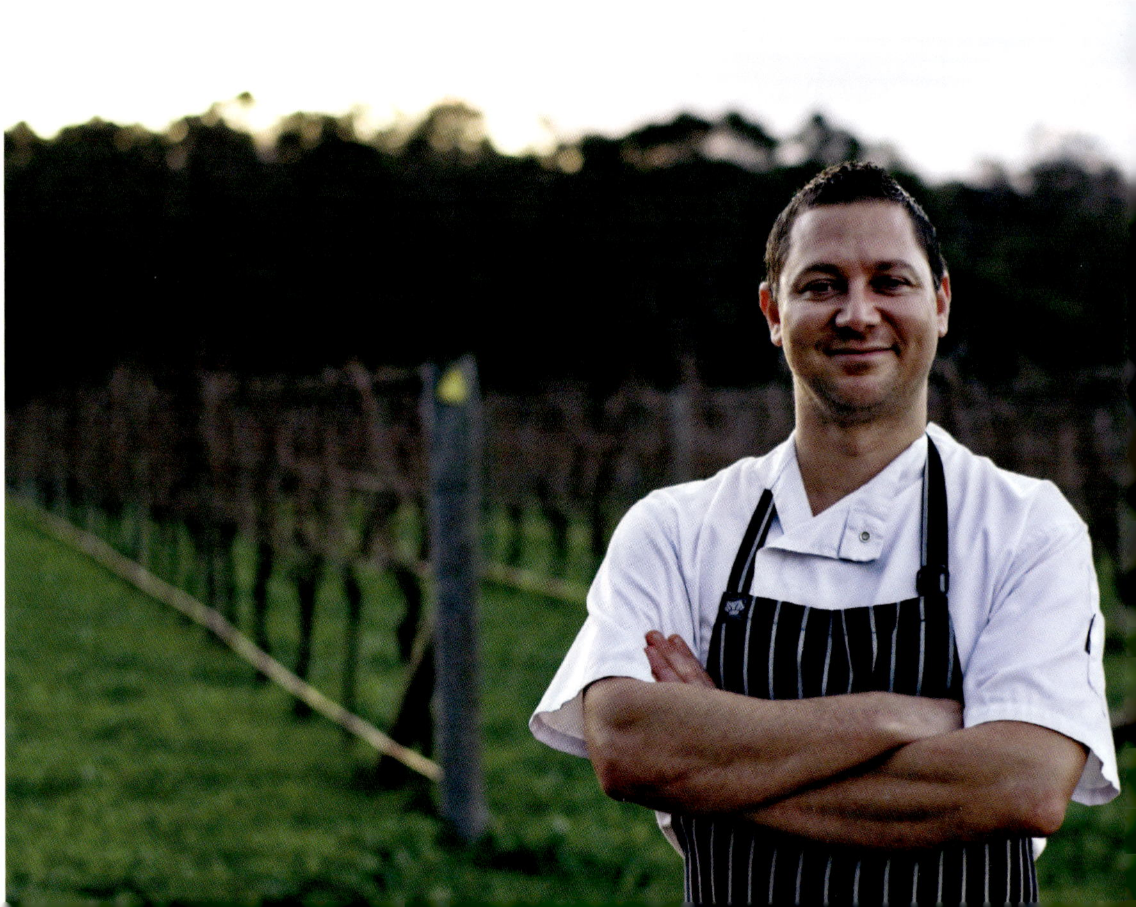

Jake Drachenberg

CLAIRAULT WINES, WILYABRUP

Jake says he enjoys the challenge of matching each season's wine with food.
"Here at Clairault, we're given each new season's wines and have to adapt our food to match them," says Jake.

Fresh produce is key to the menu at Clairault. "We spend the quieter winter months planning our menu and deciding what corresponding herbs and vegetables to plant in time for picking in the summer months," says Jake, whose belief in sustainable eating practices guides his approach to cooking. "Let's face it. If something has to travel a thousand kilometres to get to you, it's not very environmentally sustainable".

Born in Walpole, Jake grew up in one of the region's alternative shared communities. "At the weekend, us kids would knock off the chooks".

"I also learned to separate milk from cream, turn the milk into cheese and churn cream into butter. We collected duck and chicken eggs and had massive gardens. Essentially we grew everything ourselves".

Today the chef describes his style as "contemporary with a conscience. I like to use styles, produce and techniques that respect mother earth".

Not that Jake always intended to be a chef. "I kind of fell into it while I was scrubbing pots to put myself through university".

He says one of his most memorable food experiences was not at a fine diner but at an ashram in India. "I sat there and ate with thousands of other people. It was such a majestic thing".

The self-proclaimed obsessive-compulsive cites his inspirations as "my wife, mother, staff, Thomas Keller, Neil Perry, David Thompson and Anthony Bourdain".

As for career highlights, Jake says working in vintage train cars high in Canada's Rocky Mountains and private motor yachts in the far north of Australia were both special, as was working under local chefs Tony Howell (Cape Lodge) and François Morvan (Flutes at Brookland Valley).

Jake sees the nutritional value of food as being no less important than its social value. "My one-year-old's life revolves around food," he says "and reminds me everyday of its fundamental role in our lives".

Scallops, tea-smoked duck, bbq pork and masterstock

SERVES 6

SCALLOPS
- 12 plump, cleaned scallops

DUCK MARINADE
- 2 duck breasts, fat scored
- 100 g dark brown sugar
- 100 ml light soy sauce

SMOKING MIX
- 50 g dark brown sugar
- 50 g green tea leaves
- 50 g raw white rice

MASTERSTOCK
- 3 L chicken stock*
- 100 ml Chinese rice wine
- 400 ml light soy
- 50 g rock sugar
- 1 cinnamon quill
- 10 white peppercorns
- 1 tsp fennel seed
- 1 fresh red chilli
- 1 small knob ginger
- 1 bulb garlic
- 1 small bunch coriander roots
- 1 lemongrass stalk
- 1 bunch of bok choy or broccolini

PORK
- 6 x 100 g pork belly strips
- 2 tbsp hoisin (Chinese bbq) sauce

*Chicken stock recipe - see page 143

Wine Match: Clairault Estate Chardonnay.

METHOD

DUCK

Combine sugar and soy and marinate duck in this mixture for four hours. Combine all smoking ingredients and place in a metal baking tray lined with foil. Put tray directly over a hotplate and heat until mixture begins to smoke. Pat duck breast dry and place on wire rack over smoke mix. Cover with a tight fitting seal (aluminum foil works well), turn heat down to low and smoke for four minutes. Remove and cool duck.

Pre-heat oven to 180°C. Heat a frying pan until good and hot. Place duck skin side down in pan and cook for two minutes or until skin is golden brown and caramelised. Put duck in oven for three minutes, to finish cooking, remembering it should be served rare. Remove from oven and rest for 5-10 minutes before slicing.

MASTERSTOCK

Lightly roast spices, bruise fresh ingredients to release flavour and crush sugar. In a large, heavy-based saucepan, combine all ingredients except the bok choy or broccolini. Bring to the boil, skimming any foam from the surface. Simmer for one hour. Strain. Poach pork belly strips in the masterstock for approximately one hour or until tender. When cooked, remove pork from stock, pat dry and brush with hoisin sauce.

TO SERVE

Reheat masterstock to a simmer and cook bok choy or broccolini in it for a few minutes. Sear the scallops for one minute on each side, being sure not to overcook them. Arrange scallops in a bowl with the pork belly and sliced duck. Add the vegetables. Pour over the hot stock and serve.

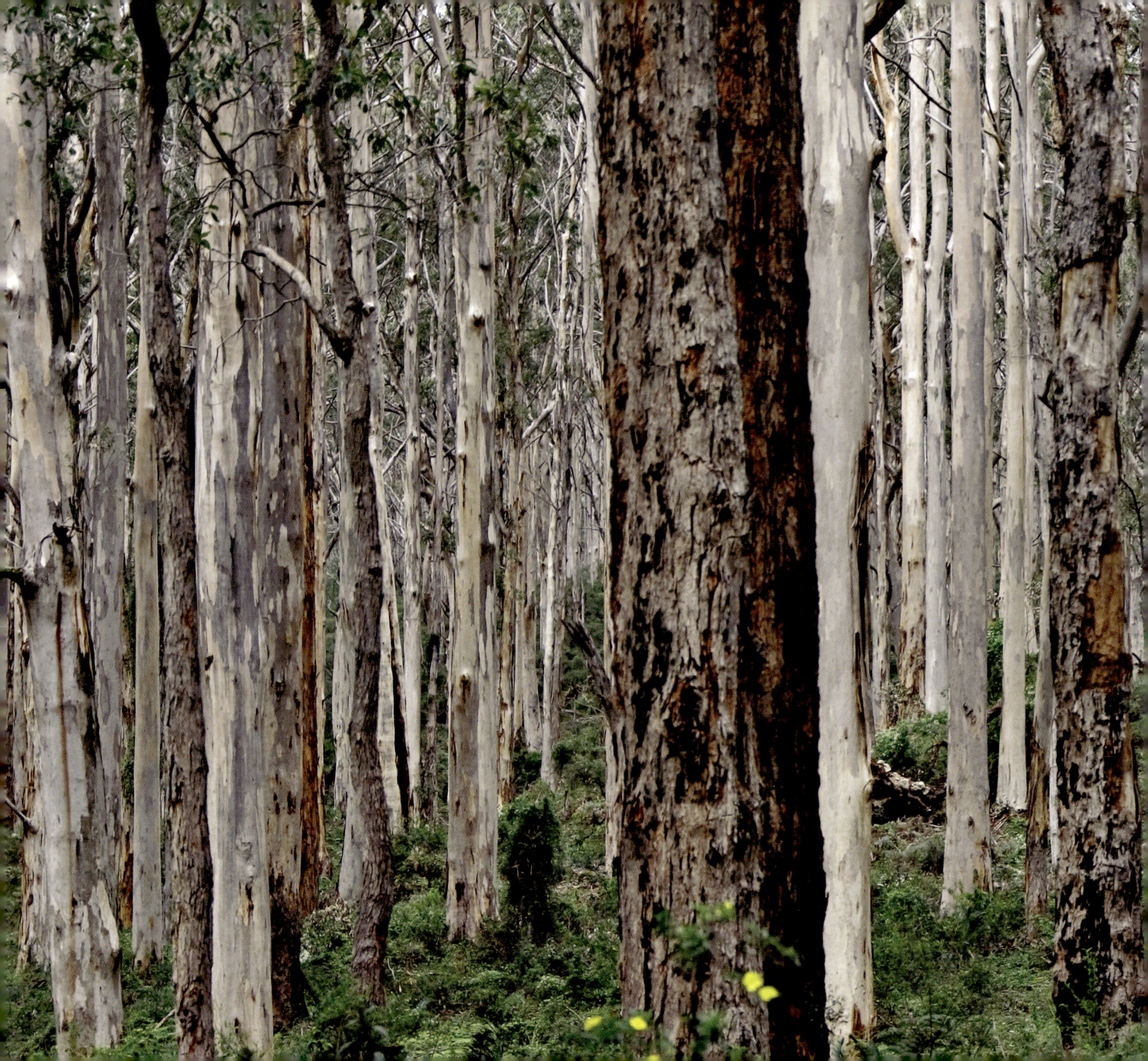

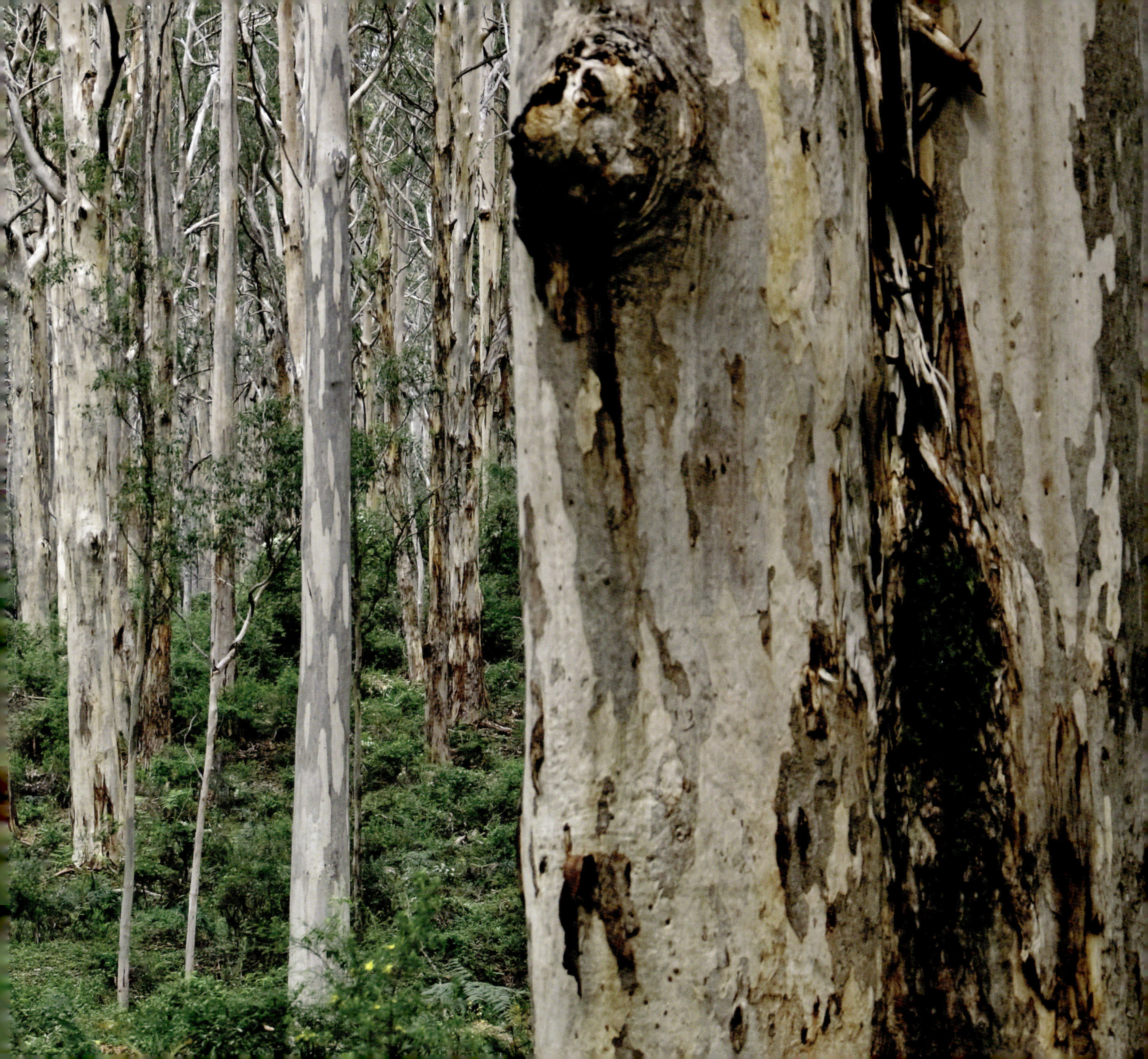

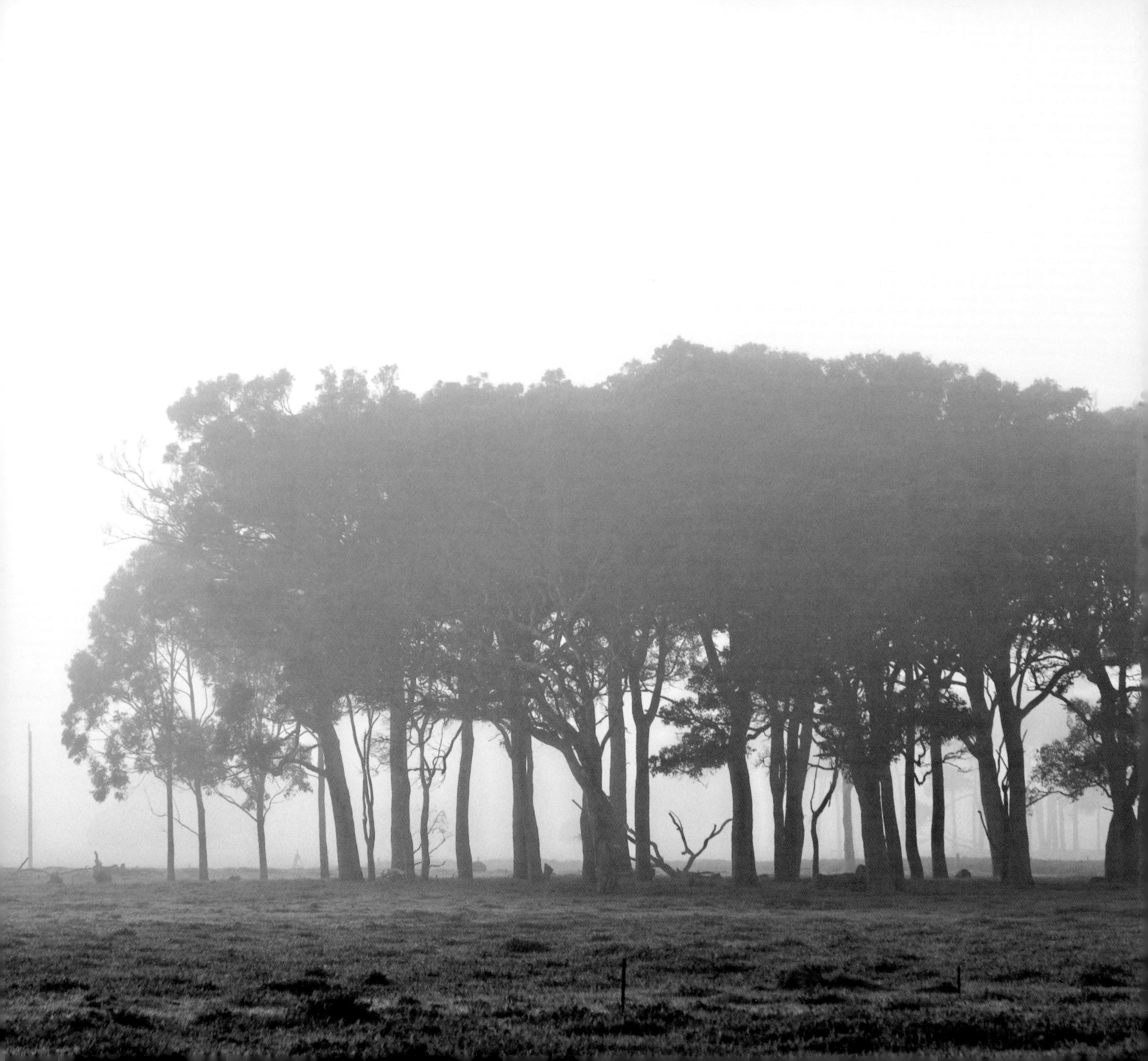

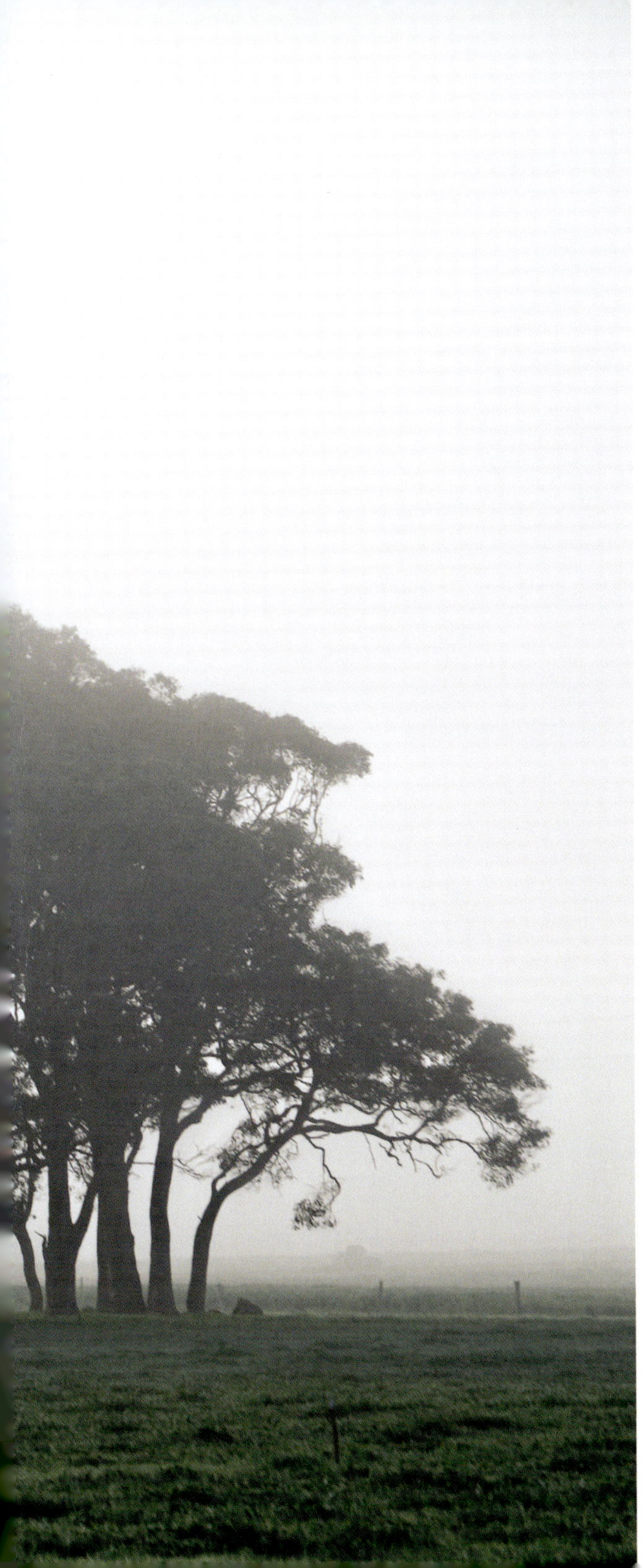
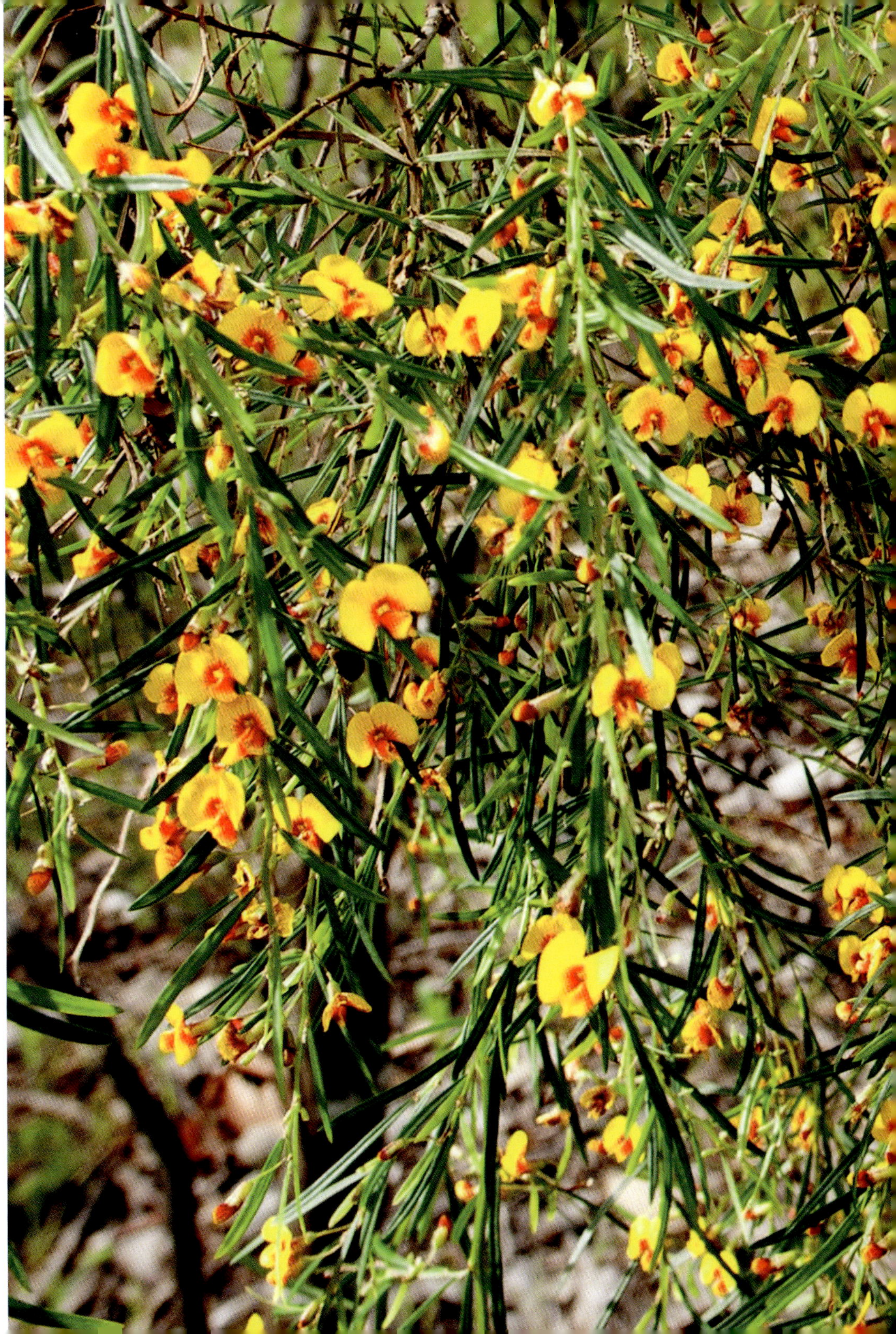

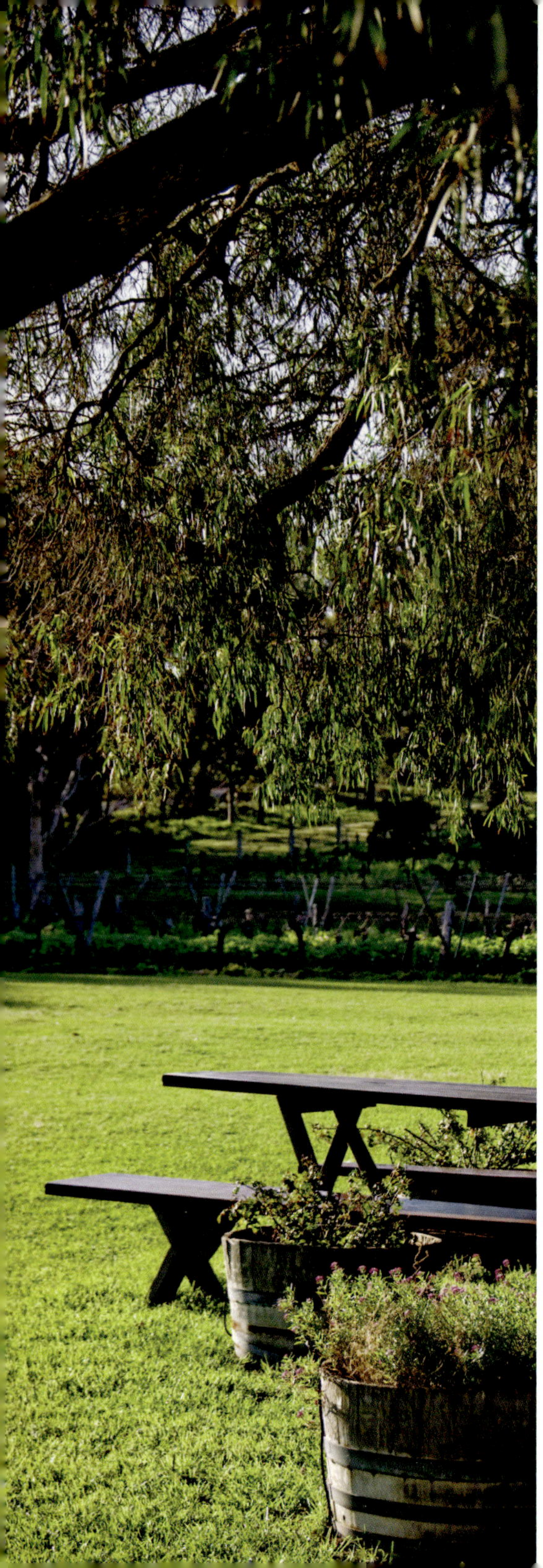

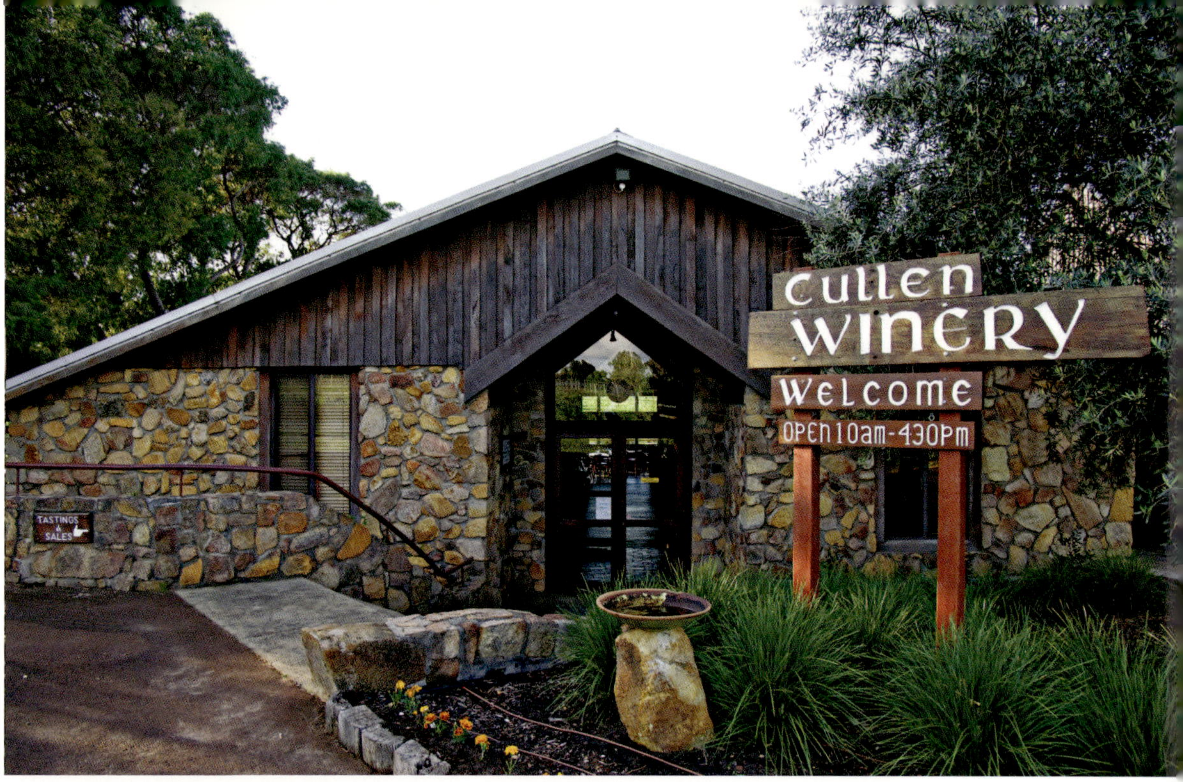
Cullen
WINERY
WELCOME
OPEN10am-430Pm
TASTINGS & SALES

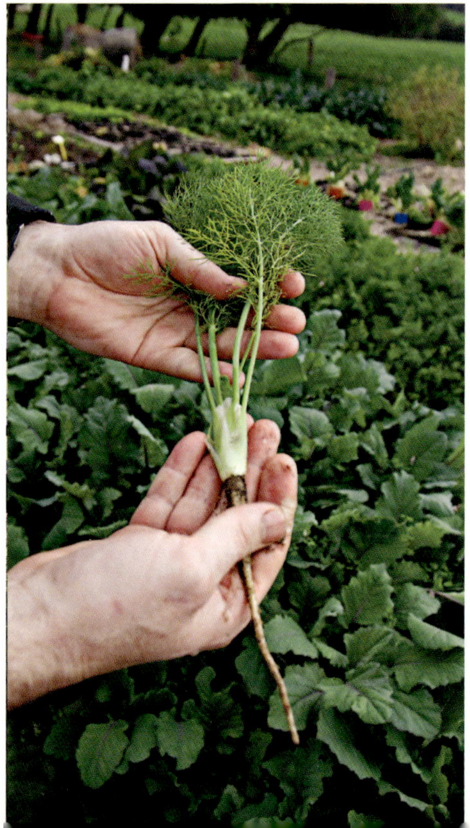

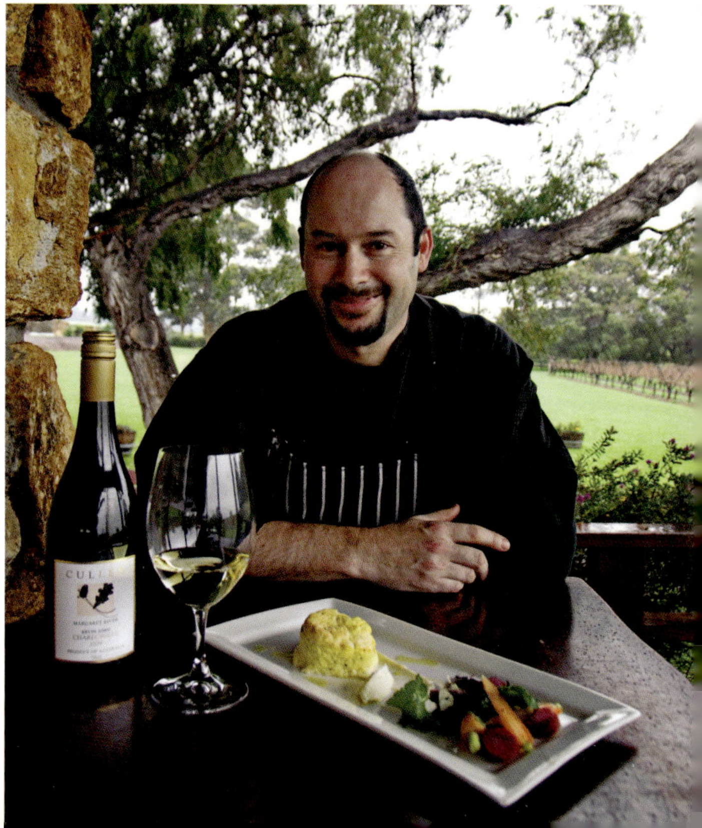

Matt Egan

CULLEN WINES, WILYABRUP

Matt grew up in New Zealand surrounded by orchards of kiwi fruit and large plots of home-grown vegetables. So the kitchen gardens at Cullen, which provide much of the fresh produce served in the restaurant, feel a lot like home.

He says his focus is on showcasing this brilliant biodynamic produce. "I don't use a lot of heavy sauces, and if I do make a jus, the flavour comes from vegetables in the stock, reduced naturally rather than thickened with flour. It's as uncomplicated as I can make it".

Matt's menu reflects whatever crops are growing on the biodynamic property. "We get watercress from the stream in winter. Broad beans, snow peas and garlic are planted in between the vineyard rows, ready for picking in spring".

The chef enjoys making the most of this own-grown produce. "Little things are coming up in the garden all the time. We pick them each day and use them in salads or to add little touches to the plate. Baby vegetables with roots on, rocket flowers, basically whatever we can find that's edible. As a chef it's fantastic to be able to do that".

Inevitably, the Cullen garden features a wide assortment of interesting vegetables. "Heritage carrots, kohlrabi, that kind of thing," says Matt. "We've even got stinging nettles and daikon radish".

Over in the chardonnay block, beehives house bees that tend to the vines and provide honey for the restaurant's own-made ice cream.

For cooking inspiration, Matt turns to his many cookbooks. "I've got five shelves of them. I should probably use the internet more, but I really love to read".

Matt lives a little south of the winery, in the picturesque coastal community of Hamelin Bay. He doesn't own a mobile phone. ("Last time I checked there was still no reception out where we live") and says it's this rich, natural environment that keeps him in Margaret River.

"Living here with my wife and daughter, surrounded by karri trees on our bush property, it's a tranquil life".

Gluten-free twice-baked goat's cheese soufflé

WITH CAULIFLOWER CREAM

SERVES 6

SOUFFLÉ
- 500 ml water
- 125 g white polenta
- 20 g finely grated parmesan cheese
- 1 tbsp extra virgin olive oil
- 75 g fresh goat's cheese
- ½ tsp lemon thyme leaves
- ½ tsp flat leaf parsley, chopped finely
- 1 tbsp melted butter
- ¼ tsp ground white pepper
- ¾ tsp pink salt
- 3 organic egg yolks
- 4 organic egg whites
- 1 L vegetable stock*

* Vegetable stock recipe - see page 143

CAULIFLOWER CREAM
- ½ an organic cauliflower
- 500 ml organic milk
- ¼ tsp cumin seeds
- ½ tsp pink salt

SALAD GARNISH
- 6 baby carrots
- 6 pink beetroot
- 100 g rocket
- A drizzle of extra virgin olive oil

METHOD

SOUFFLÉ

Pre-heat oven to 180°C. Lightly butter six 150 ml china teacups or moulds and dust with a little of the parmesan. In a small saucepan, bring the water to simmer and whisk in the white polenta. Turn down the heat and cook for 20 minutes or until polenta is thick and smooth. Whisk in extra virgin olive oil and allow to cool. Transfer polenta to a food processor, add goat's cheese, remaining parmesan, lemon thyme, parsley, salt and white pepper. Pulse the processor until combined. Add egg yolks and pulse again. Pour into a large bowl.

In another large bowl, whisk egg whites until firm peaks form. Fold half the egg white into the polenta cheese mixture until just combined. Lightly fold in the remaining egg whites, being careful to retain as much air as possible. Divide mixture between china teacups or moulds, smoothing the tops as you go. Spread a tea towel in the bottom of a baking dish and place the six cups or moulds on top. Pour in boiling water to reach ⅔ up the sides of the moulds. Bake for 40 minutes until soufflés are firm and have risen nicely. Allow to cool to room temperature before turning out into an ovenproof dish.

CAULIFLOWER CREAM

Cut cauliflower into small pieces and put into a small saucepan. Cover with milk, add cumin and simmer until soft. Strain cauliflower to separate from milk. Put milk aside. Puree cauliflower in a blender until smooth and creamy. Thin with a little of the milk if needed. Season with salt and pepper.

SALAD GARNISH

In a saucepan, cook the baby carrots with a little butter and water until tender. Toss the pink beetroot in olive oil, wrap in aluminium foil and bake in an oven at 180°C for 20 minutes or until tender. Cool and remove skin. Rinse rocket and pat dry.

TO SERVE

Pre-heat oven to 200°C. Heat the vegetable stock in saucepan and pour into the ovenproof dish until it comes quarter of the way up the sides of the turned-out soufflés. Bake for five minutes. Dollop and smear cauliflower cream on each serving plate and place the soufflé on top. Arrange beetroot and baby carrots with rocket on the plate, drizzle with olive oil and scatter with cracked pepper, salt and extra goat's cheese if desired.

Wine Match: Cullen Kevin John Chardonnay

Gluten-free twice-baked goat's cheese soufflé

WITH CAULIFLOWER CREAM

MATT EGAN
CULLEN WINES
RECIPE - SEE PAGE 30

Butter-poached Pemberton marron

TONY HOWELL
CAPE LODGE
RECIPE - SEE PAGE 36

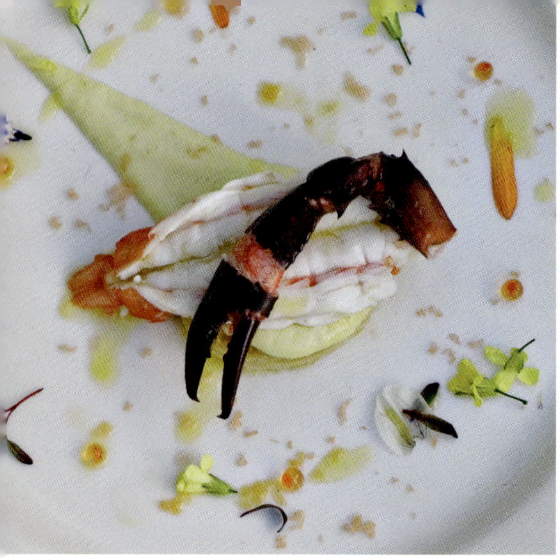

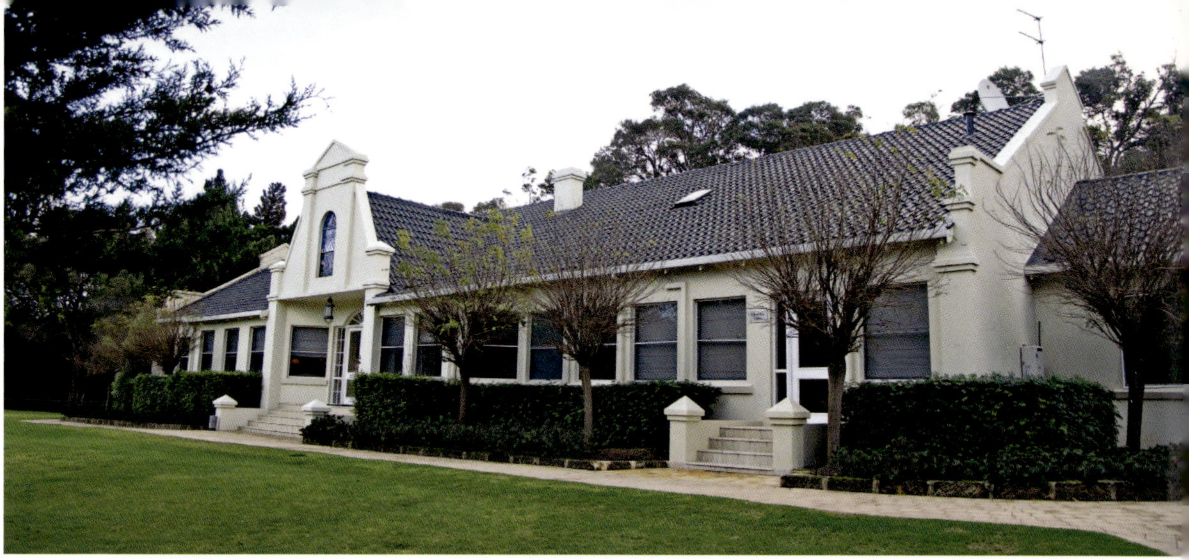

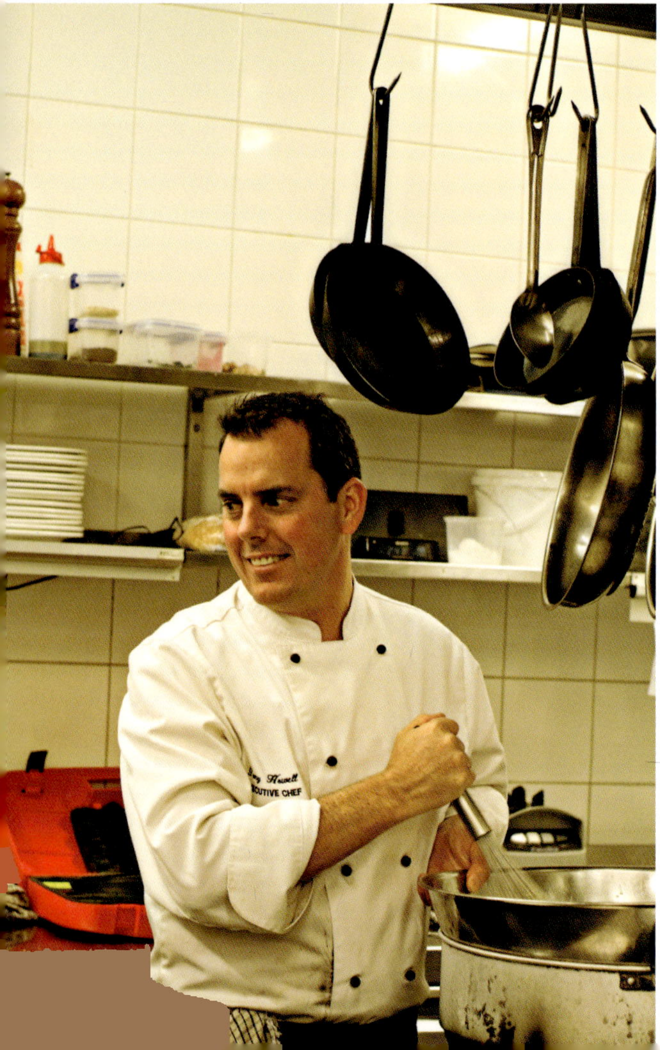

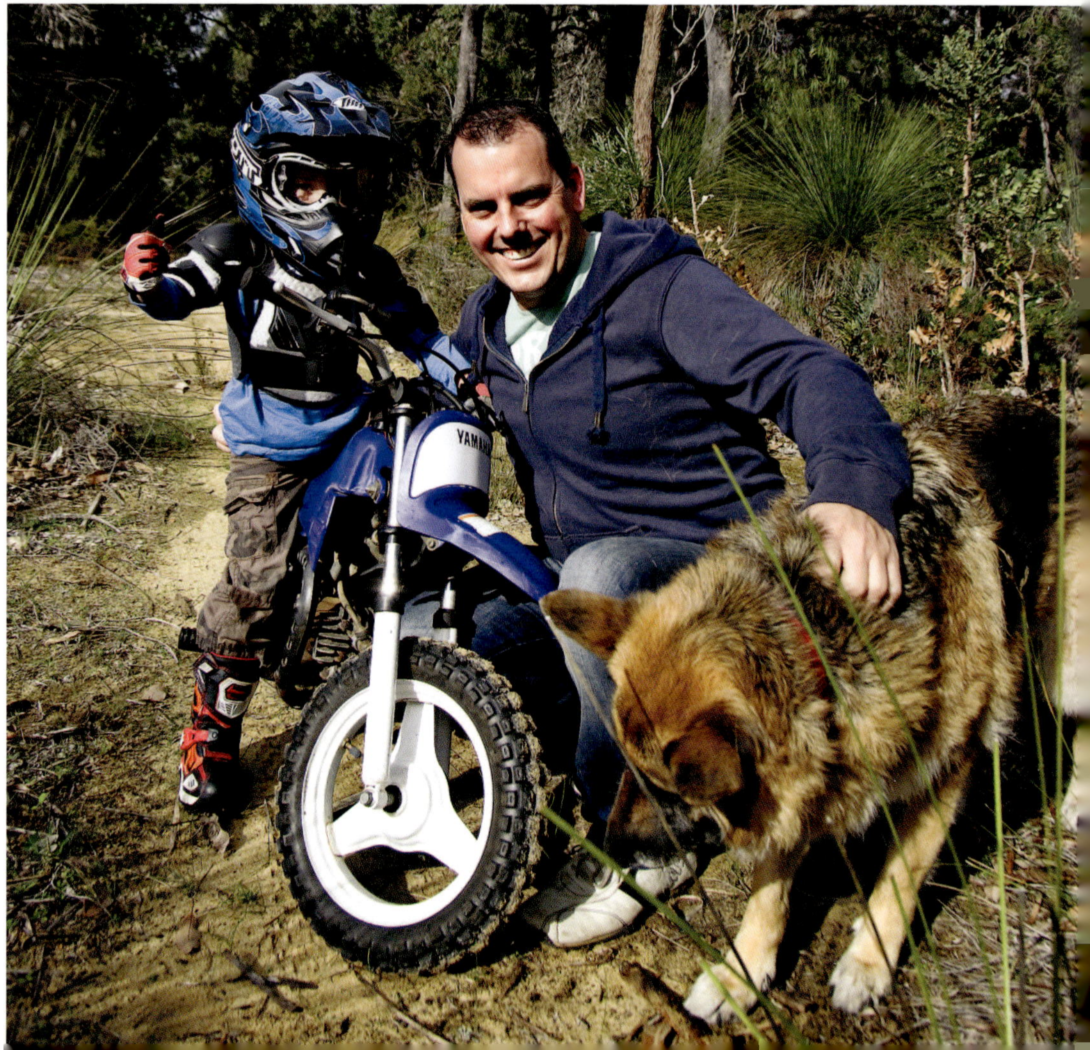

Tony Howell

CAPE LODGE, YALLINGUP

Tony's interest in food was sparked early by his best friend's family.

"They were Italians. As well as growing all their own produce, they butchered chickens, pickled pretty much everything that grew in the veggie patch and made tomato sauces and pastas," says Tony.

"They also baked pastries and bread in their own wood-fired oven, and their cellar was filled wall-to-wall with smoked meats, barrels of wine, sauces and poached fruit in jars".

Tony moved from Perth to Margaret River in 1995 planning, as so many local chefs do, to combine his love for the ocean with cooking. After three successful years as the head chef at Flutes at Brookland Valley, he moved to Cape Lodge in 1999.

Part private country estate, part resort, this luxury hotel is regularly named in the top ten finest hotel dining rooms in the world, attracting those who are seeking a private, stylish and sophisticated retreat.

Part of Tony's ethos as a chef is showcasing the region. Fresh, whole fish from Augusta is delivered to his kitchen door by the boys from 34 Degrees Blue, while seasonal catches such as dhufish and snapper are often featured on the menu.

"Here at Cape Lodge we change the menu daily," says Tony. "This means I get to play with flavours depending on what produce rocks up at my back door".

The chef also ensures his kitchen team has as much input into creating the menu as he does. "I believe it's vital to provide a supportive environment that develops young talent," he says.

Tony also enjoys sharing his passion for food with the public, and runs regular cooking classes at Cape Lodge that culminate in a five-course chef's tasting menu.

After 13 years at Cape Lodge, Tony says he's happy eating somewhere other than his own fine dining room. "My young, noisy family fits in perfectly with the hustle and bustle of a good yum cha restaurant. I also enjoy eating anywhere where the food is good and the conversation passionate".

In his spare time, Tony likes to take advantage of all that the region has to offer. A lover of the ocean and open spaces, he can usually be found fishing, diving or taking his eldest son dirt bike riding.

Butter-poached Pemberton marron

SERVES 6

MARRON
- 3 whole marron

POACHING LIQUID
- 300 ml fish stock*
- 300 g butter
- 300 ml white wine
- 2 sprigs thyme
- 5 peppercorns
- 3 sprigs dill
- 1 bulb garlic, cut in half

*Fish stock recipe - see page 142
*Creamed leeks recipe - see page 144

FOR SERVING
- Creamed leeks*
- Baked flaky pastry circles
- Shaved smoked salmon
- Salmon caviar

METHOD

MARRON
Steam marron in an Asian steamer for two minutes and cool in an ice bath. Peel the tails and remove the intestinal tracts. The marron are now ready for the poaching stage.

POACHING
Put poaching ingredients in a large, heavy-based saucepan except for the marron. Bring to a simmer. Place marron in the liquid and simmer for approximately two minutes. Remove from liquid and preserve liquid.

TO SERVE
Smear a tablespoon of creamed leek in the middle of the plate and position pastry round on top. Add a layer of creamed leeks and then half a marron. Drizzle poaching liquid around plate and on marron. Decorate plate with salmon caviar and edible flowers. Finish with marron claw on top of stack and sprinkle with shaved smoked salmon.

Wine Match:
Woodlands Chloe Chardonnay

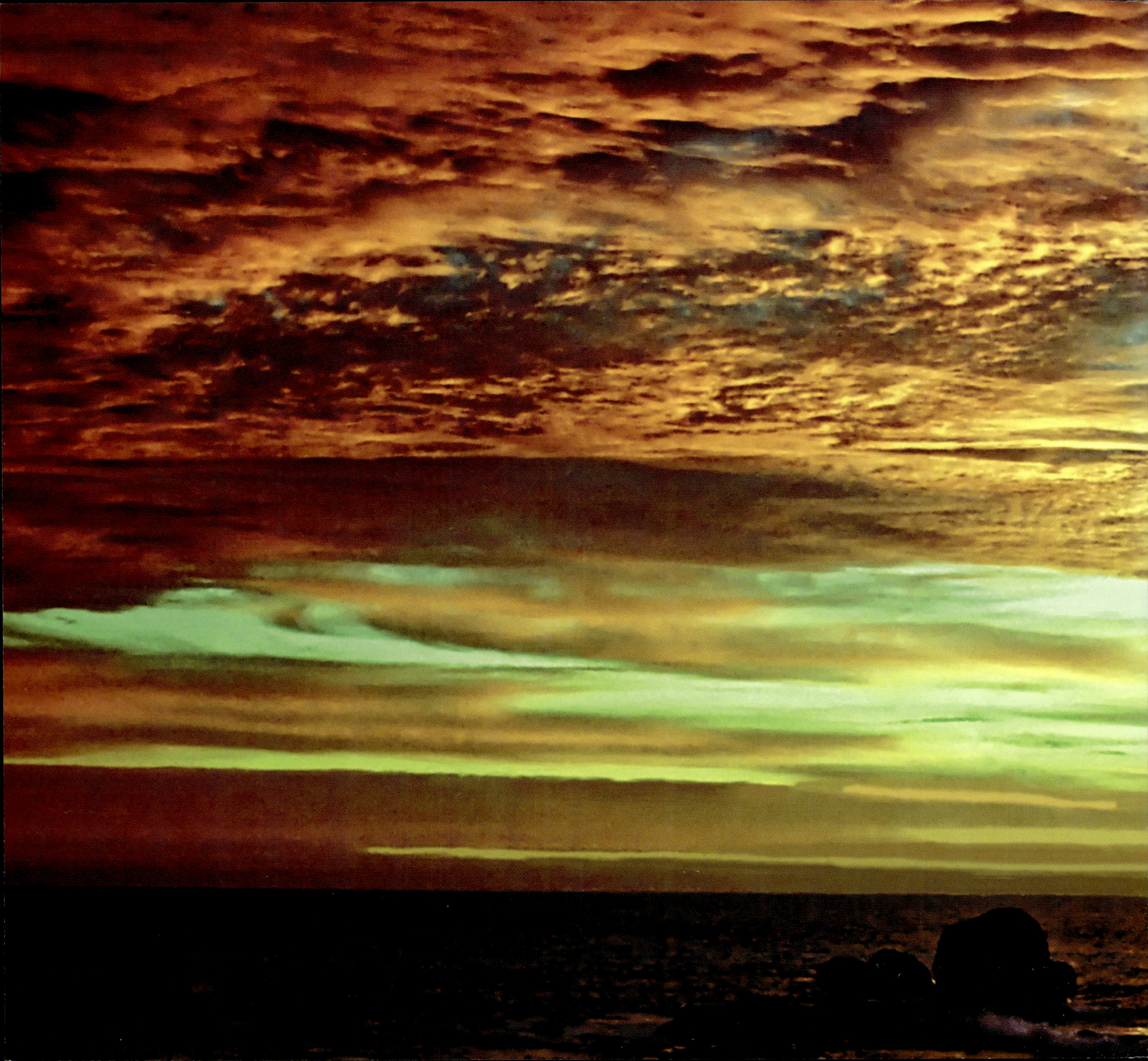

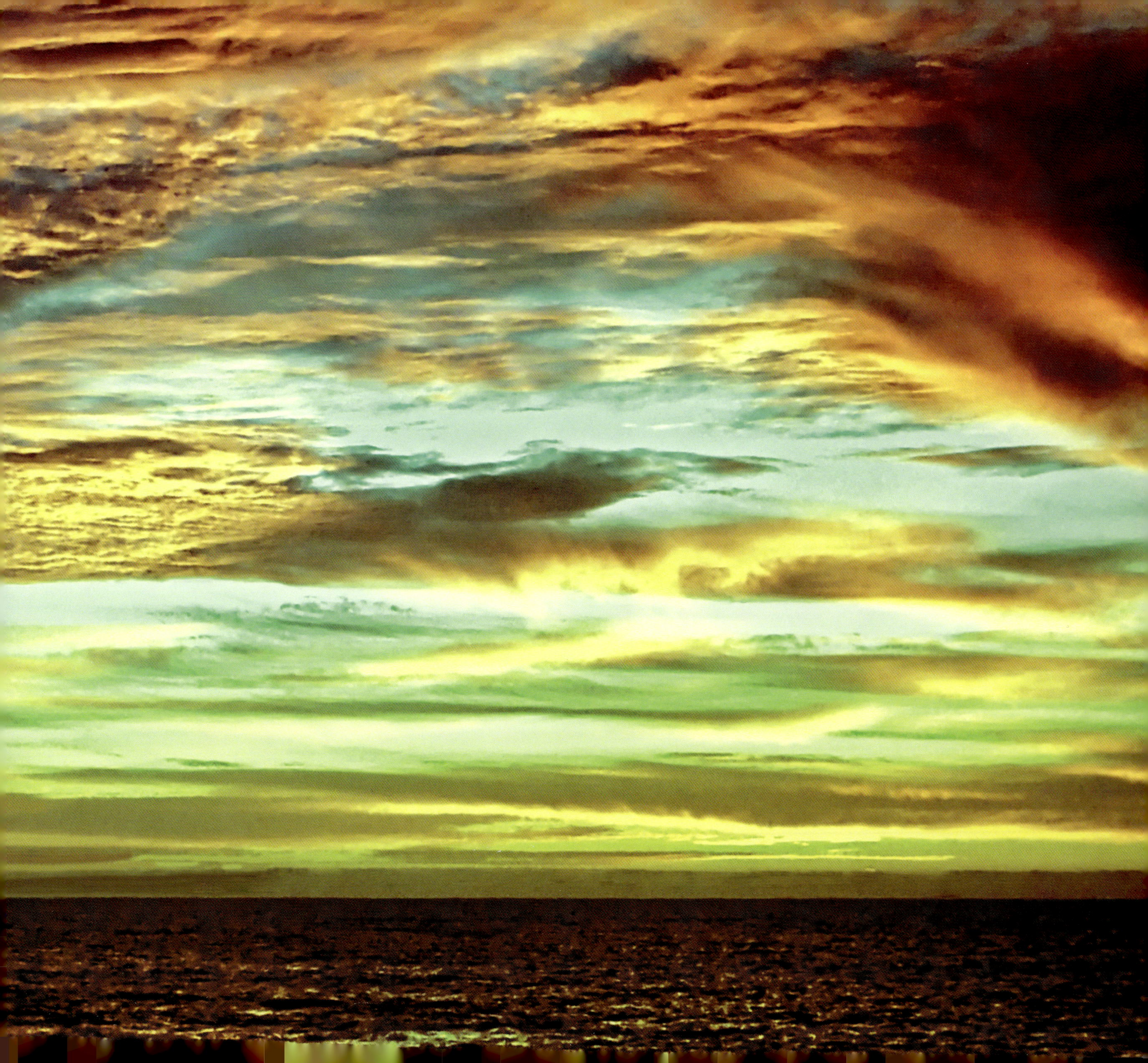

the larder
MARGARET RIVER
JAMES ROAD

OYSTER SAUCE
HEALTHY BOY BRAND

Andrea Flott

THE LARDER, MARGARET RIVER

In 1994, Andrea came to Margaret River for a week's holiday with friends and never left.

Trained in the 1980s in Perth's fine dining restaurants, she also worked at Hayman Island Luxury Resort and in Europe as a private chef for some of the world's most wealthy celebrities. Over the years, she has cooked for the Dalai Lama, Sting, The Rolling Stones, Elle MacPherson and Kelly Slater.

Andrea began the Margaret River part of her career as a sous chef at Vasse Felix. She quickly went on to become the executive chef at Clairault Wines, where she earned a reputation as one of the region's finest young chefs.

In 2006, Andrea opened The Larder on the township's main street, incorporating a cooking school, boutique catering service and well-stocked gourmet deli.

She says she's still in love with the region. "You can drive to the beach, forest or town in just 15 minutes. I love taking the tinny out on a Sunday at Quindalup with my husband and dog. We throw out the squid jig or the crab pots and come home with a seafood dinner".

Andrea is a big fan of Asian food and seeks it out both at home and while she is on holidays.

"The perfect Asian dish balances sweet, sour, salty and spice. I'm also a big fan of Middle Eastern cooking, which uses similar principles but with extremes of sweet and sour," she says.

Not surprisingly, Andrea is a regular traveller to South East Asia.

"In Bali, you can eat at a traditional warung for $3 or splurge on somewhere fancy like Sarong in Kerobokan for $100," she says, "I also love Cafe Zucchini at Zuttion in Seminyak for its fresh organic salads".

In Bangkok, Andrea goes for the big woks of noodle soup and whole bbq fish. "And then there are the hawker centres in Singapore, where you line up for one special dish such as Hainan chicken" she says.

When in Perth, Andrea heads to Viet Hoa in Northbridge for pho bo (beef soup), The Red Teapot for lacquered quail and Jade Garden for yum cha.

As for inspiration, she says she has absorbed what she can from every chef and person she has ever cooked with.

"I'm always looking for new tricks and tips".

Blue Swimmer crab rice paper rolls

SERVES 6

RICE PAPER ROLLS
- 200 g Blue Swimmer crab meat, cooked and picked (approximately 5-6 whole crabs)
- 110 g rice vermicelli noodles
- 1 cucumber, quartered and thinly sliced
- 1 carrot, peeled and grated
- 2 sprigs of coriander, roughly chopped
- 12 mint leaves
- 3 iceberg lettuce leaves, shredded
- 12 sheets medium size rice paper

NUOC CHAM DIPPING SAUCE
Makes 250 ml
- 1 fresh red chilli
- 3 cloves garlic, peeled and finely chopped
- 60 g caster sugar
- 3 tbsp fresh lime juice
- 1 tbsp rice vinegar
- 3 tbsp fish sauce
- 125 ml water
- ½ tsp salt

Wine match: Wallcliff Sauvignon Blanc Semillon

METHOD

SPRING ROLLS

Soak the vermicelli in cold water for 20 minutes. Blanch in boiling water then rinse under cold water. Drain well and set aside on a plate.

Dip the rice paper sheets in cold water a couple at a time to soften. When the sheets are pliable, place on the bench and add a pinch of lettuce to the bottom third of the rice paper. Put one small clump of noodles, some pieces of cucumber, a teaspoon of the crab meat, a few sprigs of coriander, a mint leaf and grated carrot on top. Roll the wrapper tightly until the edges seal shut. Repeat with the rest of the rolls. Place the finished rolls on a plate and cover with a damp towel to keep moist until serving time. Serve with dipping sauce.

NUOC CHAM DIPPING SAUCE

Although you can simply combine all the ingredients at once, you will get a better result by pounding the chilli, garlic and sugar together to release the flavours before adding the remaining ingredients and mixing well.

Blue Swimmer crab rice paper rolls

ANDREA ILOTT
THE LARDER
RECIPE - SEE PAGE 42

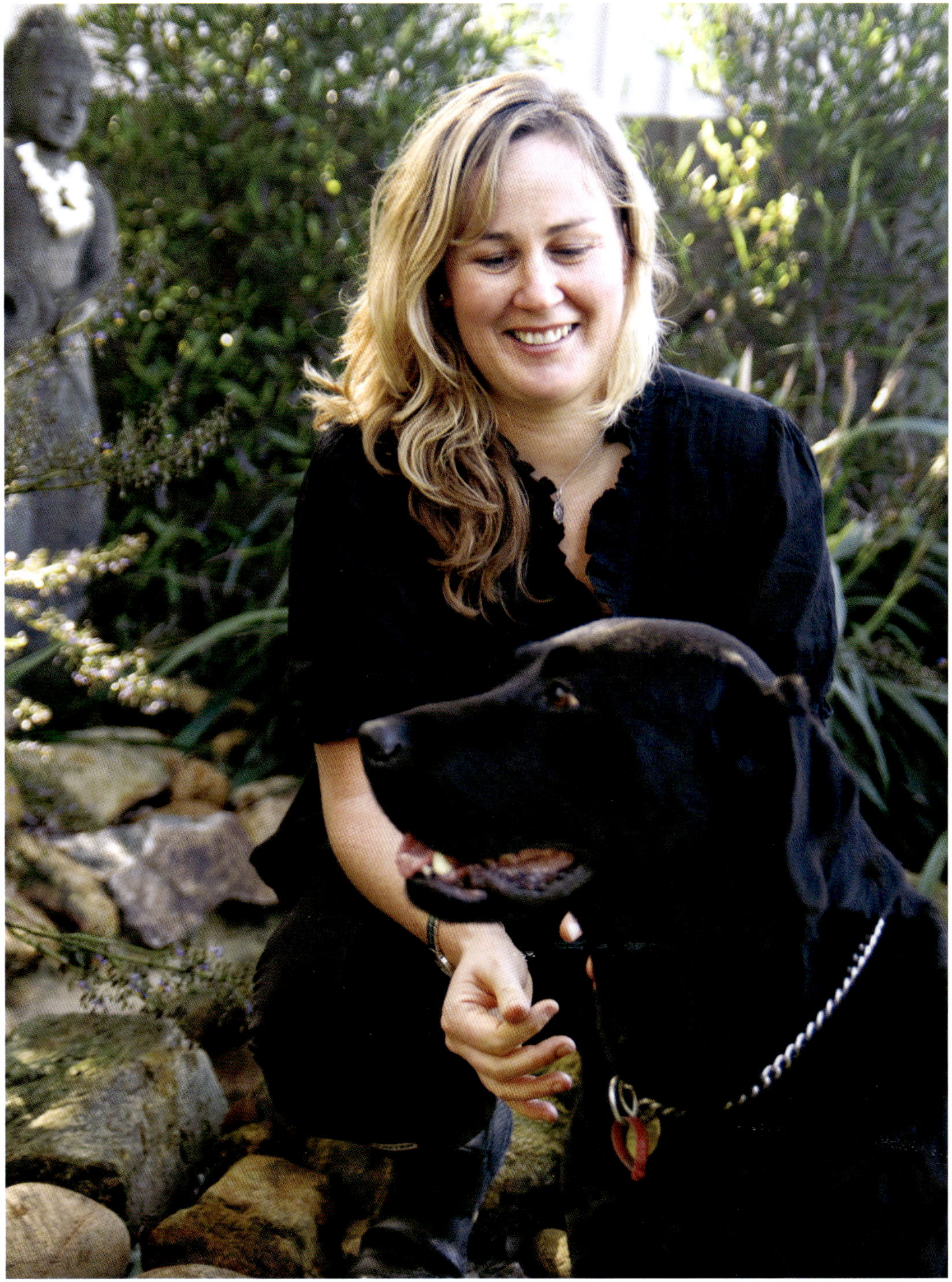

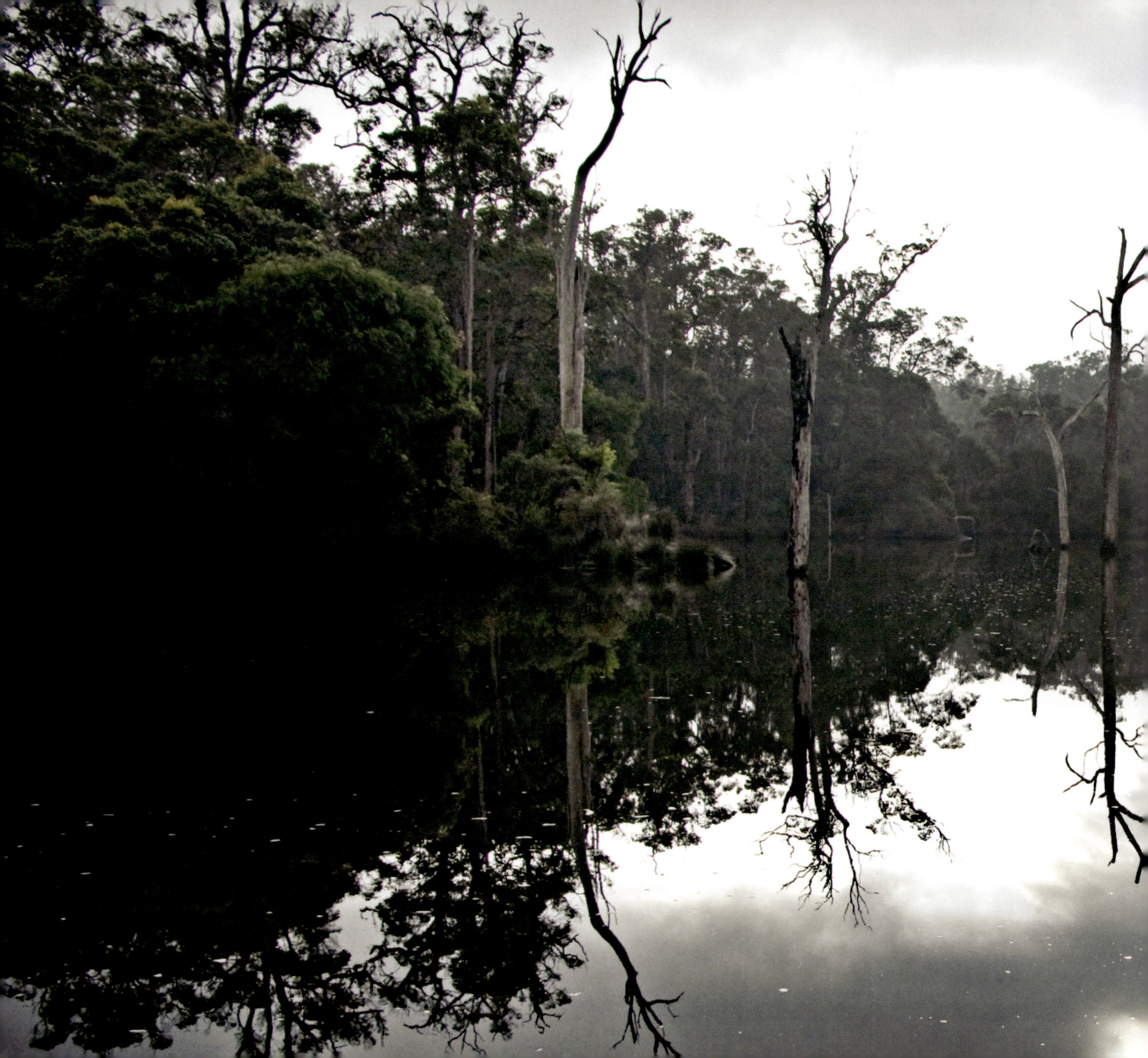

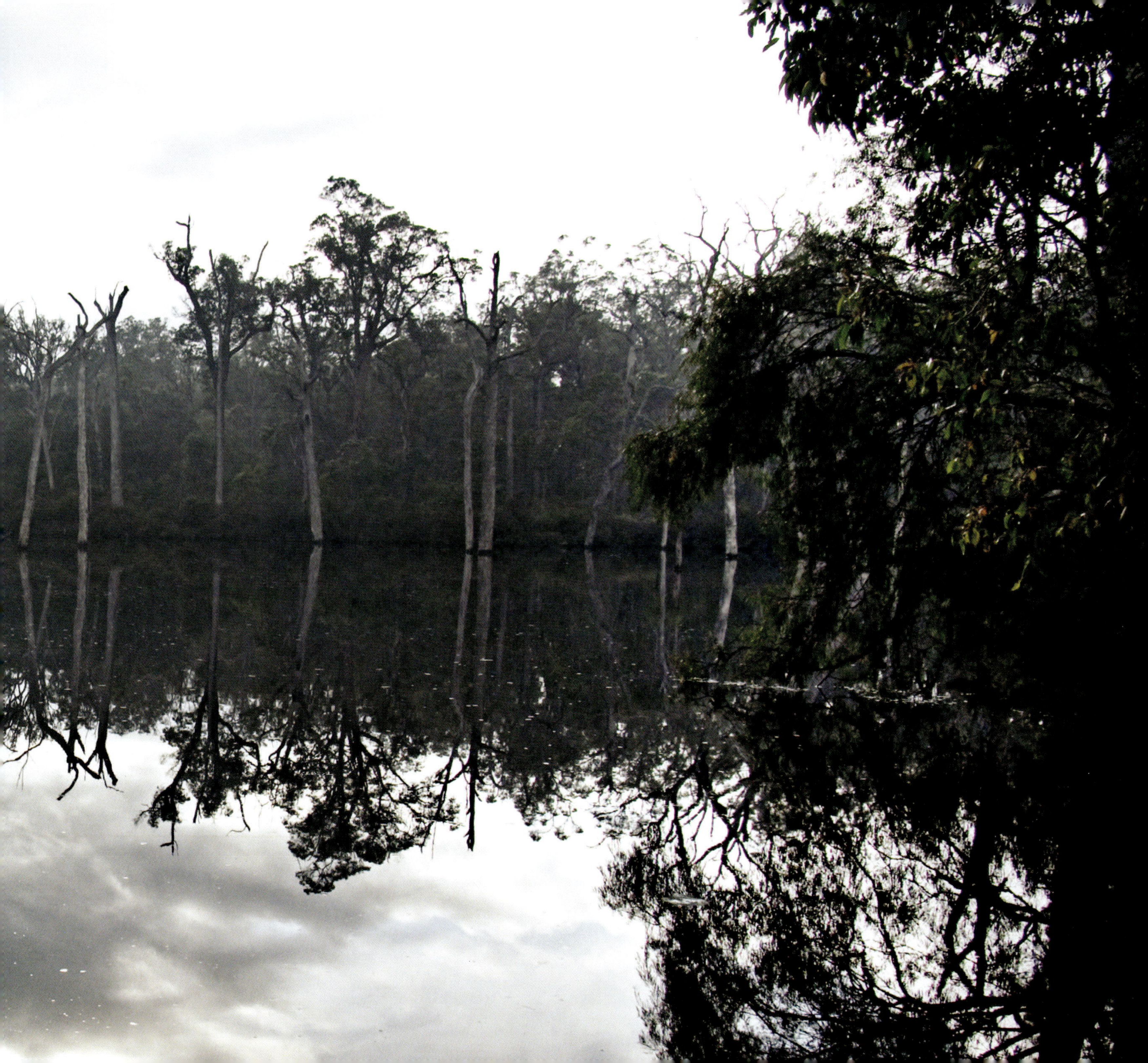

mains

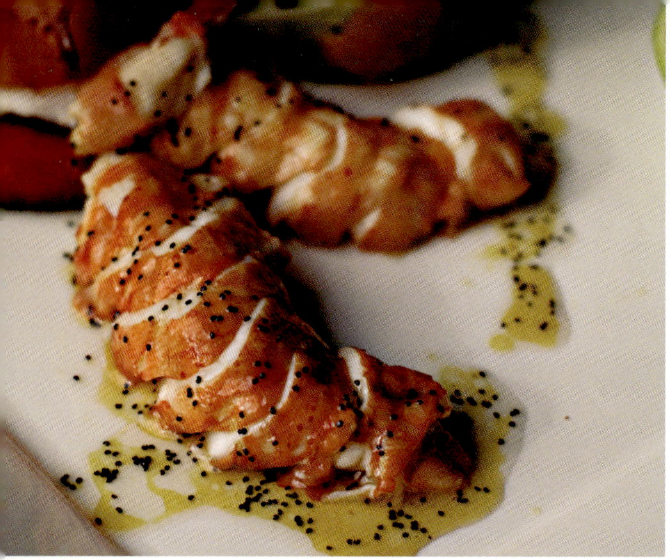

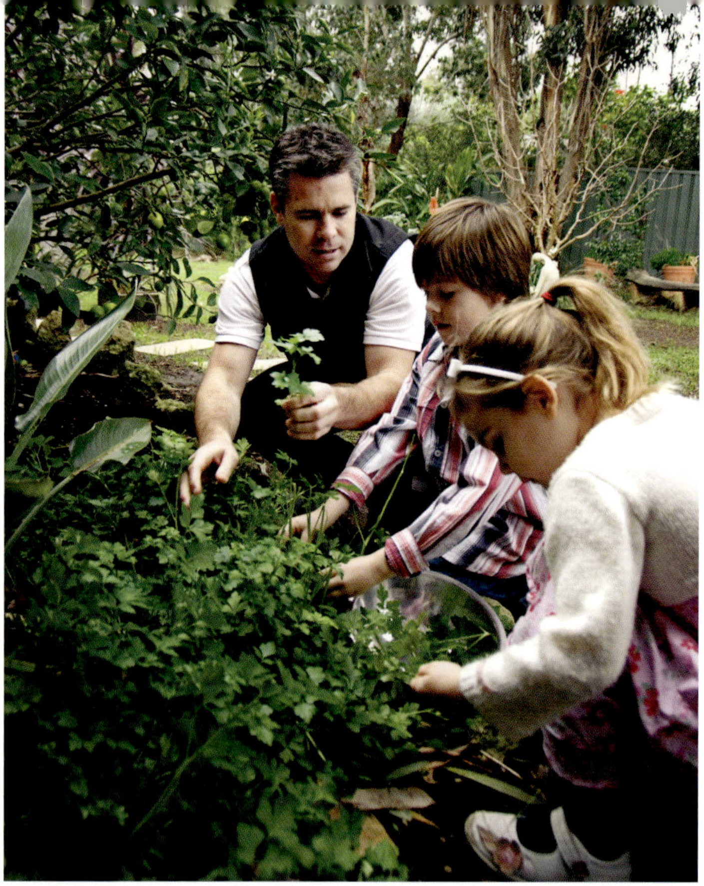

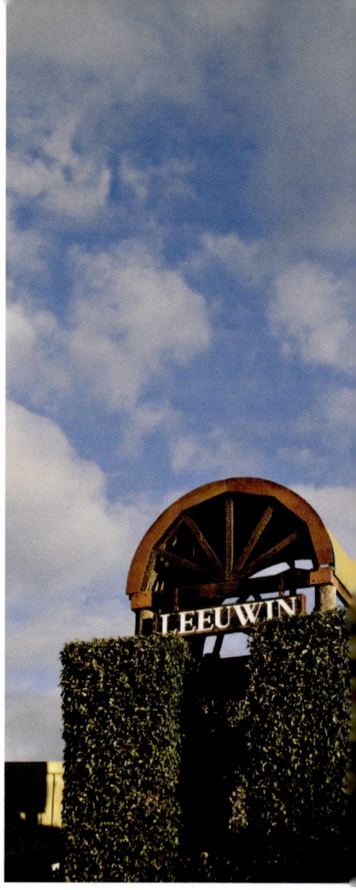
LEEUWIN

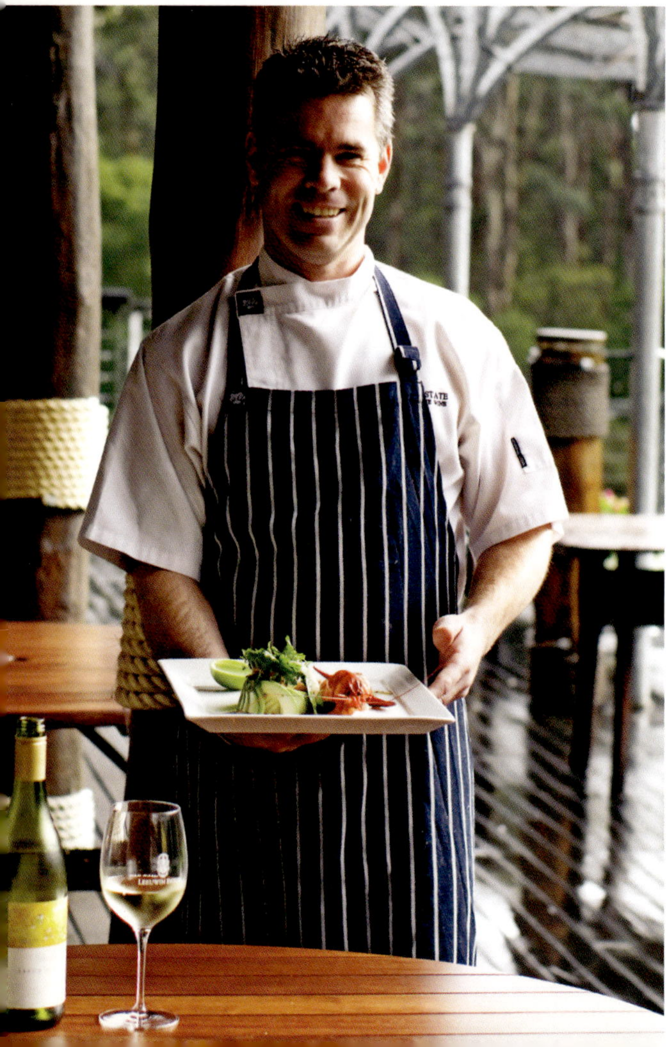

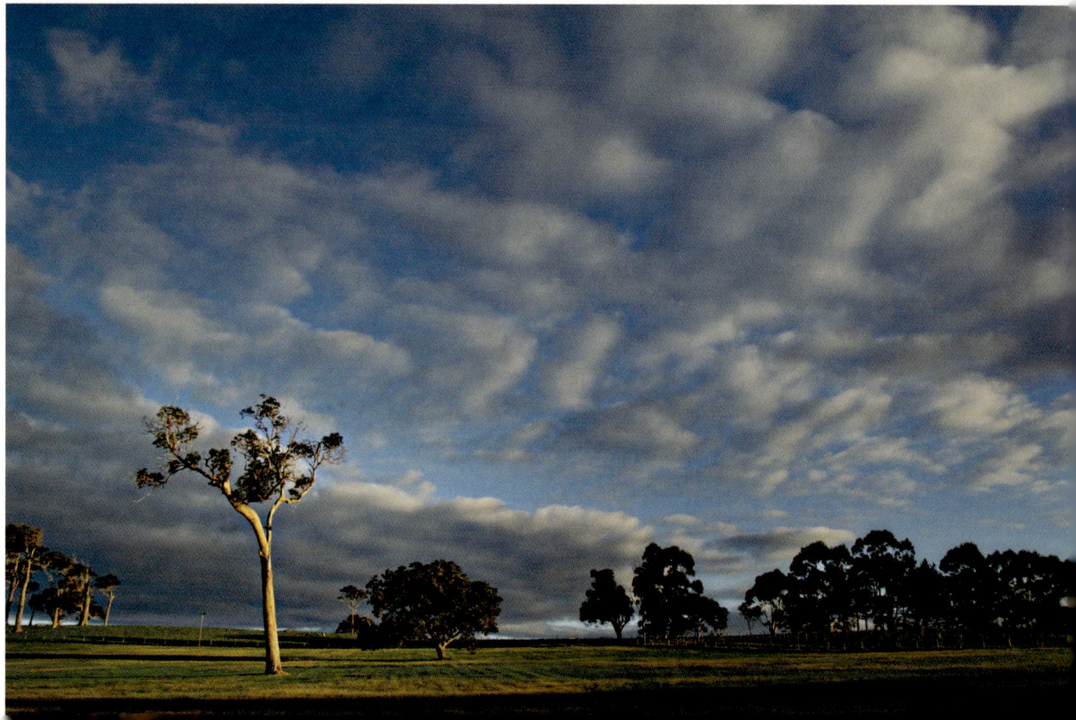

Dany Angove

LEEUWIN ESTATE, MARGARET RIVER

Dany was the first chef at acclaimed Margaret River dining room Vat 107 when it opened on the township's main street back in the late 1990s, and quickly became one of the region's most acclaimed chefs. (The property is now home to Must).

Dany has run the kitchen at Leeuwin Estate since 2007, supported by a loyal and well-trained team and matched by the company's highly-skilled and dedicated winemakers. The restaurant itself offers one of the best views in the region, overlooking manicured lawns, lush meadow and majestic Karri forest.

Since 1985, the winery has hosted an annual outdoor concert starring the likes of Diana Ross, Tom Jones, Jack Johnson and Chris Isaak.

And while Dany has appeared on television with Rockpool's Neil Perry and Margaret River resident Ian Parmenter, his star turn is undoubtedly as the guy behind the food at The Leeuwin Concert.

Faced with the mammoth task of providing 1400 hampers and 600 five-course meals, as well as looking after 100 catering staff, backstage crew and other performing artists, Dany and his team commence their preparation months ahead.

"We work out everything right down to how fast we can wash the plates," says Dany. "Everyone gets a book of tasks".

A signatory to the Greenpeace Chef's Charter for a GM-free Australia, Dany is passionate about healthy, fresh food, and he worries about the modern world's preoccupation with producing food as fast as possible. "All those preservatives and chemicals are not what I want to eat or serve," he says.

He's also concerned that too many young Australians don't know how to cook real food. "It's our responsibility as parents to reverse this in the next generation".

Dany spends as much time as he can in his home garden and kitchen, teaching his own children about food. "Finley is a pro at picking and chopping fresh herbs from the vegie patch," he reports. "As for Stella, she loves her cupcake-print apron and chef's hat!"

Dany also manages to find time to offer cooking classes, cook for friends and support SurfAid with fund-raising for its humanitarian work in the islands off Sumatra and Aceh.

Salad of Pemberton marron, smoked salmon, avocado

AND ORANGE POPPY SEED DRESSING

SERVES 4

MARRON
- 4 x 300 g whole marron
- 8 slices smoked salmon

SALAD
- 2 avocados
- 2 cups baby salad leaves
- ½ cup mixed herbs (chervil, parsley, chives, watercress, dill)

DRESSING
- 250 ml fresh orange juice
- 1 tbsp of poppy seeds
- 1 tbsp white sugar
- 50 ml chardonnay vinegar
- Sea salt
- Black pepper
- 1 tbsp extra virgin oil (optional)

Wine Match: Leeuwin Estate Art Series Chardonnay

METHOD

MARRON
Steam the marron for 12 minutes. Refresh in iced water. Peel the tail and keep the claws to one side. De-vein and then slice each tail in half lengthwise. Take the shell off the back half of claws, exposing the flesh.

DRESSING
Reduce orange juice and sugar over medium heat until there is approximately 100 ml left. Let juice cool, then add poppy seeds and whisk in the vinegar. Season to taste with sea salt and black pepper. If you prefer a richer, slightly creamier dressing, whisk in the olive oil.

TO SERVE
Halve each avocado and remove stone. Remove flesh from shell in one piece by gently sliding a large spoon between the flesh and the shell. With the cut side of the avocado face down, cut into neat slices and, using your hands, gently splay these into a circle on each plate. Cut marron tail halves into slices and neatly place them next to avocado. Mix together salad ingredients and smoked salmon, lightly toss in the dressing and place on top of the avocado. To finish, drizzle marron tails with dressing and place two marron claws and the head next to marron flesh.

Salad of Pemberton marron, smoked salmon, avocado

AND ORANGE POPPY SEED DRESSING

DANY ANGOVE
LEEUWIN ESTATE
RECIPE - SEE PAGE 52

Roast barramundi, Puy lentils,

CHARRED BABY LEEK, SMOKED BONE MARROW, POTATO FONDANT AND JUS GRAS.

AARON CARR
VASSE FELIX
RECIPE - SEE PAGE 58

VASSE FELIX
4357
Cellar Door, Restaurant,
Gallery, Sculpture Walk

DEUS

Aaron Carr

VASSE FELIX, COWARAMUP

One of Margaret River's original surfing chefs, Aaron moved to the coastal region in his early 20s. For the past 15 years he has worked as executive chef at the iconic Vasse Felix restaurant.

"I just fell into cooking," he says. "School wasn't interesting to me, but I did some work experience in a kitchen and I liked all the excitement and commotion".

Juggling a young family with work means that these days Aaron doesn't have as much time for surfing as he once did. Mind you, he still pays the occasional visit to his favourite surfing spot, Three Bears, which lies on his route to work.

"I can't complain," he says. "I don't have to cook a dinner service, which means I work substantially fewer hours than many of my colleagues in the industry. Plus we get a lot of freedom to cook what we want".

The internet has revolutionised the way Aaron and his team work in the kitchen.

"I get home at night and spend hours online watching everyone do such different things," says Aaron. "It's very exciting".

He is particularly taken with the sous vide ("under vacuum") technique, where food is sealed in bags and cooked very gently in a hot water bath.

"We've been doing it at Vasse Felix for about five years," says Aaron. "It's gives a really nice, slow heat and means you can consistently cook to exact temperatures, which takes away a lot of the guesswork".

When it comes to remaining at the top of his game, Aaron says there's no substitute or way around hard work. "There's a lot of trial and error on the way to perfecting a new dish".

He believes that television cooking shows like Masterchef have their negatives and positives, says Aaron. "While I like how they've made people realise ours isn't an easy job, they also offer an unrealistically glamorous short cut to the world of being a chef".

"In the real world, you've got to do it the hard way. If someone came here from Masterchef, they'd start from the bottom and work their way up. They'd have to prove themselves, just like everyone else".

Roast barramundi, Puy lentils,

CHARRED BABY LEEK, SMOKED BONE MARROW,
POTATO FONDANT AND JUS GRAS.

SERVES 4

BARRAMUNDI
- 4x 180 g portions of barramundi, skin on

JUS GRAS
- 250 g chicken wings, roughly chopped
- 2 shallots, roughly chopped
- 1 carrot, peeled and roughly chopped
- 2 celery sticks, roughly chopped
- 100 ml port
- 100 ml sherry
- Sprig of thyme
- 1 bay leaf
- 1 tbsp vegetable oil
- 1 L water

To be added later to the jus gras:
- 100 g salted butter
- Juice of ½ a lemon

SMOKED BONE MARROW
- 4x4 cm centre-cut bone marrow (ask your butcher to do this)
- 200 g vine cuttings
- 1 L water
- 70 g salt
- 50 g jasmine rice
- 50 g brown sugar
- 25 g jasmine tea leaves (optional)

LENTILS
- 200 g Puy lentils
- 1 carrot, peeled and roughly chopped
- 1 stalk celery, roughly chopped
- 1 leek, white part only, washed and roughly chopped
- 2 bay leaves
- 1 brown onion, finely diced
- 2 cloves garlic, minced
- 100 g pancetta, finely diced
- 350 ml chicken stock*
- olive oil
- salt and pepper

*Chicken stock recipe - see page 142

POTATO FONDANT
- 400 g potatoes, peeled and cut into 12 barrel shapes approximately 3cm x 2cm
- 100 g butter
- 300 ml chicken stock
- 2 sprigs of thyme
- 2 garlic cloves

LEEKS
- 8 baby leeks, washed and trimmed

TO FINISH
- Olive oil
- Sea salt
- Baby herbs (celery, mustard cress, basil)

METHOD

JUS GRAS
Pre-heat your oven to 200°C. In a large baking tray, roast the chicken wings until they are golden brown. Meanwhile, heat a large saucepan, add vegetable oil and fry the shallots, carrots and celery until golden brown. Add the roasted chicken wings. Remove as much fat as possible from the baking tray. Pour remaining cooking juices and tray scrapings into a small saucepan and place onto a high heat. Add the port and reduce by ½, stirring constantly. Add the sherry and reduce by ½ again. Pour liquid into saucepan with the vegetables and chicken wings. Add water and herbs and bring to the boil. Reduce heat to a simmer and skim any impurities that rise to the top. Reduce the jus until you have approximately 200 ml. Strain the jus through a cloth and refrigerate until needed.

SMOKED BONE MARROW
Soak the bone marrow overnight in the refrigerator in cold salted water. Remove from the fridge and push the bone marrow centres out of the bone using the top of a wooden spoon (they should slide out easily). Mix together the rice, sugar and tea leaves and place them on a sheet of aluminum foil in the bottom of a wok. Put the bone marrow on a small cake rack and place this above the smoking mix. Cover with more foil. Heat the wok on the stove. Once the mix starts smoking, cook the marrow for four minutes. Remove from the wok and place immediately into the refrigerator. When cold, cut each piece of marrow into three. Cover and reserve for later use.

POTATO FONDANT
In a small saucepan, melt the butter on medium heat. Add the potatoes and cook slowly, shaking the pan so they don't stick. Once potatoes are golden, add the stock, thyme and garlic and bring to a simmer. Cook for 30-40 minutes or until the potatoes are tender. Keep warm for later use.

LENTILS
In a sieve, wash the lentils over the sink then place them into a large pot with enough water to cover the vegetables and lentils. Bring to the boil and simmer for four minutes. Drain and remove the vegetables. Place lentils into a large pot with a little olive oil and cook on high for 30 seconds or so. Add the onion, garlic and pancetta. Reduce heat to low and cook until onions are tender and the pancetta crisp. Add the chicken stock and simmer for a further 4-6 minutes or until the lentils are cooked but still firm. Remove from the heat and keep warm.

Wine Match: Vasse Felix Heytesbury Chardonnay

LEEKS
Blanch the leeks in a pot of boiling salted water for 30 seconds. Remove from the heat and refresh in iced water.

TO FINISH
Pre-heat your oven to 200°C. Remove the jus from the fridge and scrape off any fat that may have set on top and discard. In a small saucepan, add the butter and place onto a high heat. Cook until the butter stops frothing and starts to turn golden brown. Remove from the heat. Add a good squeeze of the lemon juice and then stir in the jus. Place the sauce back onto the heat and warm through. Reserve in a warm spot. Lay the leeks flat onto a baking tray and, using a blowtorch, char until they are evenly colored. Heat an ovenproof frying pan big enough to hold the four serves of fish. Add a pinch of sea salt and a good drizzle of olive oil. When hot, place the fish skin side down and cook for one minute. Transfer the pan into the oven and cook for four minutes. Remove from the oven and turn the fish over. Place back into oven for a further two minutes or until the fish is just cooked. Place the smoked bone marrow into the hot pan to allow it to warm through, stirring occasionally.

TO SERVE
Place two leeks in the centre of each serving plate and top with a spoonful of the lentils. Arrange three potato fondants and bone marrow around the plate. Remove barramundi from the pan and place on top of the lentils. Drizzle a little jus gras around the plate and sprinkle with some of the micro herbs.

Serve to your guests and pat yourself on the back!

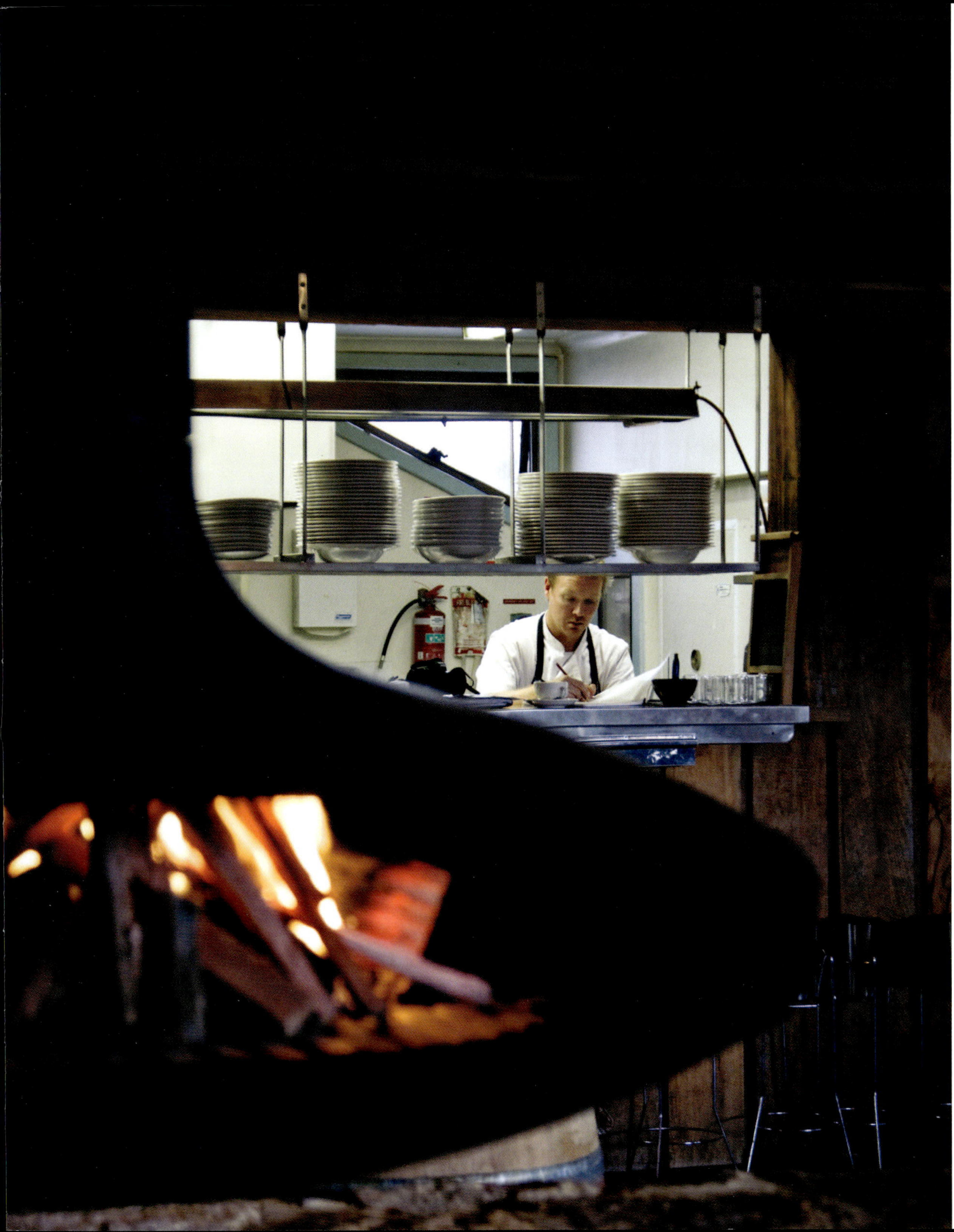

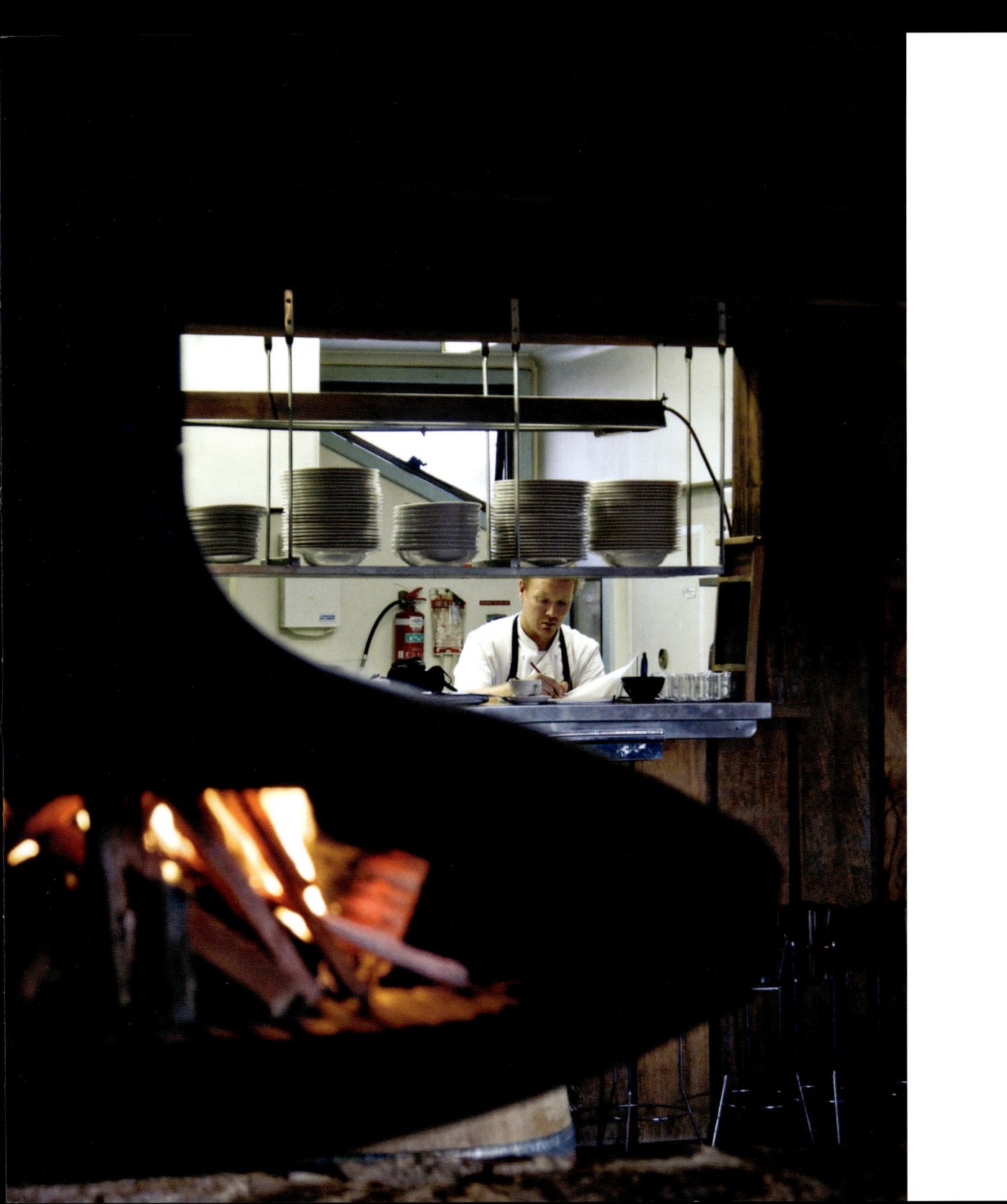

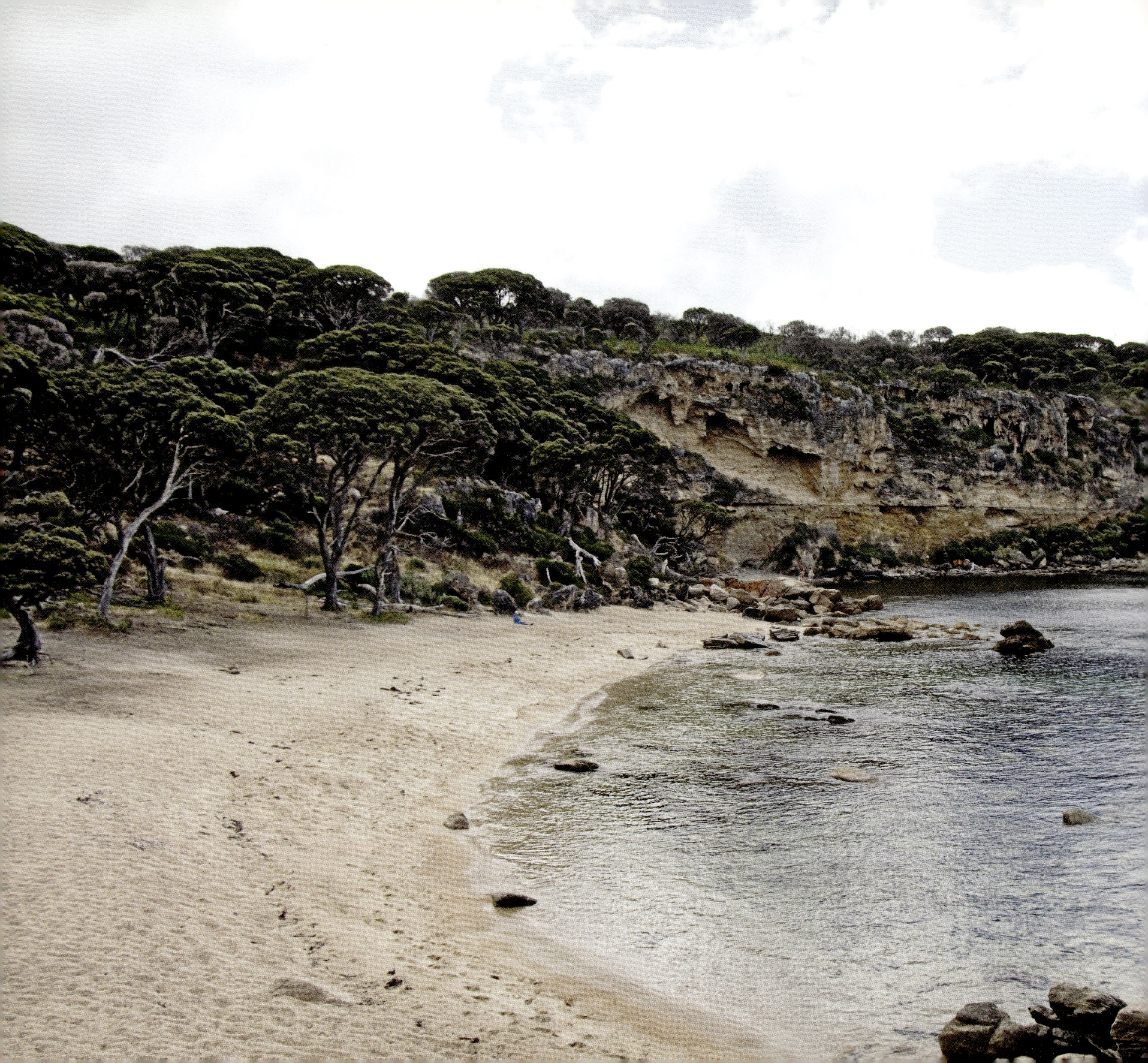

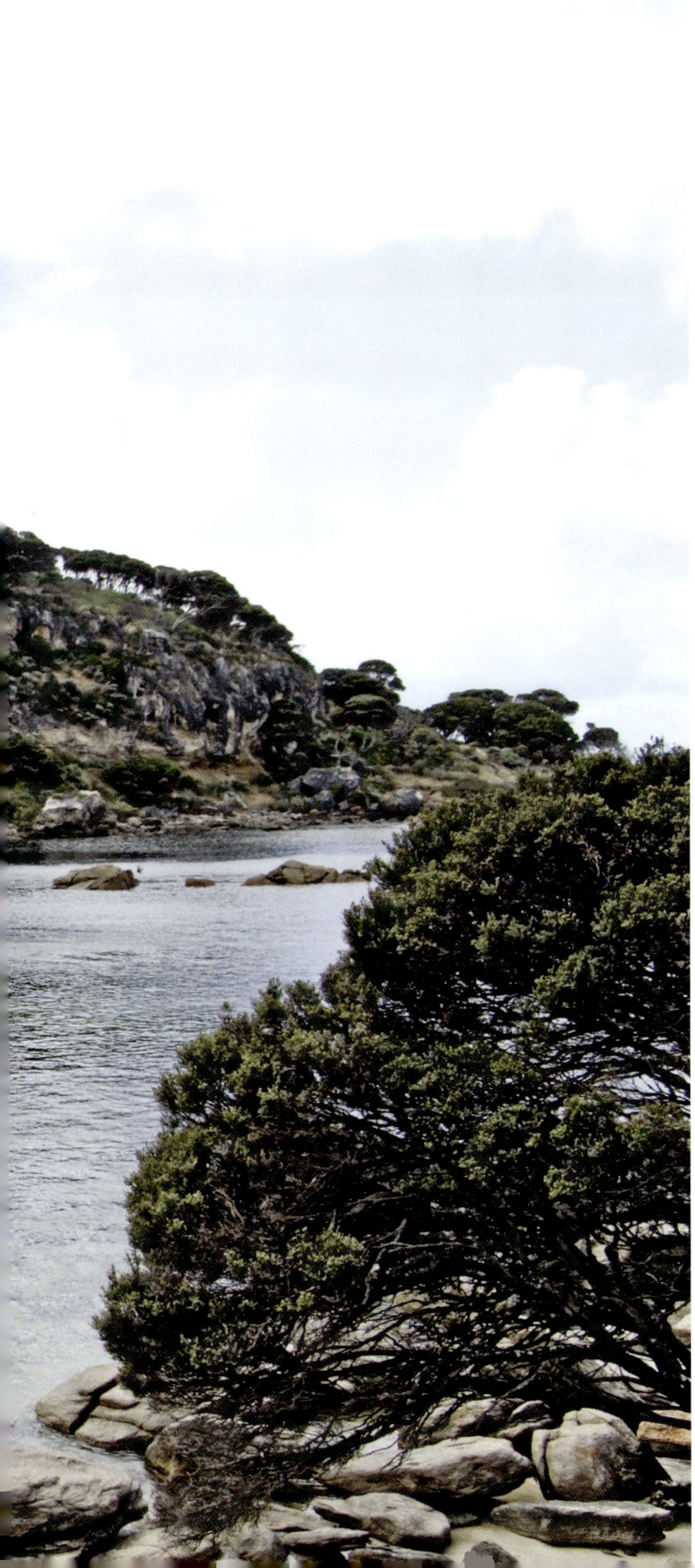

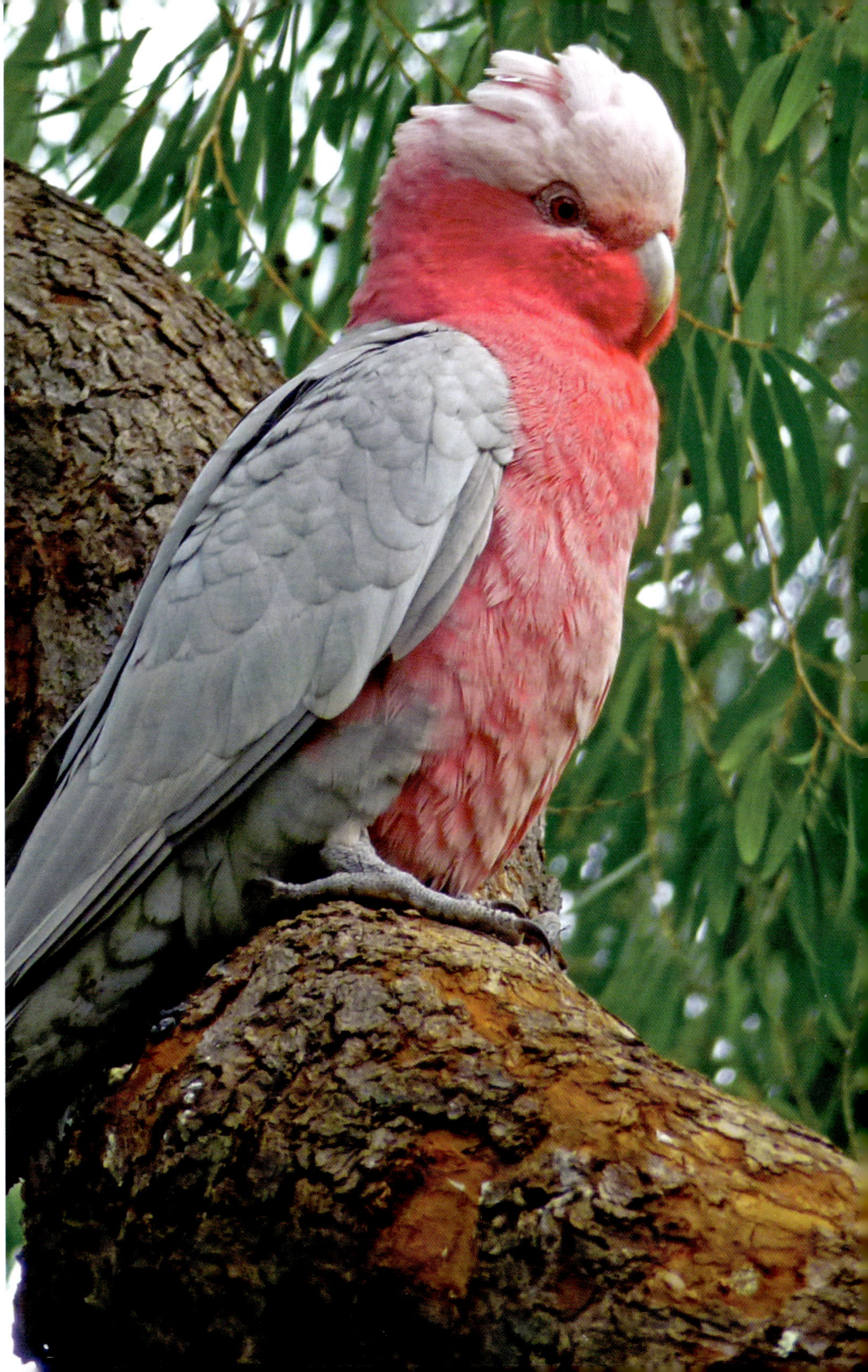

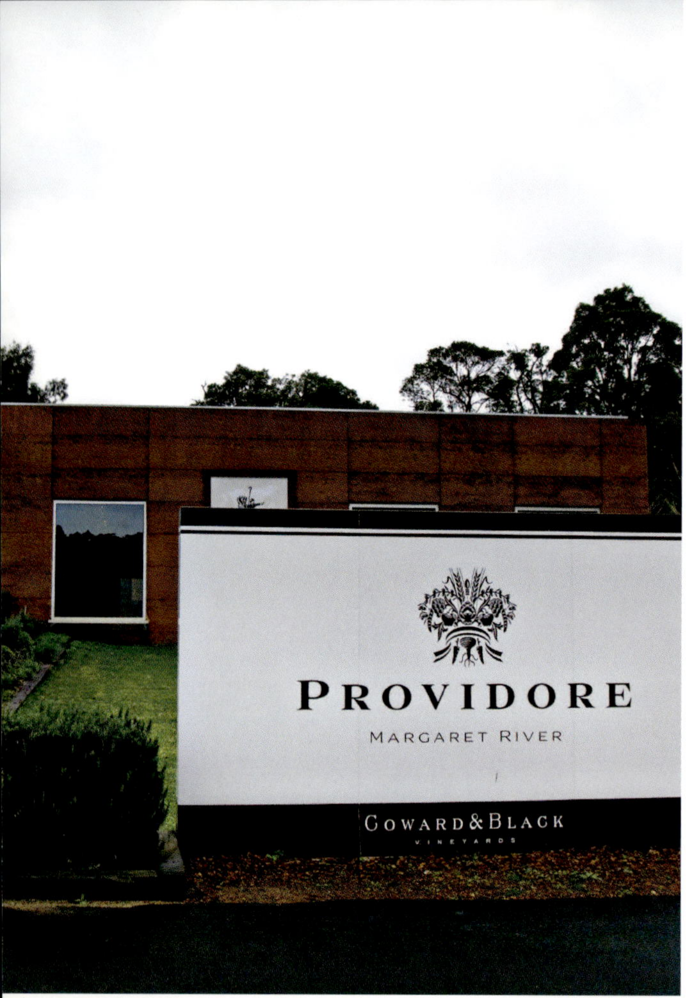
PROVIDORE
MARGARET RIVER
COWARD&BLACK

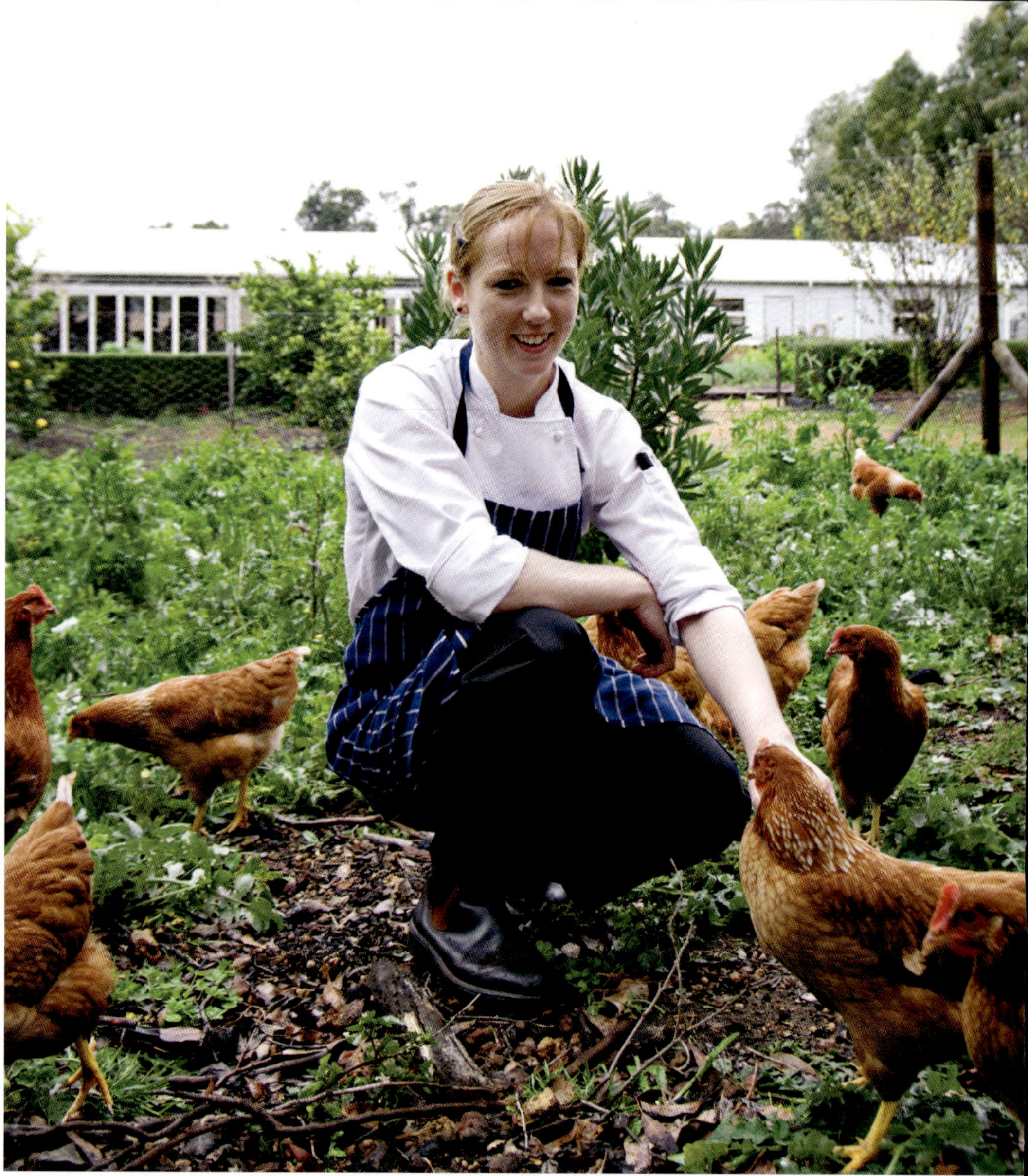

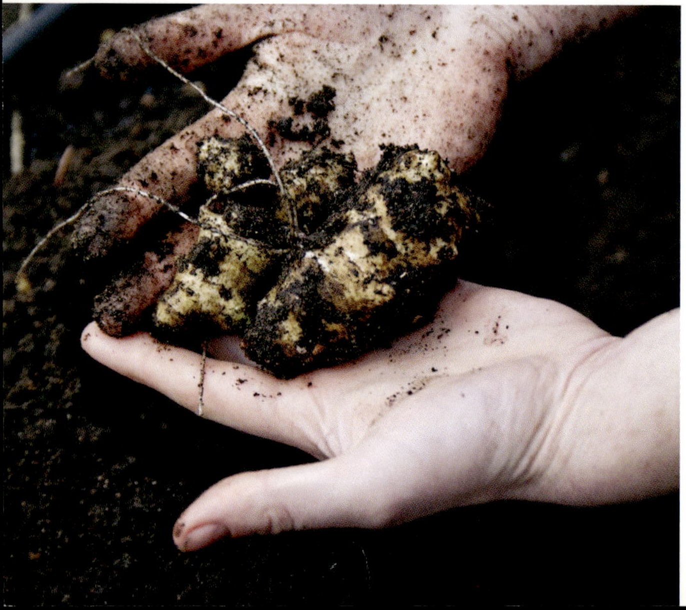

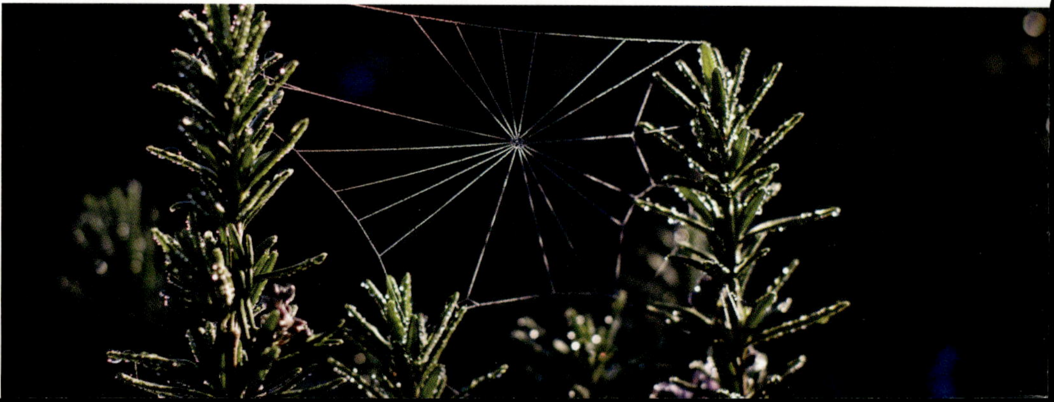

Claire Donohue

PROVIDORE, WILYABRUP

Claire moved from New Zealand in 2010 to work at Providore. And while she draws her culinary inspiration from a wide range of people, top of her list is Trixie Timney, an 80-year-old neighbour from back home in Auckland.

"Trixie used to bake up a storm, spoiling us kids with pikelets, pinwheel scones and delicious pastries," says Claire, "I'm still using a 100 year-old recipe for Worcestershire sauce she gave me".

Having grown up in New Zealand, a country famed for its natural beauty, Margaret River seemed an obvious choice for Claire's next career move. What's more, she says she's set to stay. "When your surroundings are forests, vineyards and beaches, why would you want to leave?"

A graduate of Auckland University of Technology, Claire received on-the-job training as a cold larder chef at Carriages Cafe in Auckland, where she worked her way up to acting head chef. Set in the heart of Kumeu Wine Country, this classic 1930s style restaurant is an institution. Claire went on to be sous chef at nearby Gracehill Vineyard Estate, where she specialised in weddings and private functions.

Today she uses produce from the Providore garden to make an array of own-made jams, preserves, sauces, salad dressings and vinegars.

"From my kitchen I can see the half-acre organic vegetable garden, our small orchard and 40 free-range chickens. Their organic eggs go into baked treats served in the cafe".

Claire loves this closeness to the ground. "One day you're picking eggplants and fresh herbs, the next day you're digging up Jerusalem artichokes. I couldn't ask for more from my job".

When she's not in the garden trying to get to the figs before the birds, or coming up with new ways to distract the parrots from her strawberries, Claire enjoys watching Providore's many visitors enjoying the garden.

"I often find myself lingering to chat about the types of plants we're growing here. It's great to see people getting inspired enough to grow their own garden at home," she says.

Crispy confit duck

WITH ORGANIC SPINACH AND BEETROOT SALAD, PERSIAN FETA AND POMEGRANATE GLAZE

SERVES 4

CONFIT DUCK
- 50 g sea salt
- 3 sprigs of thyme
- 3 garlic cloves, crushed
- 4 duck legs
- 750 g duck fat

ROAST BEETROOT
- 200 g whole beetroot (reserve and use leaves for the salad)
- ½ cup water
- 20 ml oil
- Salt and pepper

SPICED PUMPKIN SEEDS
- 100 g pumpkin seeds
- 1 tsp smoked paprika
- ½ tsp garlic powder
- ½ tsp salt
- 1 tsp oil

POMEGRANATE GLAZE
- 250 ml pomegranate molasses
- (As an alternative to pomegranate molasses you can use vincotto)
- ¼ cup brown sugar

ORGANIC SPINACH & BEETROOT LEAF SALAD
- 200 g organic baby spinach
- Beetroot leaves
- 150 g Persian feta
- Small handful of Italian parsley

BALSAMIC VINAIGRETTE
- 50 ml good quality balsamic vinegar
- 75 ml extra virgin olive oil
- Salt and pepper to taste

Wine Match: Coward & Black Cabernet Sauvignon. Enjoy!

METHOD

CONFIT DUCK

Combine salt, thyme and garlic in a large dish. Add the duck legs in a single layer and rub all over with the salt mixture. Cover and refrigerate overnight or for at least 12 hours. Brush salt off the duck legs, pat dry and place in a single layer in a deep roasting dish. Pre-heat the oven to 100°C. Melt the duck fat over a low heat, then pour over the duck legs until they are totally submerged. Bake until the meat is just about to fall of the bone – this usually takes 1-2 hours. Let the duck cool but remove from the fat before it solidifies.

ROAST BEETROOT

Pre-heat the oven to 175°C. Cut the beetroot into 2 cm dice and place in a roasting pan with the water, reserving beetroot leaves for the salad (see below). Cover with foil and steam until just tender. Remove foil, drain and toss beetroot in oil. Season with the salt and pepper and roast for 10 minutes or until nicely coloured.

PUMPKIN SEEDS

Pre-heat oven to 170°C. Toss all the ingredients together and place in a shallow roasting dish. Bake for five minutes.

POMEGRANATE GLAZE

In a small saucepan on a low heat, stir the two ingredients together until the brown sugar has dissolved. Leave to cool.

SALAD

Wash and pat dry spinach, reserved beetroot leaves and parsley. Toss together with Persian feta.

TO SERVE

Place the salad into a bowl and lightly dress with balsamic vinaigrette . Sprinkle with the spiced pumpkin seeds and roast beetroot. Divide onto four plates. Heat a pan with a little of the duck fat. Place the duck skin side down and sear until golden and crisp. Place the crispy duck on top of the salad and drizzle lightly with pomegranate glaze.

Crispy confit duck

WITH ORGANIC SPINACH AND BEETROOT SALAD, PERSIAN FETA AND POMEGRANATE GLAZE

CLAIRE DONOHUE
PROVIDORE
RECIPE - SEE PAGE 66

Margaret River venison

WITH ROASTED PUMPKIN, PAPARDELLE, BEETROOT PUREE, SAUTÉED SPINACH AND CHOCOLATE-INFUSED JUS.

NIGEL HARVEY
VOYAGER
RECIPE - SEE PAGE 72

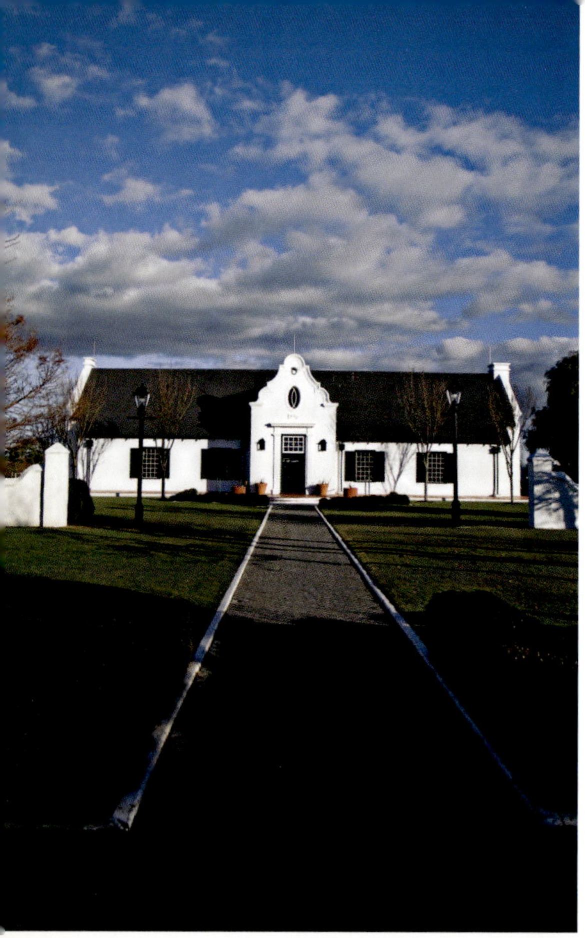
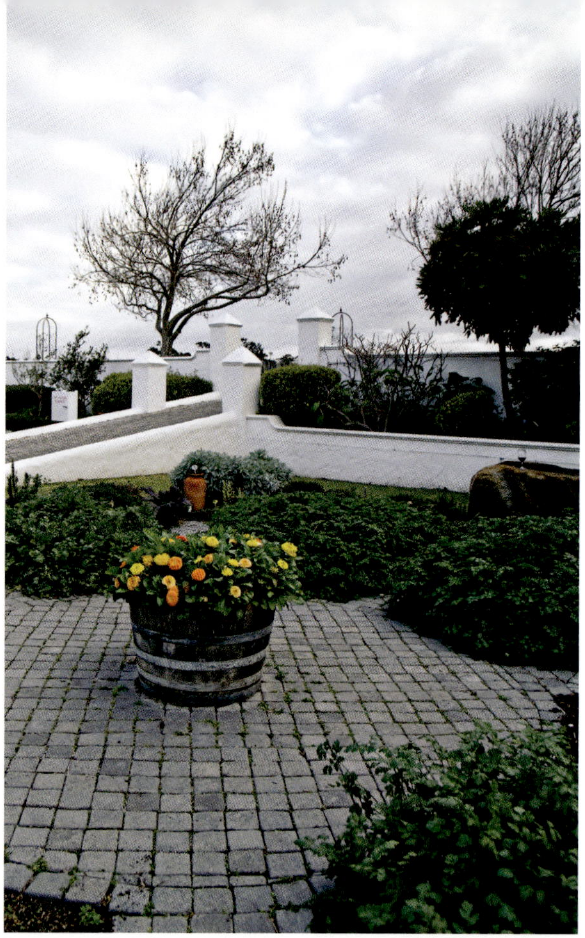
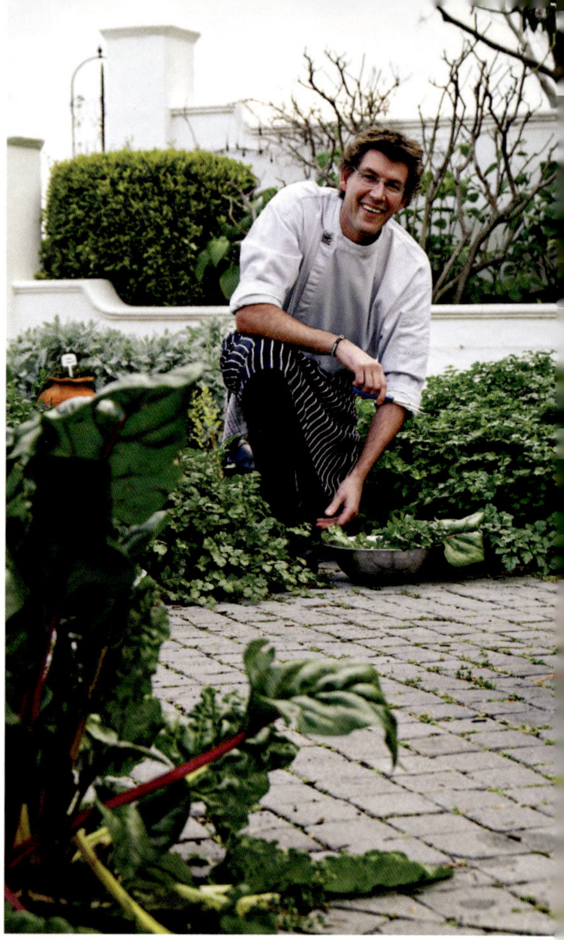
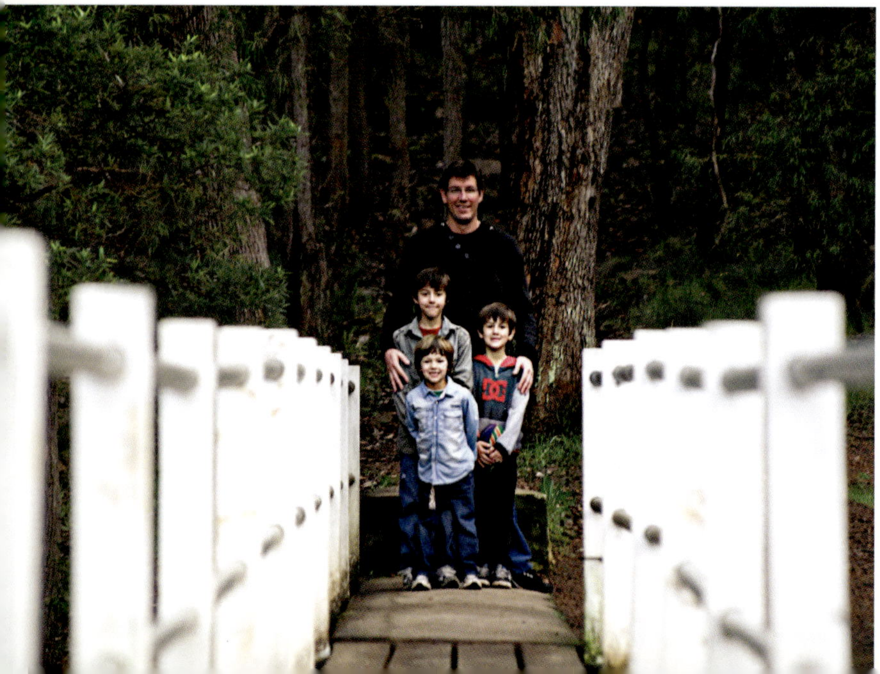
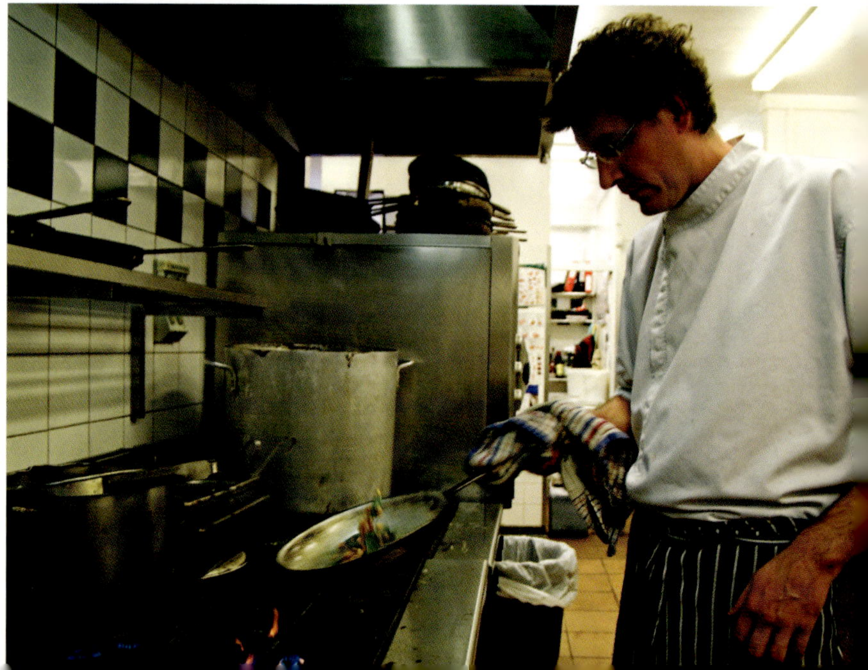

Nigel Harvey

VOYAGER ESTATE, MARGARET RIVER

A doting father of three young boys, Nigel relocated his family from the east coast to Western Australia in search of a better work-life balance.

"It's such a beautiful place to live," he says. "My wife Kellene and I take our kids down to the beach and we often go kayaking at the weir. I love getting the kids out of the house, away from the electronic games and televisions to have some quality time together".

Since joining Voyager in 2004, Nigel has played a key role in establishing the winery restaurant's reputation as one of Australia's best. He says he's lucky to be surrounded by people who share his passion for taking the finest ingredients and turning them into something special to share.

"Every aspect of Voyager, from the Cape Dutch architecture to the gardeners who maintain our stunning gardens and meticulous vineyards, inspires me".

The acclaimed chef says his greatest lesson is that success depends on dedication and passion. "Being a chef is tough and stressful. The hours are long, it's always a hands-on role and to be good you have to constantly seek ways to improve and vary the food you produce".

Nigel's favourite chefs include renowned Sydneysider Tetsuya Wakuda and Alain Fabregues, owner-chef of The Loose Box in the Perth Hills.

Nigel says he has also learned and drawn inspiration from kitchen teams past and present.

"I've worked with some of the most amazing people, who bring out the best in each other. Being involved in their ideas and enthusiasm is great".

The chef has won many awards during his time at Voyager, notably the 2006 Premier's Award for best restaurant in Western Australia. But it's the smile on a customer's face that drives him to produce food of the best standard possible.

"Above all, hearing someone say 'That was the best meal I've ever eaten' continues to be my most significant achievement".

Margaret River venison

WITH ROASTED PUMPKIN, PAPARDELLE, BEETROOT PUREE, SAUTÉED SPINACH AND CHOCOLATE-INFUSED JUS.

SERVES 4

VENISON
- 700 g venison silverside

PASTA
- 350 g 00 flour
- 3 whole eggs
- 4 egg yolks
- 25 ml olive oil
- Pinch of sea salt

BEETROOT PUREE
- 4 whole beetroot
- 1 garlic clove
- 50 ml sherry vinegar
- 15 g caster sugar
- Salt and pepper to taste

ROAST PUMPKIN
- ½ butternut pumpkin
- Olive oil

CHOCOLATE INFUSED JUS
- 500 ml good beef stock*
- 1 Spanish onion
- 1 tsp soft brown sugar
- 100 ml red wine
- 50 g 70% dark chocolate

SAUTÉED SPINACH
- 250 g baby spinach
- Small ladle of clarified butter
- 1 thinly sliced purple eschallot
- Salt and pepper to taste

*Beef stock recipe - see page 142

METHOD

PASTA
Add all ingredients to a bowl mixer fitted with a dough hook. Mix until just coming together. Turn out onto floured bench and knead for 10 minutes, then rest in the fridge for at least ½ an hour. Run the rested dough through a pasta machine until it reaches gauge 5. Lay out on a floured bench and cut into wide strips, using the edge of a ruler to keep strips the same width. Lay on greaseproof paper until needed.

BEETROOT PUREE
In a saucepan, cover the unpeeled beetroot with water, bring to the boil and cook until soft. Run under cold water, peel and cut into rough dice. Place cubed beetroot into food processor with garlic and blitz until pureed and smooth. Return to saucepan. Add sherry and sugar. Season to taste. Cook for 10 minutes, until flavours are mellow and sweet.

ROAST PUMPKIN
Peel pumpkin and cut into 1-2 cm dice. Place on a baking tray and toss with olive oil. Season with salt and pepper and cook in oven for eight minutes or until just tender. Place to one side until needed.

CHOCOLATE-INFUSED JUS
In a heavy-based pot, gently sauté the onion and sugar in a little oil until soft and caramelised. Add red wine, scraping up any bits from the pan. Reduce by ¾. Add beef stock, bring to the boil and reduce again by ½. Add chopped chocolate and reduce until jus starts to thicken.

TO SERVE
Pre-heat oven to 200°C. Sauté venison quickly on both sides to seal, then place in oven and cook to desired tenderness (Nigel recommends medium). In a large pan of salted boiling water, cook pasta for three minutes or until tender. In a heavy-based pan, melt butter and sauté sliced eschallot, spinach and the roasted pumpkin. Season to taste. Place cooked pasta in a circle on plate using a large biscuit cutter or circular mould. Smear warm beetroot puree on the plate. Cut rested venison in half and let any excess blood run free before placing on puree. Drizzle with jus. Enjoy!

Wine Match:
Voyager Estate
Cabernet Sauvignon
Merlot

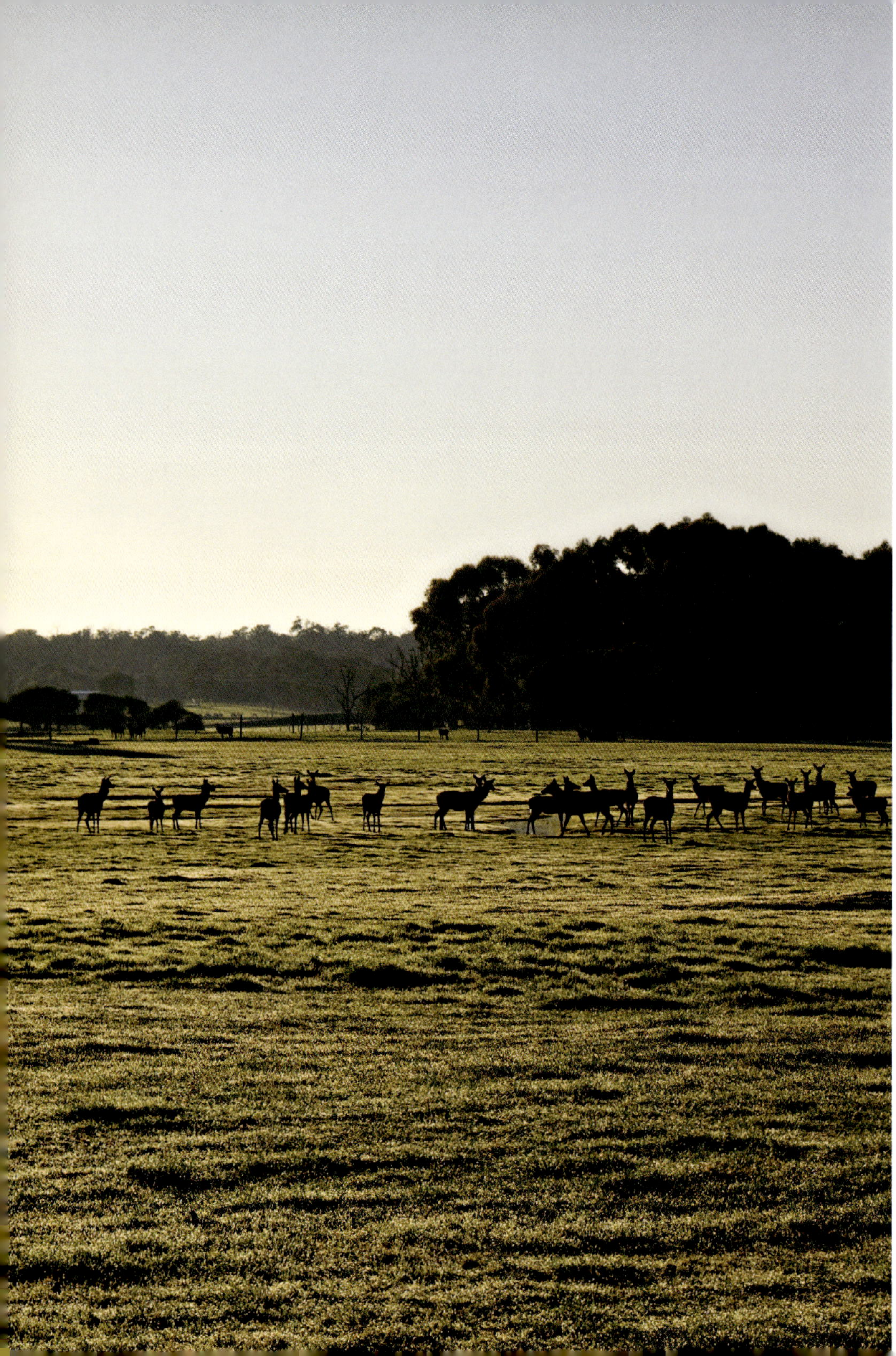

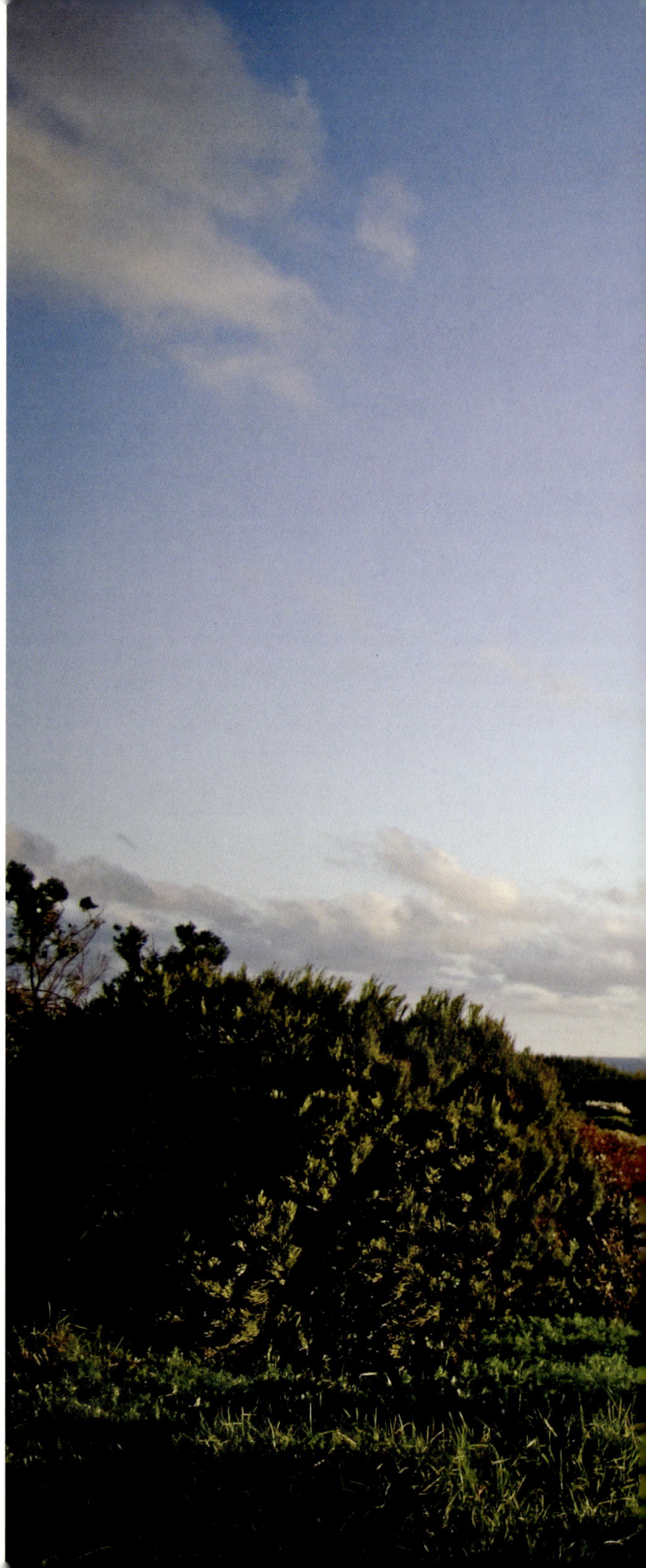

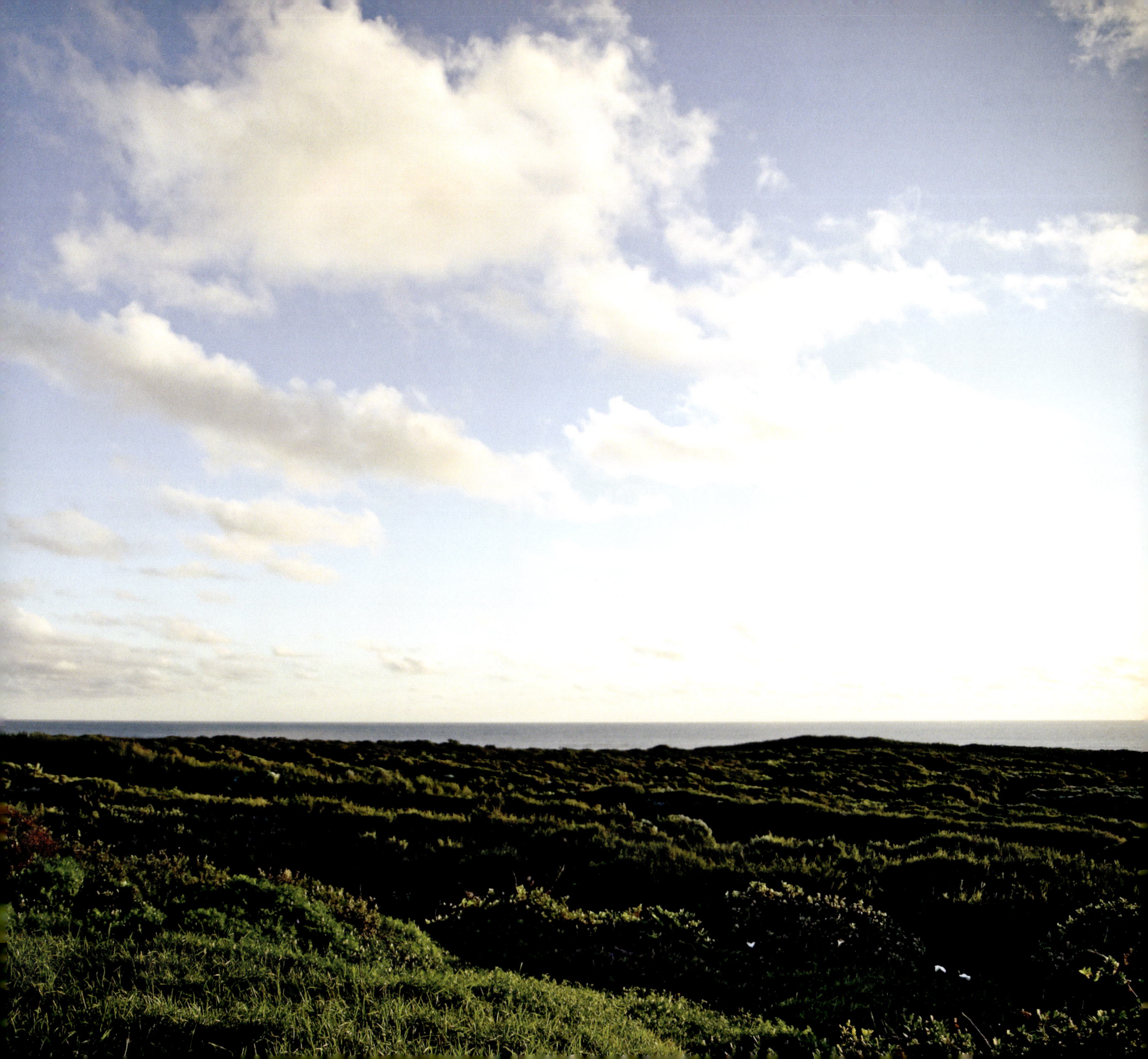

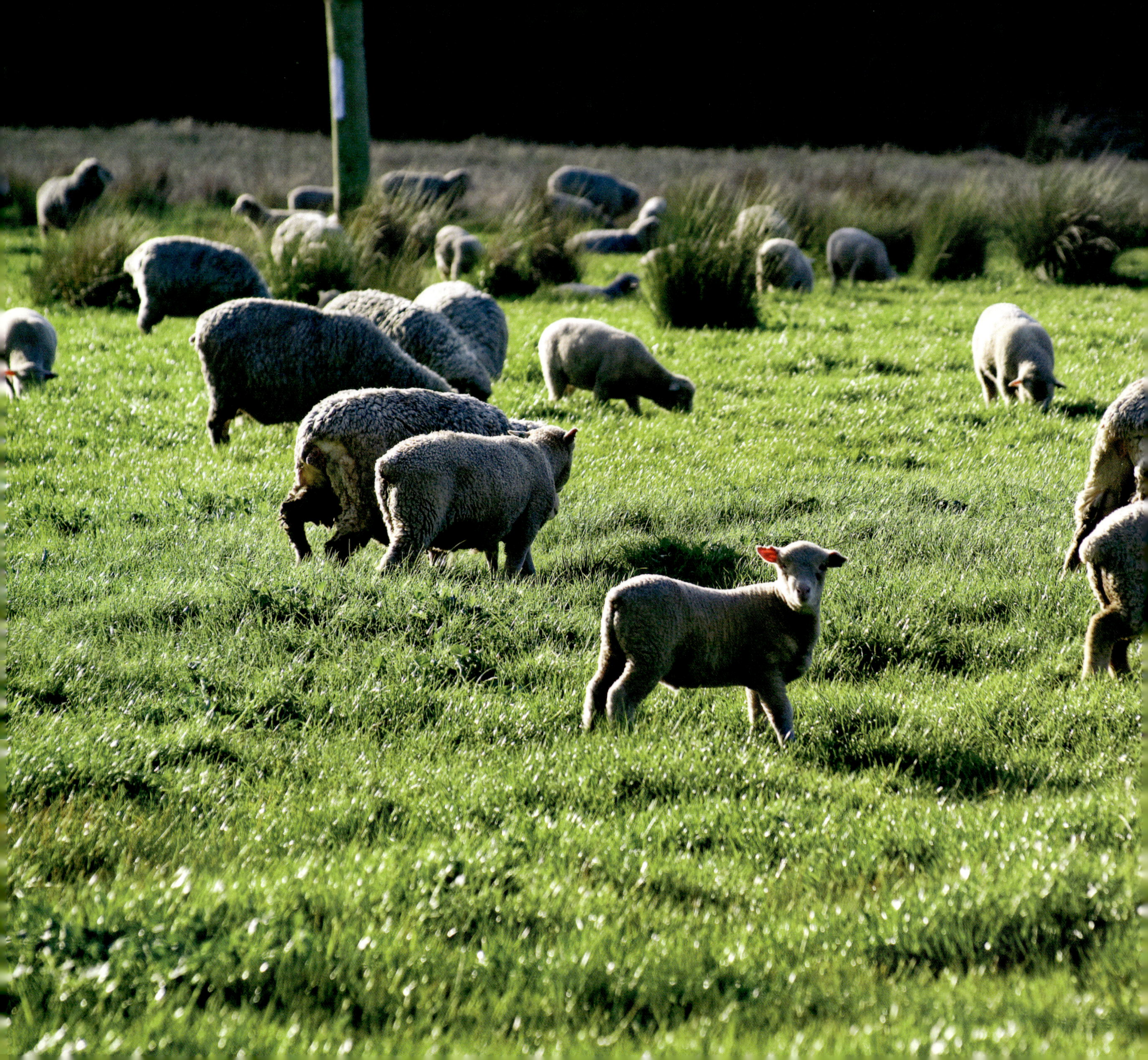

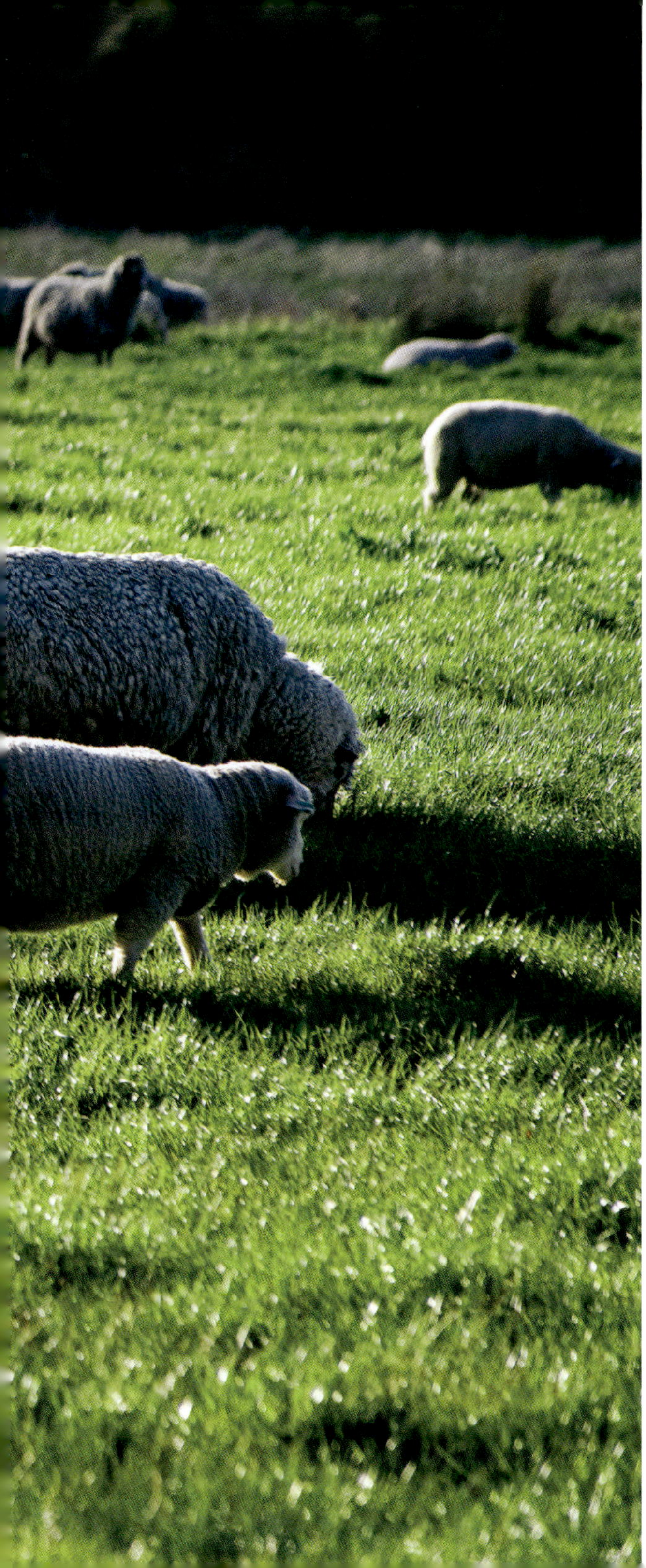
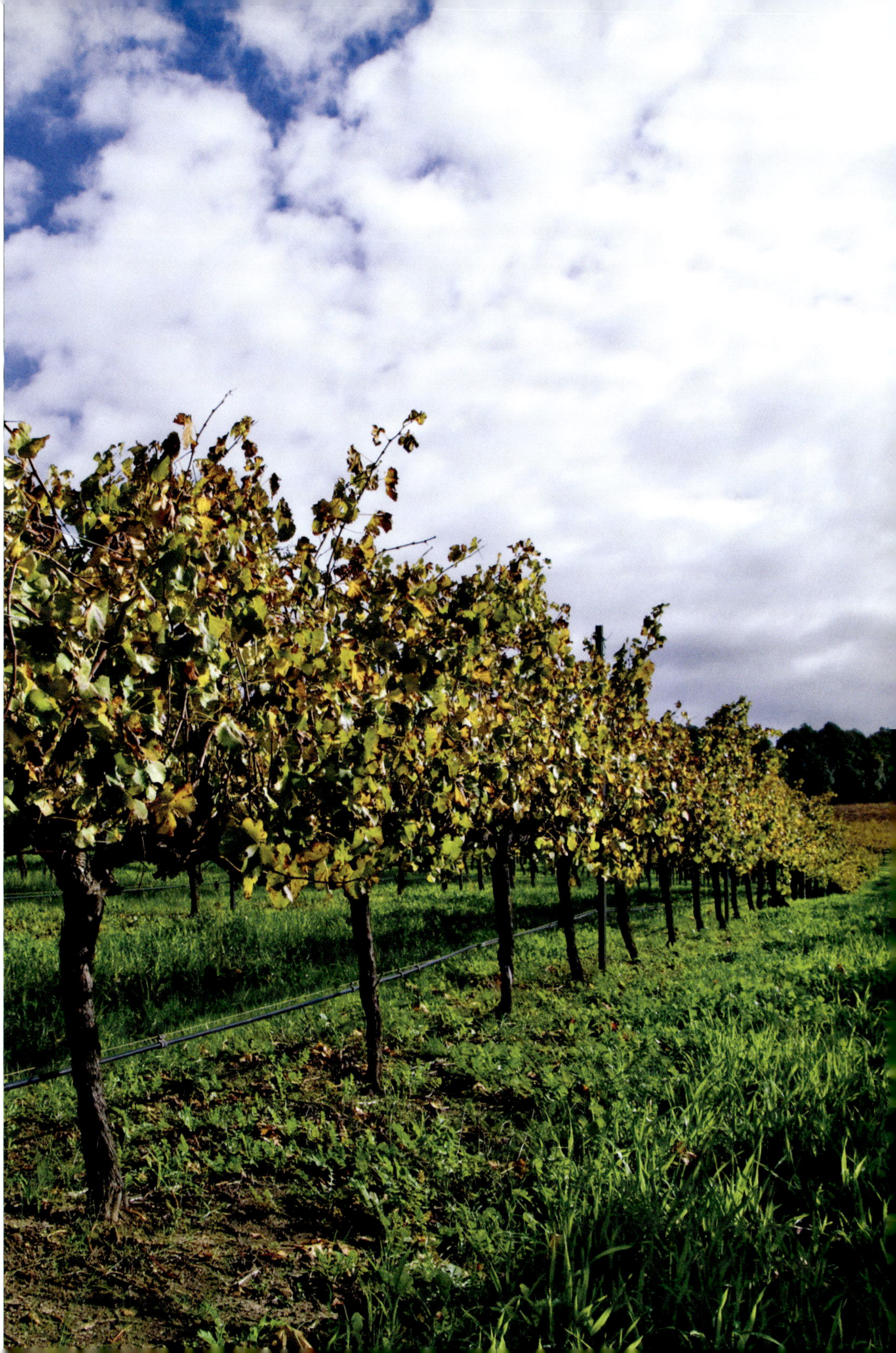

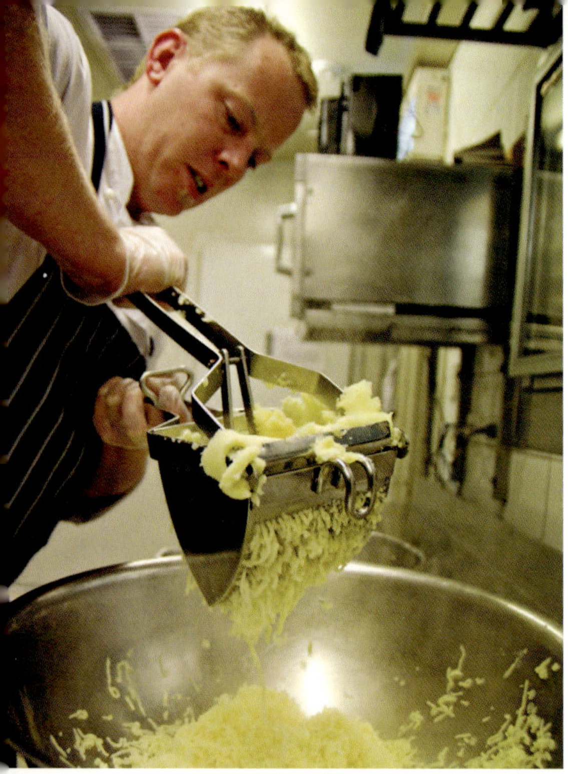
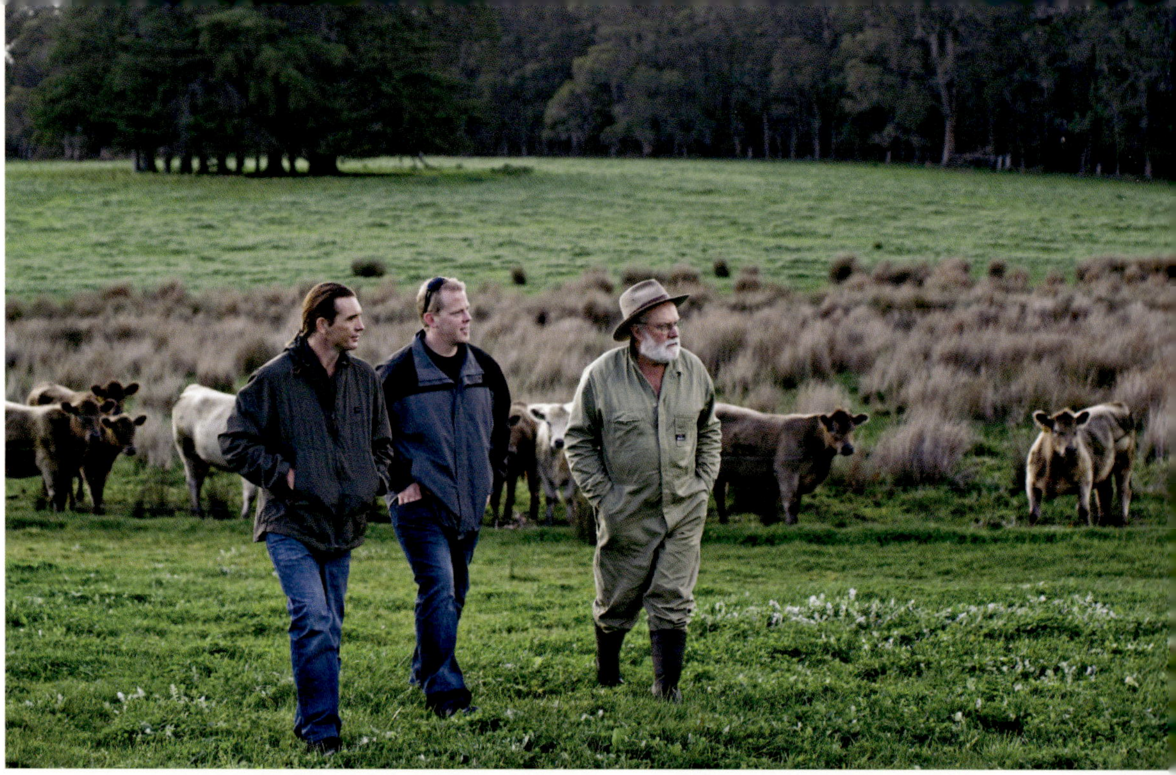
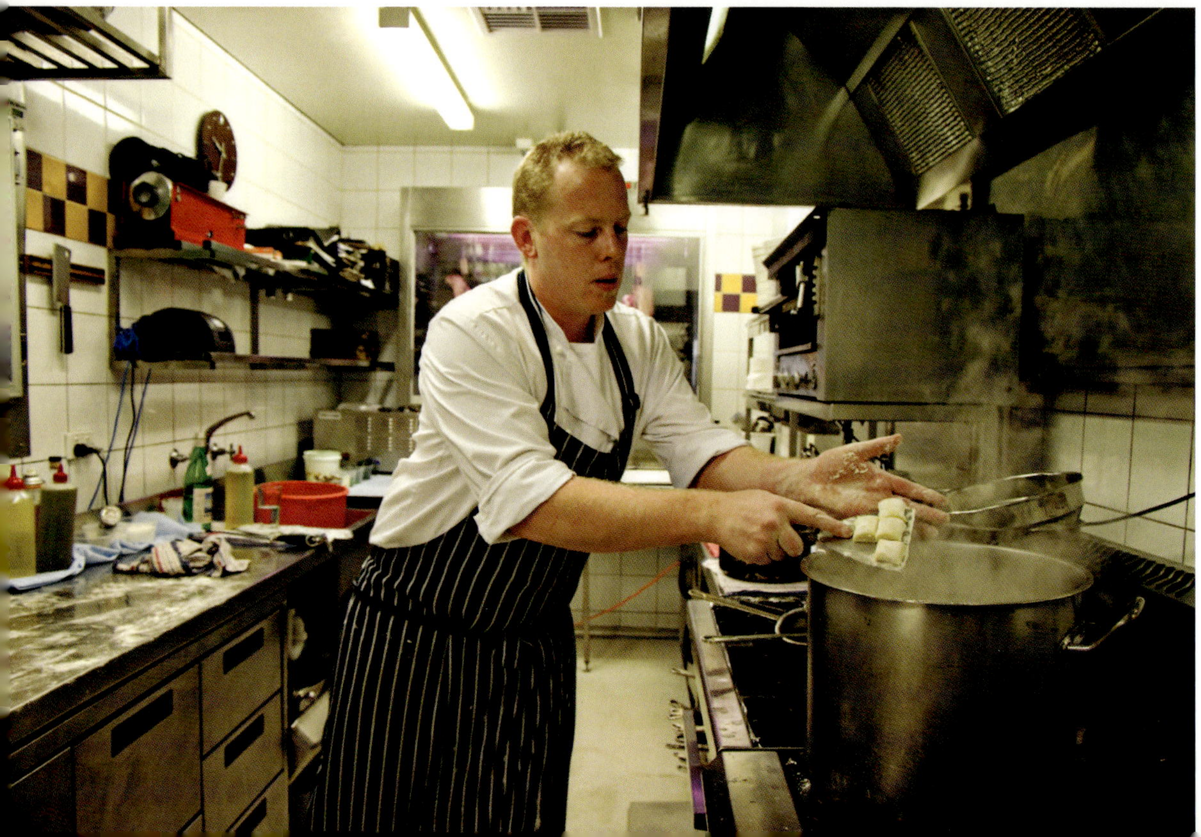
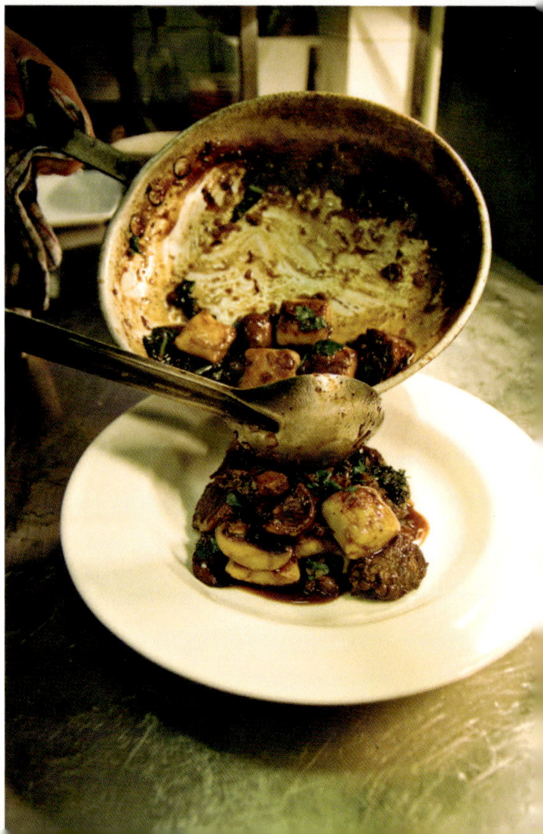

Rick Houston

MUST, MARGARET RIVER

A football injury at the age of 15 saw this Bunbury athlete make an early choice to turn an interest in food into a career and lifestyle. That decision sees Rick at the helm of Must, located on the main street of Margaret River and an offshoot of Must Winebar in Perth.

Rick's enthusiasm for playing team sports has stood him in good stead in the kitchen. "There's nothing you can't do with a good team" he says, attributing much of Must's success to his kitchen staff. "I particularly get a big thrill seeing young apprentices contribute to the menu and build up their talent in the kitchen".

Now a Cowaramup local, Rick makes the most of the region's freshest produce. "The big key for me is to get that perfection out of your produce. If you start with the best, you finish with the best".

Early on in life, Rick took control of his food world. "I used to make my own lunches during home economics at school rather than settling for my mum's lunchbox sandwiches!"

Rick's apprenticeship training included working at a Thai restaurant, where he spent whole days laboriously grinding curry pastes from fresh ingredients. "It taught me about the complexity of combining flavours and the importance of balance".

These days, Rick likes to get out of the kitchen and onto the farms, where he can talk directly with suppliers about what he wants.

"When you have one hundred per cent confidence in your produce and staff, then you are doing something that feels right".

This appreciation of quality is something Rick plans to nurture in his own children. "I'm looking forward to teaching my young son how stuff changes through the seasons so that nothing's set in stone," he says. "I already get the biggest thrill seeing him out there in the paddocks, getting in touch with animals".

Slow-braised Burnside beef cheeks

WITH HANDMADE GNOCCHI

SERVES 6

GNOCCHI
- 600 g (peeled weight) Royal Blue potatoes
- 125-150 g bread-making flour, plus extra flour to roll gnocchi
- A pinch of freshly-grated nutmeg
- 1 tsp table salt
- Pinch of ground white pepper
- 1 egg, lightly whisked

BEEF CHEEKS
- 5 x 250 g Burnside beef cheeks*
- 500 ml shiraz
- 2 carrots, peeled and cut into large dice
- 2 brown onions, peeled and cut into large dice
- ½ head celery, cleaned, leaves removed and diced
- 2 garlic heads, halved horizontally
- 1 bunch thyme
- 1 stick rosemary
- 1 bay leaf
- 10 black peppercorns
- 3 L good beef stock*

TO FINISH
- 100 g shaved Parmesan
- 18 small Swiss brown mushrooms, halved
- 1 small bunch cavolo nero (black-leafed kale), cut into 2 cm strips
- 4 shallots, finely diced
- 1 small bunch baby flat leaf parsley leaves, picked from stems
- 2 heaped tbsp of butter
- Olive oil
- Salt and pepper

* Burnside beef cheeks, are available from Burnside Organic Farm.
* Beef stock recipe - see page 142

METHOD

GNOCCHI
Pre-heat oven to 190°C. Chop potatoes into 4 cm chunks and place into a large saucepan of salted water. Simmer until tender. Pour the potatoes into a strainer placed over the sink and drain for five minutes. Arrange on an oven tray in a single layer and dry in the oven for another five minutes. The idea is to remove as much excess moisture as possible. Pass the potatoes through a potato ricer or push through a coarse sieve into a large bowl. Add nutmeg, salt, pepper, egg and most of the flour. Using your hands or a wooden spoon, mix lightly for no more than 30 seconds. You want smooth but soft dough. If it is very sticky, add a little extra flour and gently work through. Flour a large board or the back of an oven tray. In small batches, gently roll the mixture into long sausages. Cut into 2 cm lengths, regularly dipping your knife into flour to prevent it sticking. Fill your largest saucepan with salted water and bring to the boil. Carefully roll the gnocchi off the tray or board and into the pot and cook at a very slow simmer for 7-8 minutes. Unless your pot is very large, you may need to cook the gnocchi in several batches. The gnocchi will float to the top of the pot as they are cooking. Firmly tapping the side of the pot with a wooden spoon will help release any gnocchi that may be stuck to the bottom. Leave floating gnocchi to simmer for five minutes then remove from the pot with a slotted spoon and drop into a large bowl of cold (preferably iced) water. Once cool, drain and refrigerate until required.

BEEF CHEEKS
Pre-heat oven to 190°C. Remove any loose fat from beef cheeks. Place the beef, shiraz, vegetables, herbs, garlic and peppercorns in a bowl, making sure the beef cheeks are fully submerged. If needed, cover with a plate and top with something heavy (several big cookbooks or a house brick covered in foil work well.) Cover and store in the fridge overnight. Take beef cheeks out of marinade and pat dry. Strain herbs and vegetables from wine and reserve both. On the stove, heat a heavy-based ovenproof casserole and seal the beef cheeks. Remove cheeks, add a splash of oil and the reserved vegetables, cook them until beginning to colour. Add the reserved wine, bring to boil and simmer, uncovered, until syrupy and the vegetables are coated. (this should take about 15 minutes). In a separate saucepan, warm 3 L of beef stock. Return cheeks to ovenproof dish and add beef stock. Cover tightly and bake in oven for three hours. Once cooked, carefully remove beef cheeks, strain stock and reduce by ½ on a stovetop, skimming fat off the surface. Place cheeks in fridge until cool and firm. Keep stock for later use.

Wine Match: Windance Shiraz

TO FINISH
Once beef cheeks are cold, cut into 3 cm cubes. Place beef in a pan and add enough stock to cover the cheeks. Heat gently until beef is soft. Heat a large, non-stick fry pan until smoking. Melt the butter and add small quantities of gnocchi spreading them out evenly. Brown on one side for two minutes. Once you turn the gnocchi over, add the mushrooms and cook for a further two minutes. When both sides are golden brown and the mushrooms have softened, turn up heat and add the kale, shallots and a splash of olive oil. Cook until edges of kale start to go crispy. The pan must still be really hot otherwise it will stew.

TO SERVE
Carefully remove beef from stock and add to gnocchi pan, tossing lightly. Add enough stock to form a coating sauce. Add salt and pepper to taste. Serve immediately in bowls, garnished with the shaved Parmesan and parsley. Serve with crusty bread to mop up the sauce.

Slow-braised Burnside beef cheeks

WITH HANDMADE GNOCCHI

RICK HOUSTON
MUST MARGARET RIVER
RECIPE - SEE PAGE 80

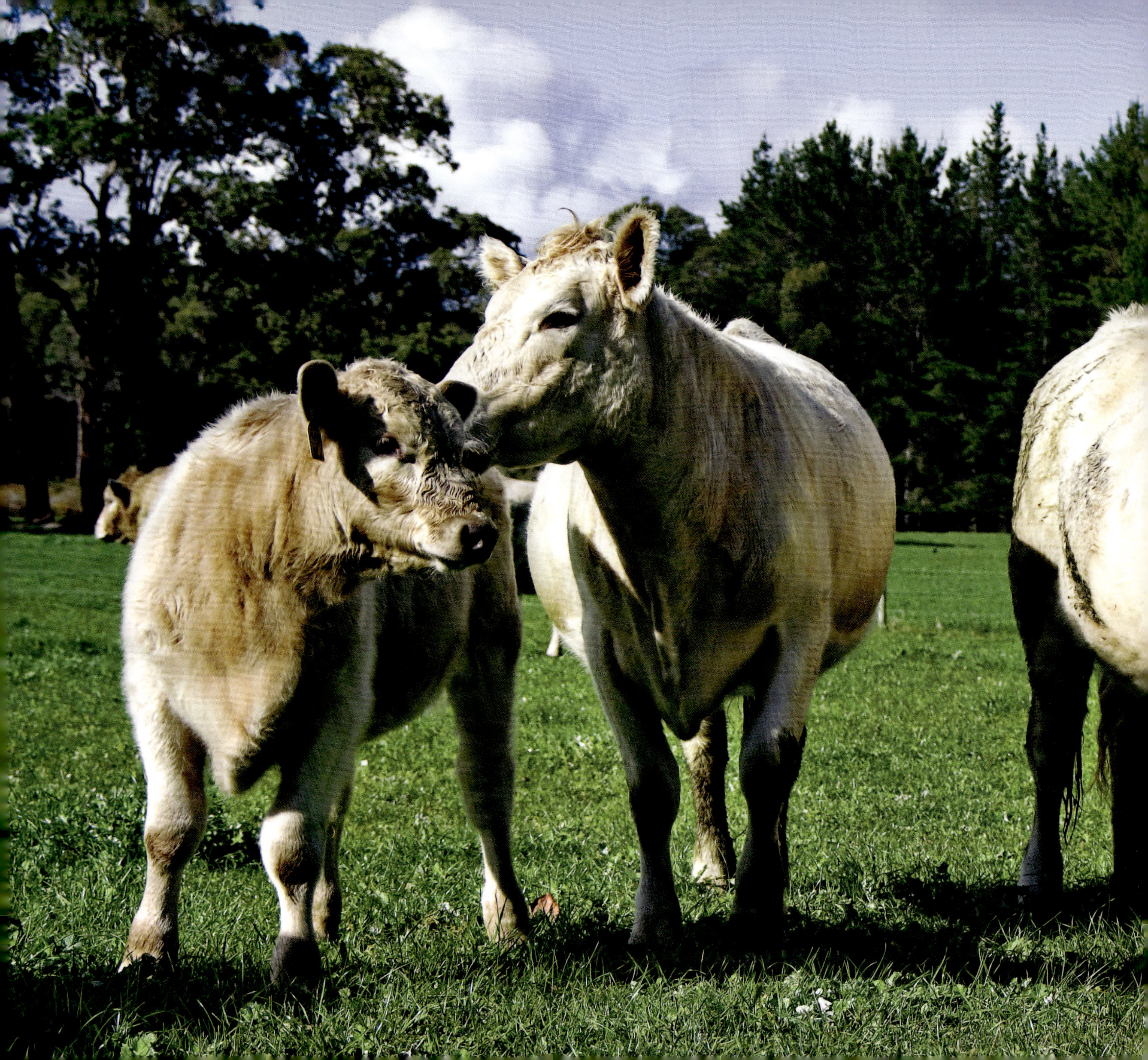

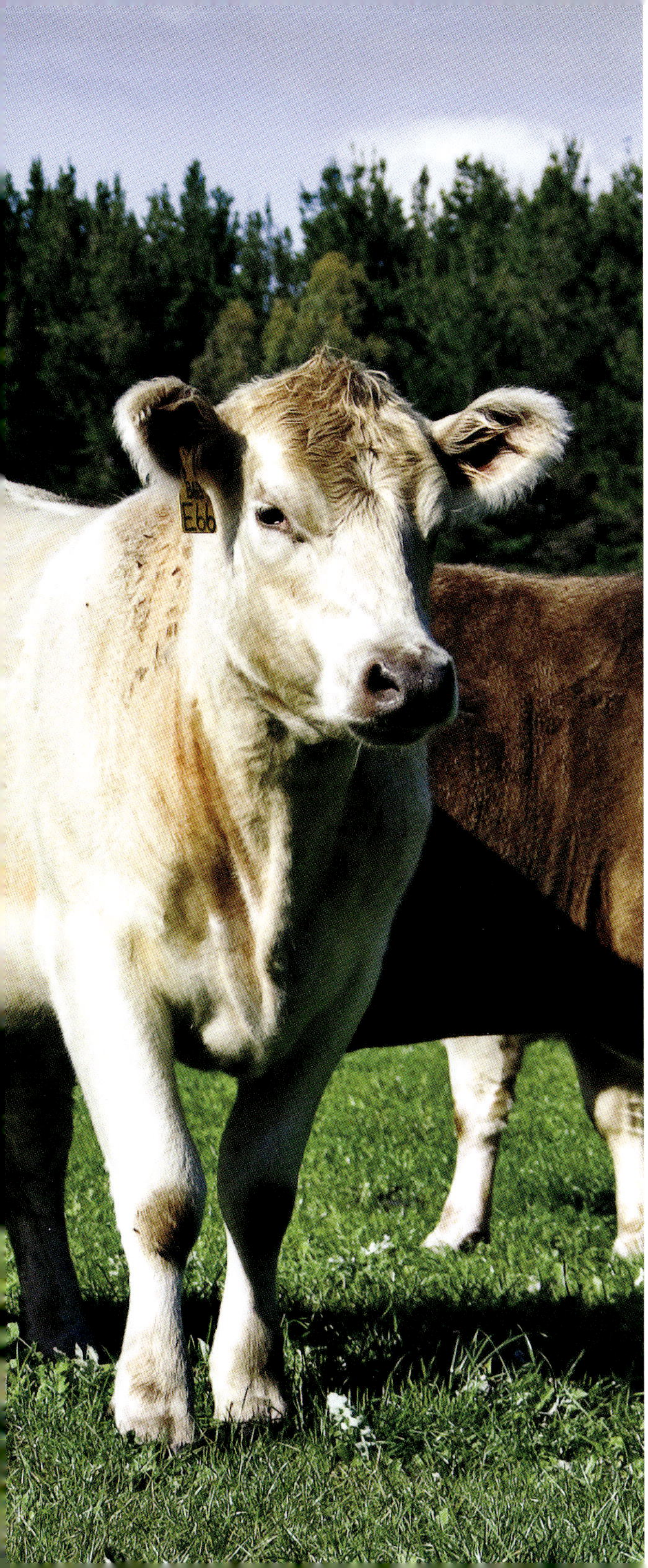
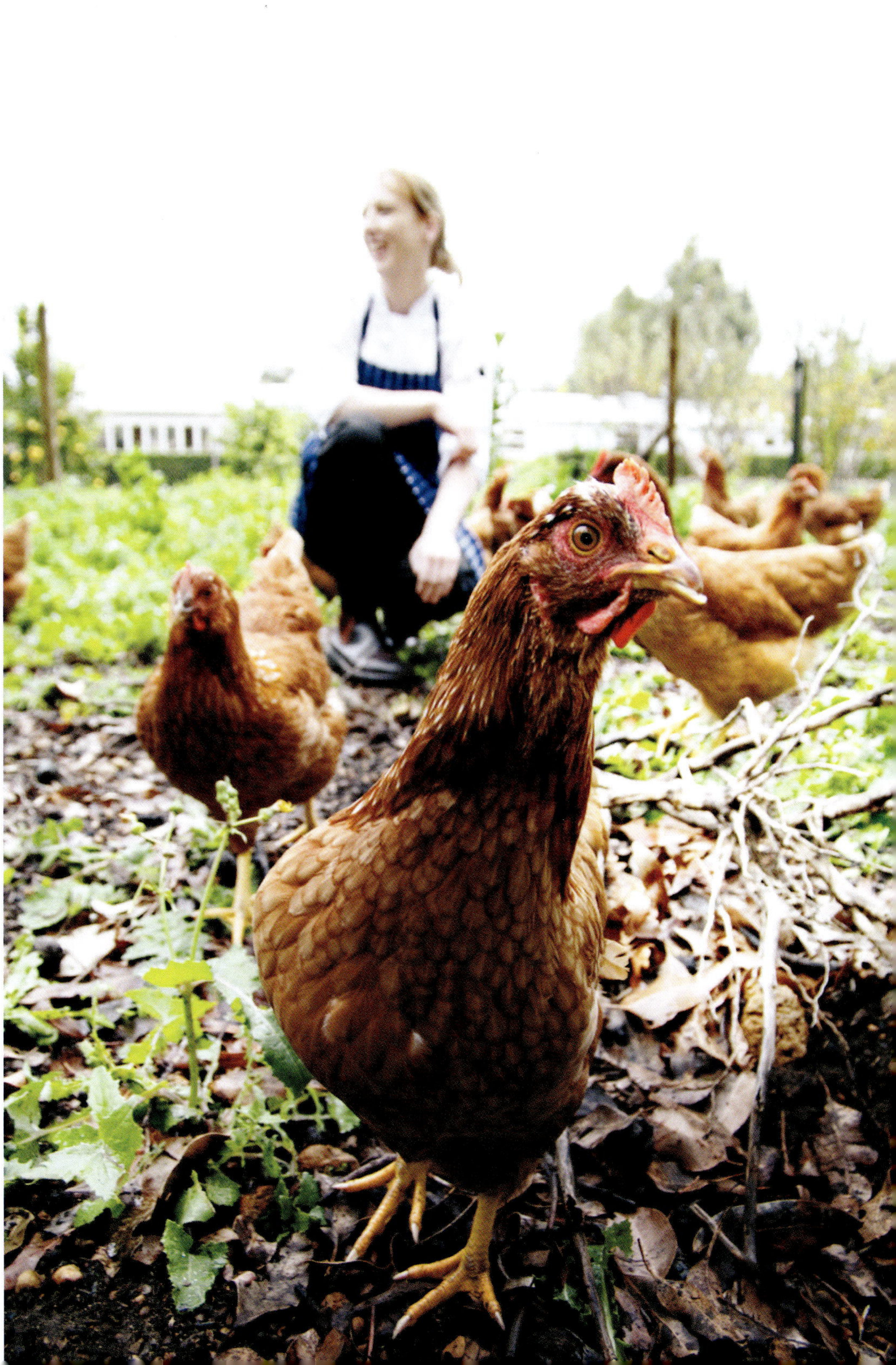

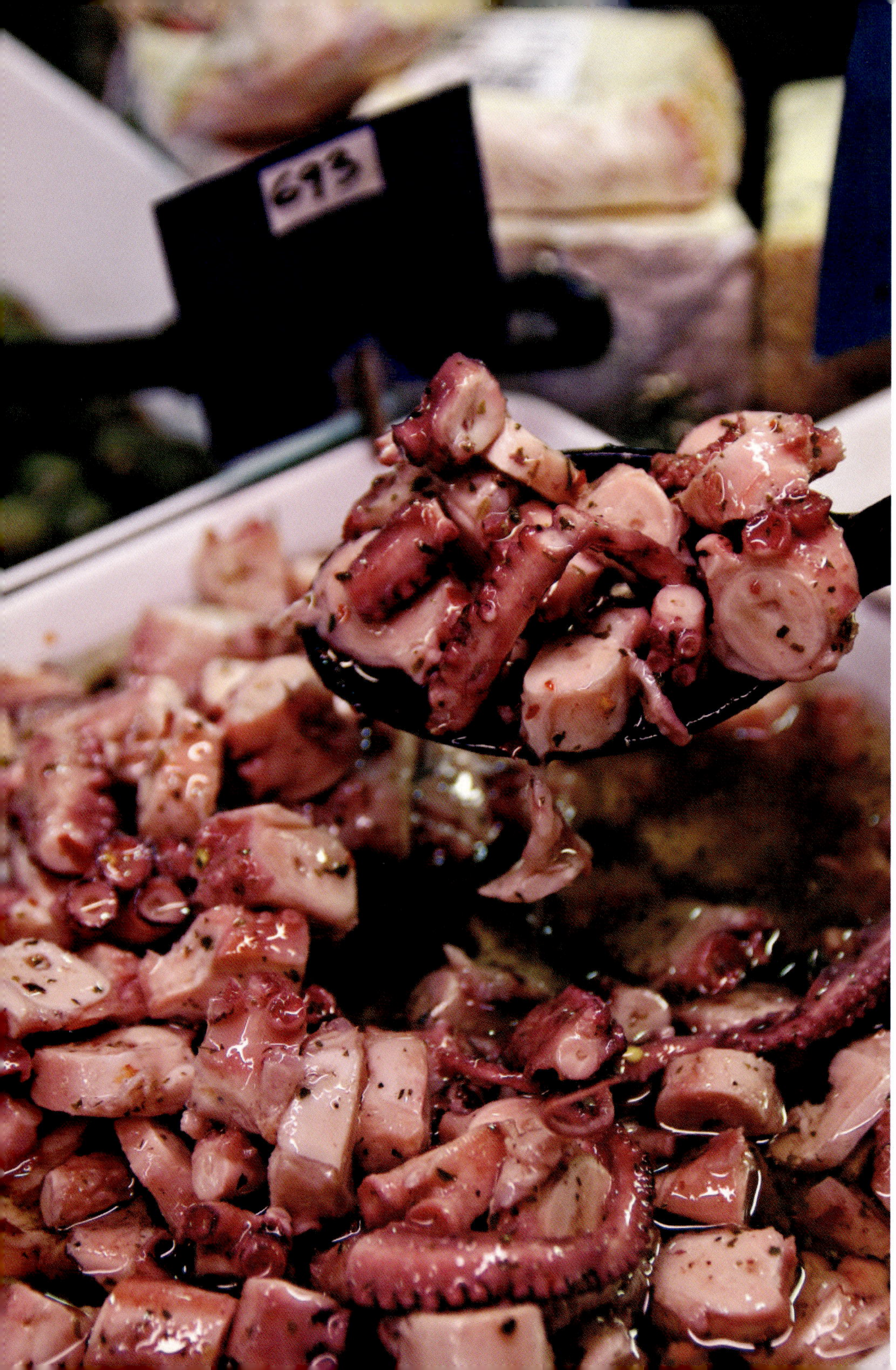

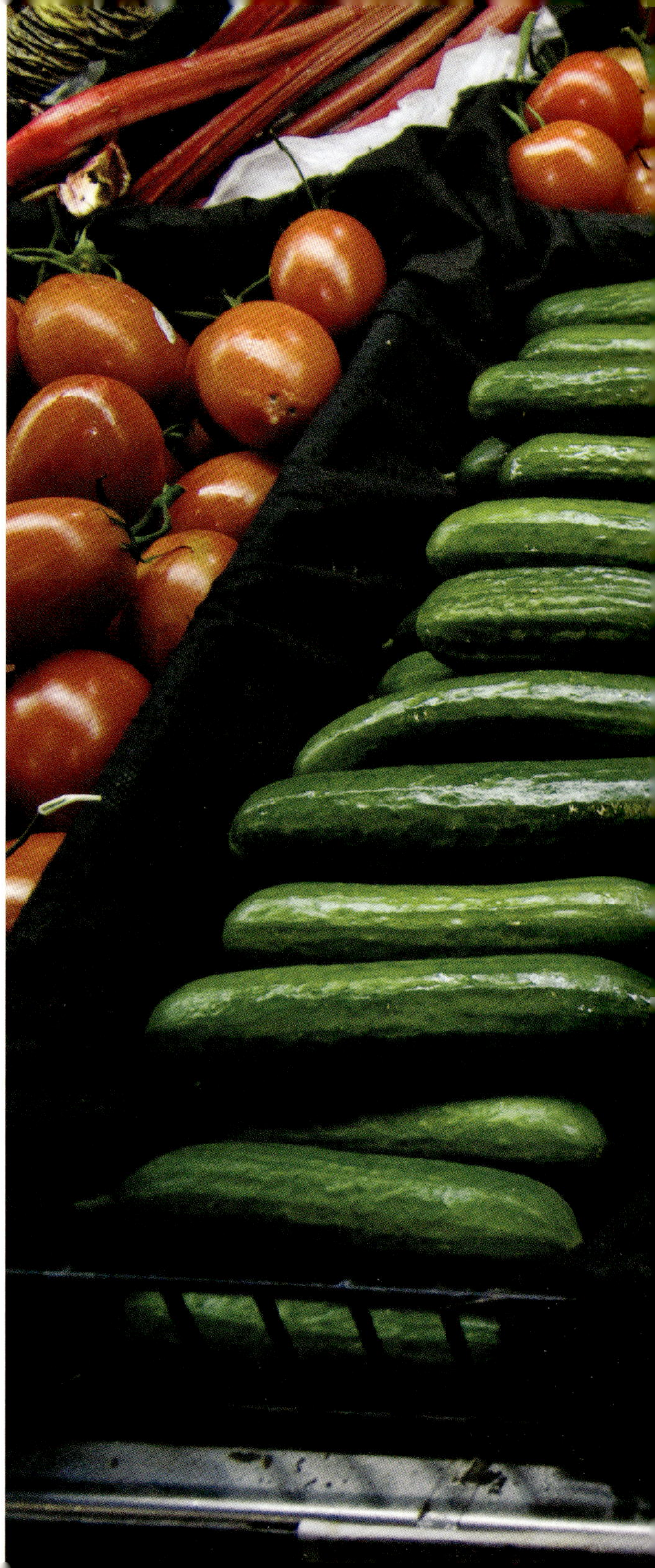

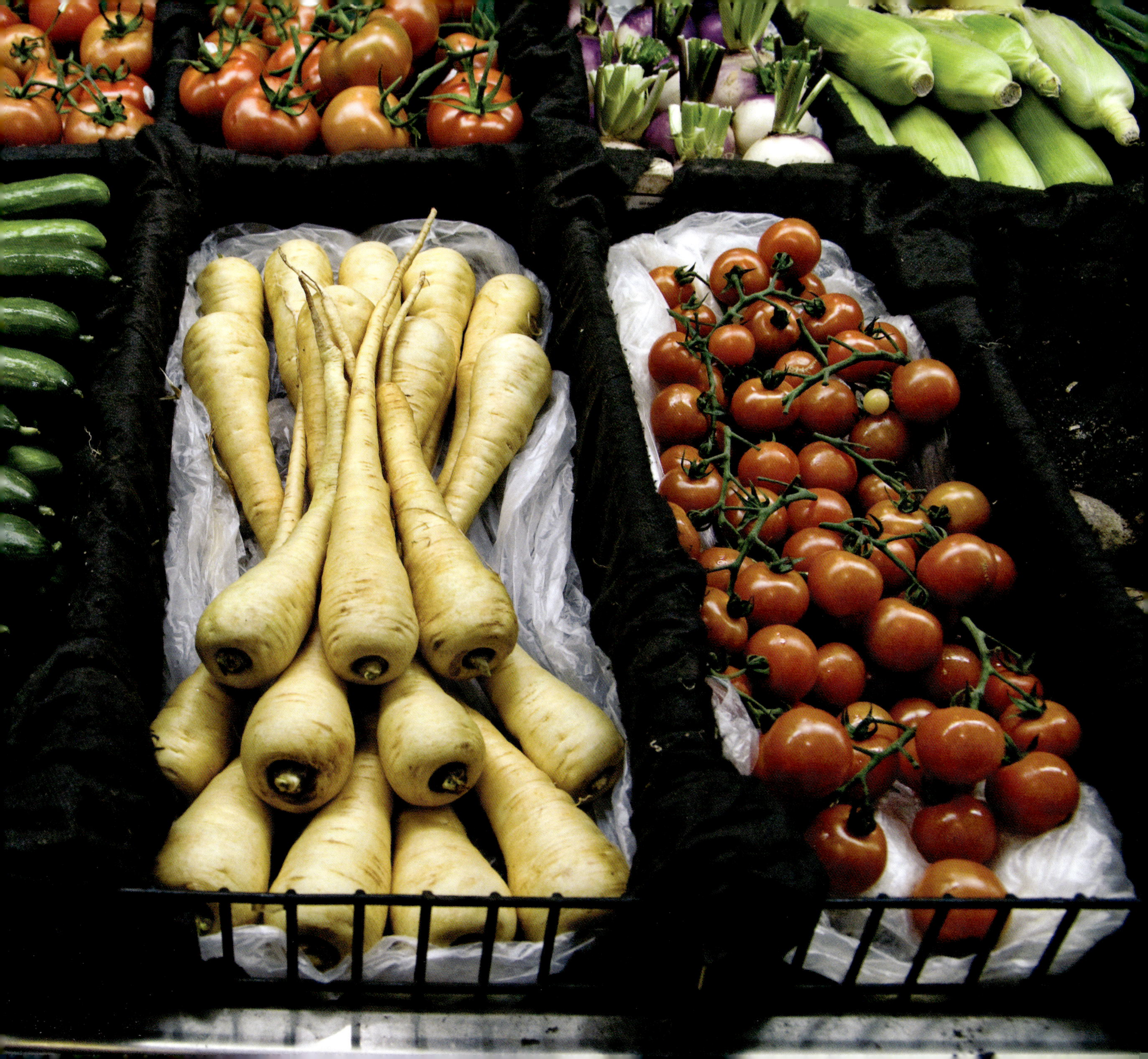

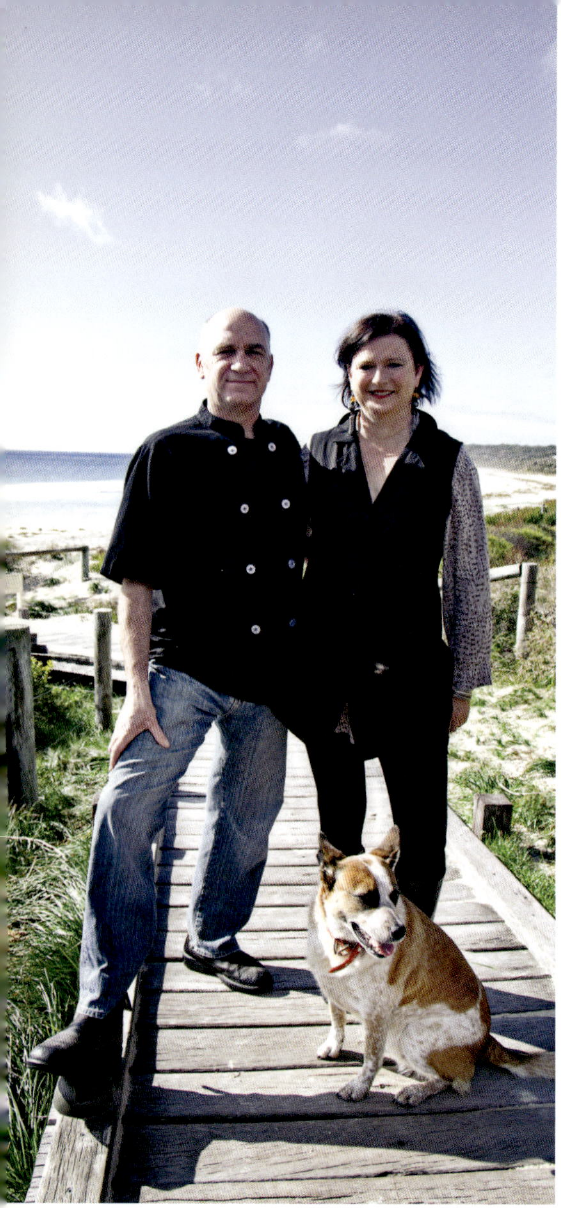

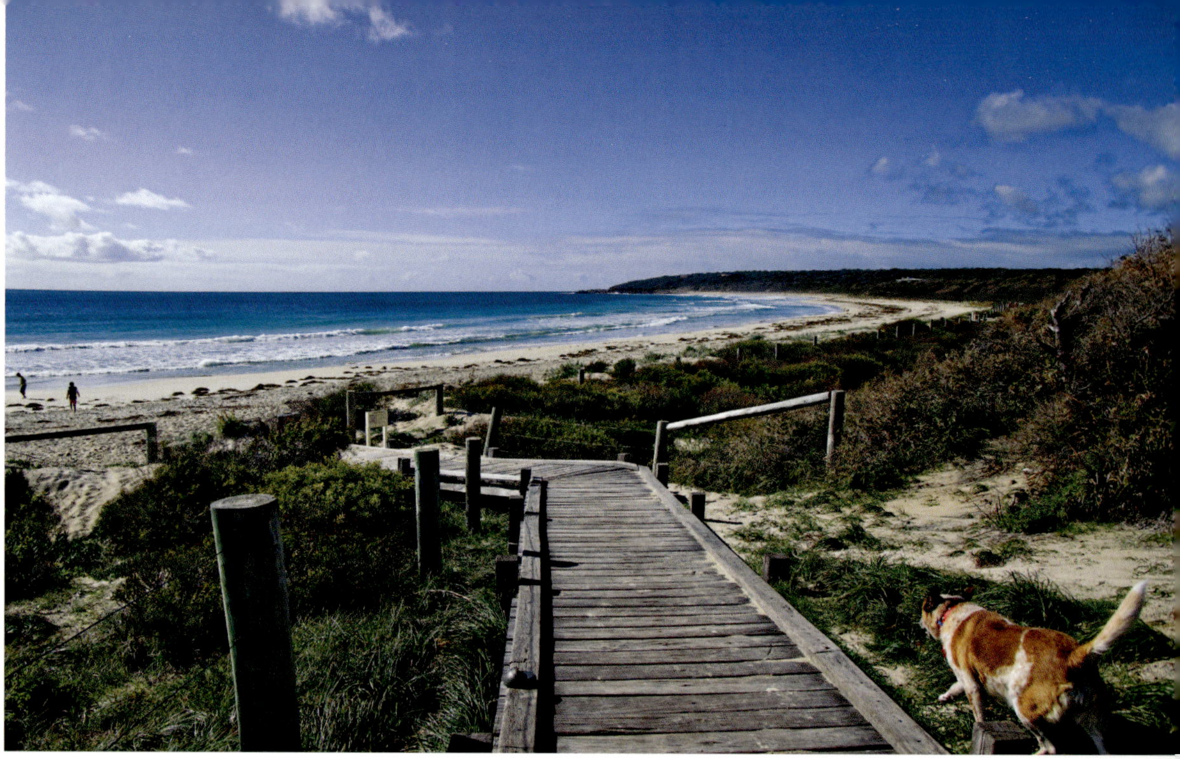

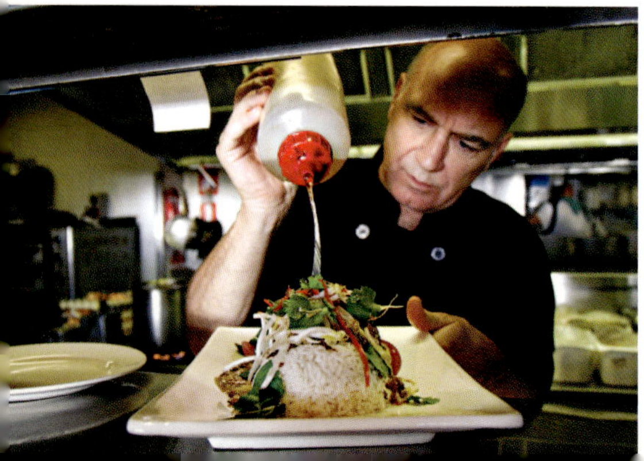

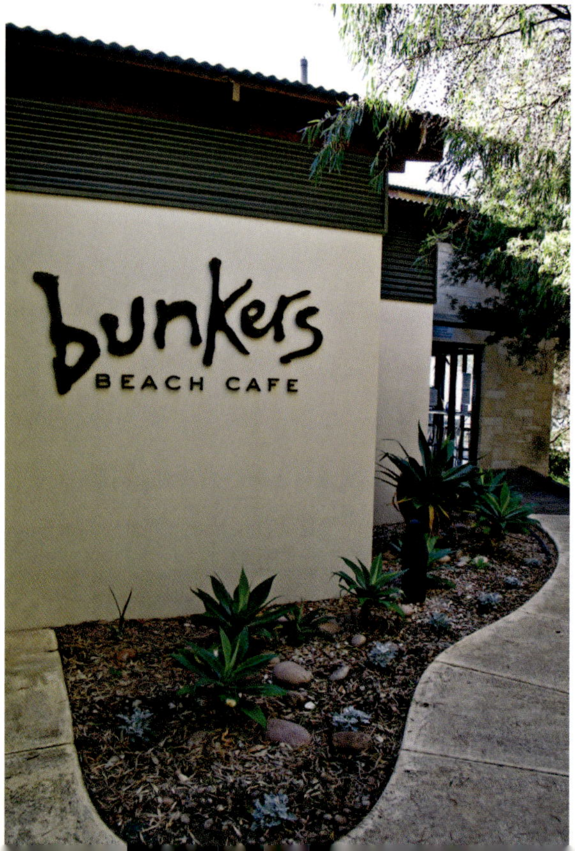
bunkers
BEACH CAFE

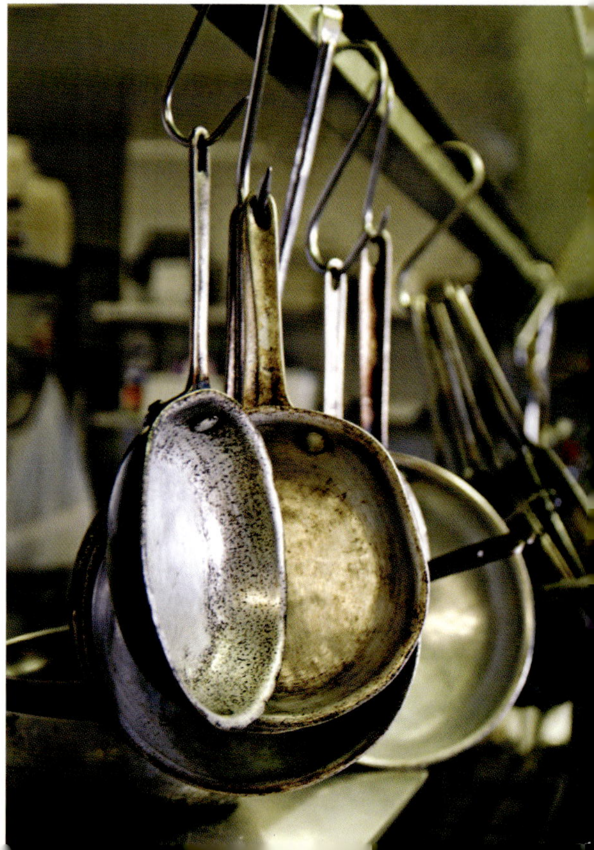

Hamish McLeay

BUNKERS BEACH CAFE, BUNKER BAY

Like so many good chefs, Hamish grew up in New Zealand surrounded by an abundance of great produce. His family's emphasis on the benefits of fresh food, whether grown in the garden or caught in local waters, fundamentally influenced his approach to cooking.

After leaving school and studying architecture, Hamish cooked and trained at several top Wellington restaurants, learning classic French techniques. He then went on to develop his ongoing interest in Asian food.

In 1986, Hamish left New Zealand to travel the world but didn't get very far. Given his strong passion for surfing and the ocean, Western Australia's South West captivated him. That it came with a budding food and wine industry was an added bonus.

"Here I could surf, return to my childhood days of fishing, draw on my culinary experience and work in an environment that provided an abundance of local produce," he says. "What more could I want?"

Hamish helped establish several of Margaret River's most popular dining rooms, the first of which was The Flametree in Cowaramup, well-known for its modern Australian cuisine. Hamish sold the business to run the kitchen at Cullen Wines, where he was instrumental in developing the restaurant and organic garden.

After seven successful years and numerous accolades, Hamish left Cullen for Indonesia to cook on charter boats and pursue his love of surfing. "Not only did I get to cook and go surfing," he says, "I also got to learn more about a culture that inspired me".

When Hamish returned to the South West, he was offered the role of manager and head chef at Bunkers Beach Cafe.

"We get all sorts of patrons here," he says. "Often they've been in the car for a while and are looking for something nice to eat and drink but don't want to get dressed up. Others simply rock up from the beach barefoot in their boardies. Regardless we offer them great service, interesting food and a good atmosphere".

The casual, relaxed beachside dining room features glass bi-fold doors that open onto a spectacular view of the white sands of Bunker Bay. "We've got a boardwalk that leads straight down to the beach," says Hamish. "Even better, I get to watch the ocean while I work".

Lupin tempeh, coconut rice and satay sauce

SERVES 6

TEMPEH
- 250 g Margaret River tempeh (lupin variety), cut into 1 cm slices

RICE
- 1 L jasmine rice
- 1 can (400 ml) coconut milk
- Add water to coconut milk to bring liquid to 1.2 L
- 1 piece cassia bark
- 2 star anise

PEANUT SAUCE
- Spice mix
- 1 onion
- 50 g ginger
- 5 garlic cloves
- 2 red chilli
- 4 coriander stalks
- 1 lemongrass, cut into small pieces
- 2 kaffir lime leaves

SAUCE
- 2 cups roasted peanuts, pounded
- 2 cans (400ml each) coconut cream
- 75 ml shao hsing wine
- 50 ml light soy sauce
- 6 cm block of palm sugar, shaved
- 50 ml fish sauce
- 30 g chilli jam
- Lime juice to taste

SALAD
- 1 red chilli, chopped
- 1 small bunch spring onions, sliced
- 1 cup of bean shoots, rinsed
- ½ cup each mint and coriander leaves, stems removed

PAK CHOY
- ½ bunch pak choy
- 1 tsp sesame oil
- 1 tsp sesame seeds

GARNISH
- 100 g deep-fried shallots

Wine Match: Deep Woods or McHenry Hohnen Semillon Sauvignon Blanc or Millbrook Sauvignon Blanc.

METHOD

RICE
Wash rice thoroughly and soak in cold water for 14 minutes. Drain rice and leave in strainer for 14 minutes. Bring coconut milk and water to the boil. Add the drained rice and the spices. Return to the boil, cover tightly and reduce to the lowest possible heat. Cook for 12 minutes. Remove from heat, leave lid on and sit for 12 minutes more. Turn onto a tray and, using a fork, gently separate the grains. Remove cassia and star anise.

PEANUT SAUCE
In a food processor, blend spice mix ingredients to a smooth paste. Heat oil in a fry pan. Add the paste and fry until fragrant. Add all of the sauce ingredients and cook until thick. Adjust seasoning to ensure a rich flavor and add lime juice to taste.

SALAD
Wash and mix all the salad ingredients together.

PAK CHOY
Blanch and then grill pak choy until tender. Season with sesame oil and sesame seeds.

TO SERVE
Fry sliced tempeh until golden brown. Place a bowl of rice on plate. Place tempeh pieces on rice. Position grilled pak choy on side of the plate, ladle peanut sauce over the tempeh and rice and top with the salad. Garnish with the fried shallots.

Lupin tempeh, coconut rice and satay sauce

HAMISH MCLEAY
BUNKERS BEACH CAFE
RECIPE - SEE PAGE 90

Maltese rabbit stew

(STUFFAT TAL-FENEK)

DENNIS MIFSUD
VEDA CATERING
RECIPE - SEE PAGE 96

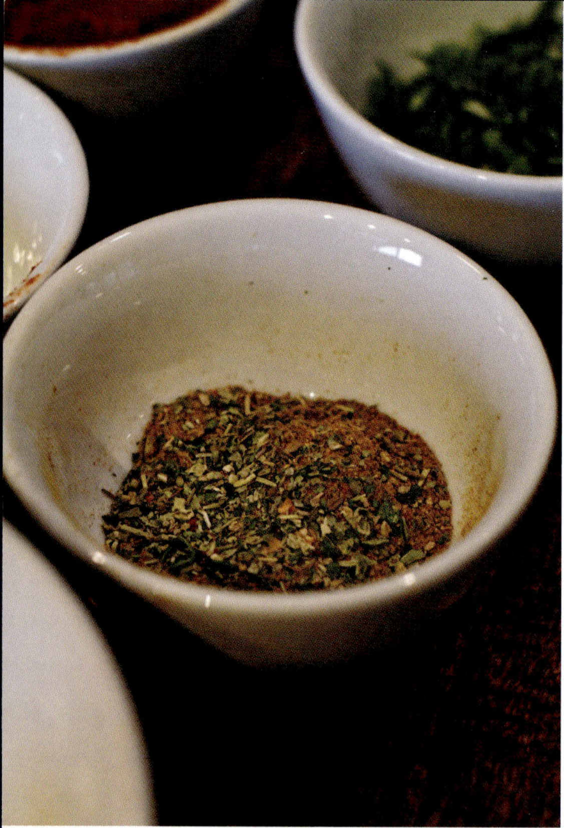

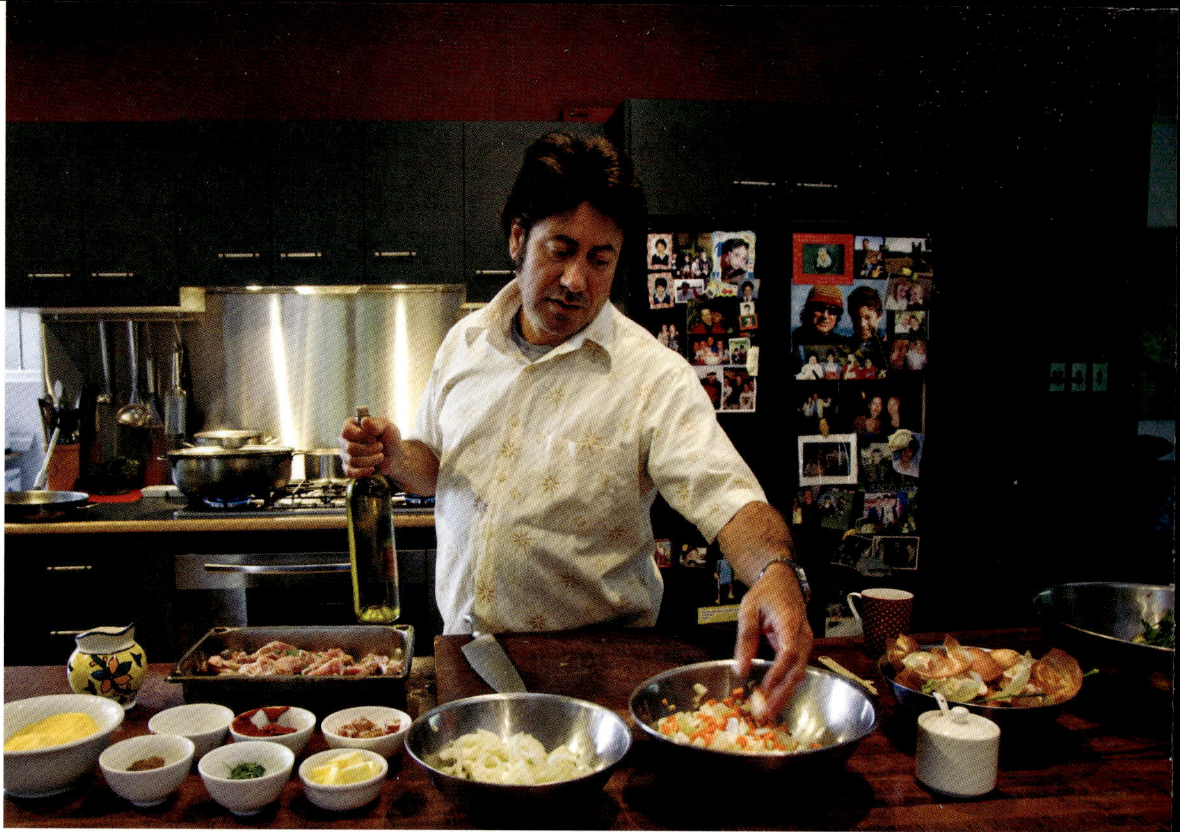

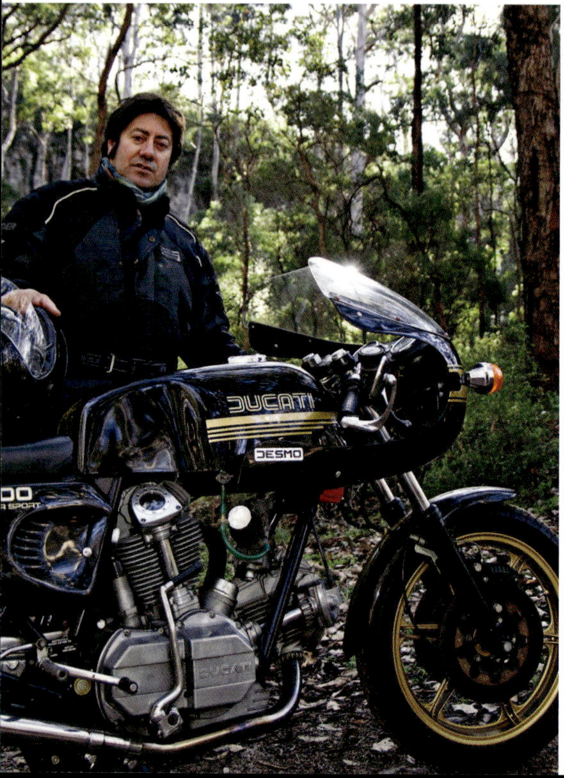
DUCATI
DESMO

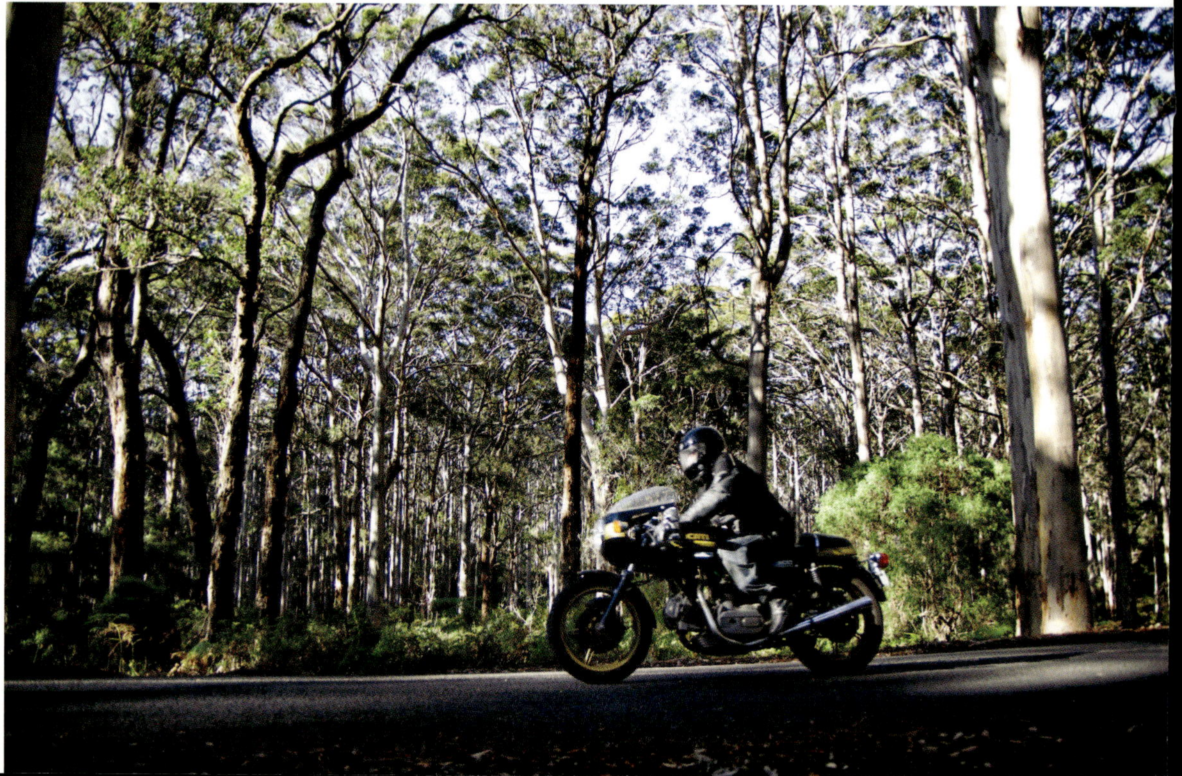

Dennis Mifsud

VEDA CATERING, MARGARET RIVER

A self-confessed wanderer, Dennis once backpacked across Asia, funded by the sale of his first 1979 Supersport Ducati motorbike.

Dennis' family were originally from Malta. He grew up in the Perth suburb of Bassendean and remembers back when nearby Morley was all bush. "We would go shooting rabbits there," he says. "It was great. It seemed so wild and free".

One of Dennis' earliest influences was his grandmother. "I used to watch her making gnocchi," he says. "There were 10 kids on my mother's side and 14 on my father's, so big family feasts were very much part of my upbringing".

Having flirted with the idea of being an engineer, Dennis always had a passion for food and knew he would cook no matter what else he did. A big fan of Asian food, he says he's as happy sitting at a warung on the side of a street as in a fine diner. "It would be great if we had warungs here," he adds. "Imagine all that free enterprise! "

In 2001, Dennis helped established Wino's wine bar on the main street of Margaret River. He soon developed a reputation for showcasing South West produce.

Since leaving Wino's he has focused on his catering business. "I love the flexibility of not being attached to a restaurant anymore," he says. "I have much more fun".

"When you create a restaurant you're stuck with it. You've got to come up with a theme and a target market, and once you've got a good business plan, you'll stick to it.

"You can't then go 'I'll be a French restaurant' and if that doesn't work change your approach and say 'I'll be Spanish'. It takes a long time for people to know who you are and you can't keep changing on them".

Dennis chose to share a family recipe for stewed rabbit in memory of his late father, "I have chosen this dish because dad was very fond of it" he says. "It's very warm and made for sharing," he says. "For me that's what Maltese food is all about".

Maltese rabbit stew

(STUFFAT TAL-FENEK)

SERVES 6

RABBIT
- 12 hind legs of rabbit

MARINADE
- 1 cup (250 ml) olive oil
- 3 onions, chopped
- 2 medium carrots, chopped
- 2 celery sticks, chopped
- 2 bay leaves
- A few peppercorns
- 6 pimentos

STEW
- 6 garlic cloves, chopped
- 2 extra onions, chopped
- 1 cup smoked pork belly or smoked pancetta, chopped
- 4 cloves
- 1 tsp ground cinnamon
- ½ tsp allspice
- 1 cup (250ml) red wine
- 2 cups seeded and peeled tomatoes
- 2 tbsp tomato paste
- 3 bay leaves
- 2 rosemary sprigs
- 3 cups (750ml) chicken stock*
- 1 cup (155g) shelled peas
- Salt and pepper to taste
- A handful of flat-leaf parsley, roughly chopped

*Chicken stock recipe - see page 143

Wine match: Borrisokane Cabernet Sauvignon, Merlot and Cabernet Franc

METHOD

Mix together the marinade ingredients. Marinate the rabbit legs for at least two hours (preferably overnight). Remove the rabbit from the marinade, retaining the oil for later use. Fry the rabbit in a heavy-based pan over medium heat until golden brown. Remove from pan. Add the olive oil from the marinade to the pan then fry the remaining chopped onions, chopped garlic, pork belly and spices. Fry (without burning) the spices until fragrant. Add the wine, tomatoes, tomato paste, bay leaves, rosemary and rabbit. Add chicken stock and cook over a low heat until tender, about 1½-2 hours. Alternatively, the stew can be placed in a deep dish, covered with greaseproof paper and a lid and bake in the oven at 175°C for about 1½ to 2 hours. Add shelled peas, continue cooking for 10 minutes or until peas are tender. Season to taste.

TO SERVE
Sprinkle with the parsley. Serve with a grilled polenta cake (see recipe - page 144), white bean puree or potatoes (either boiled or mashed), plus green salad and a crusty loaf of bread, broken at the table to mop up the juices.

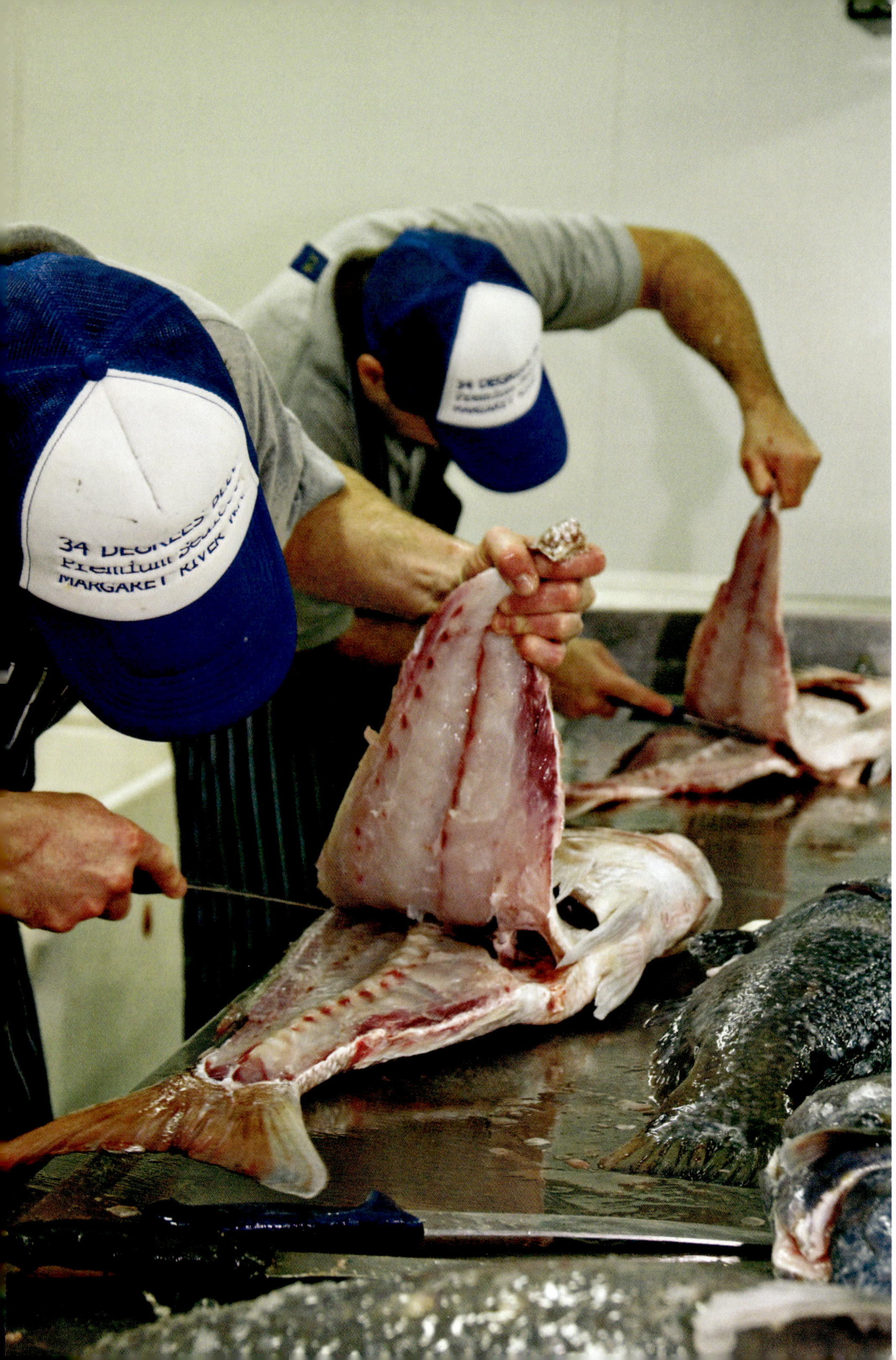
34 DEGREES
MARGARET RIVER

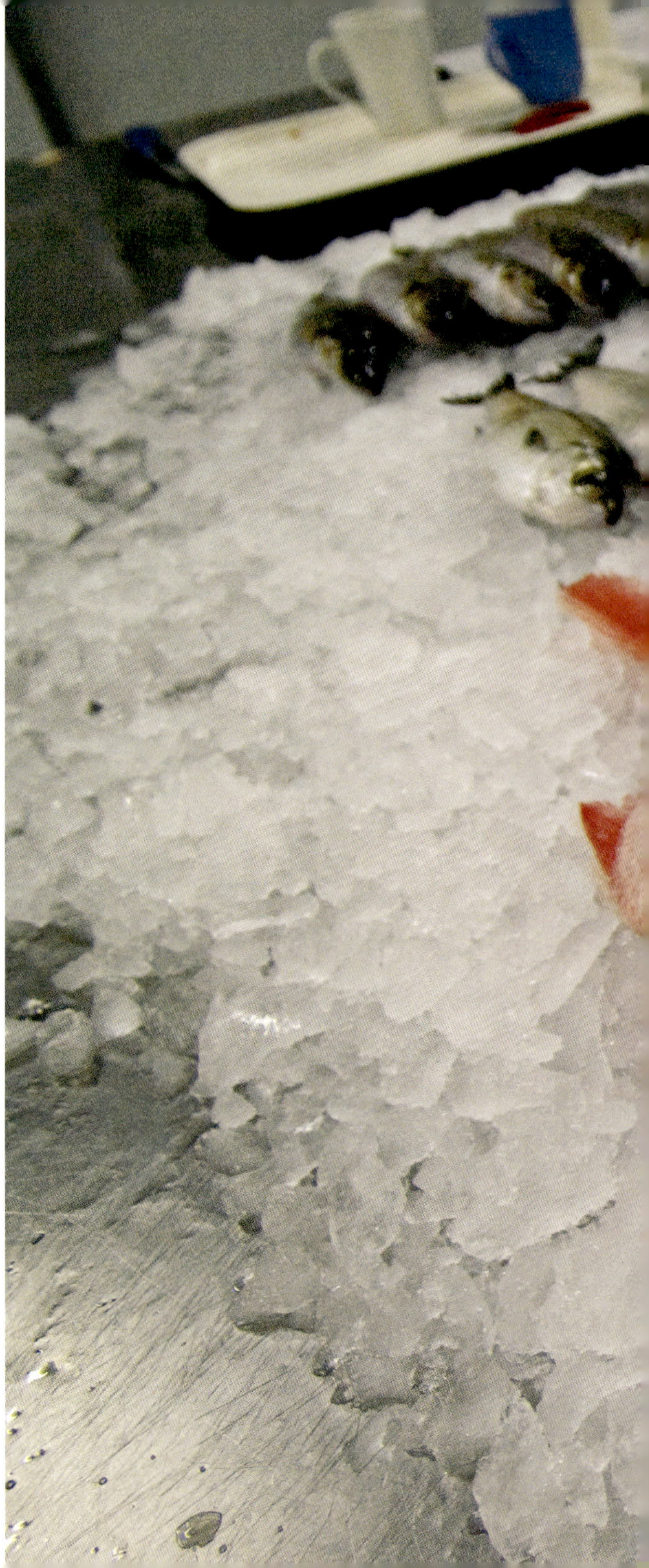

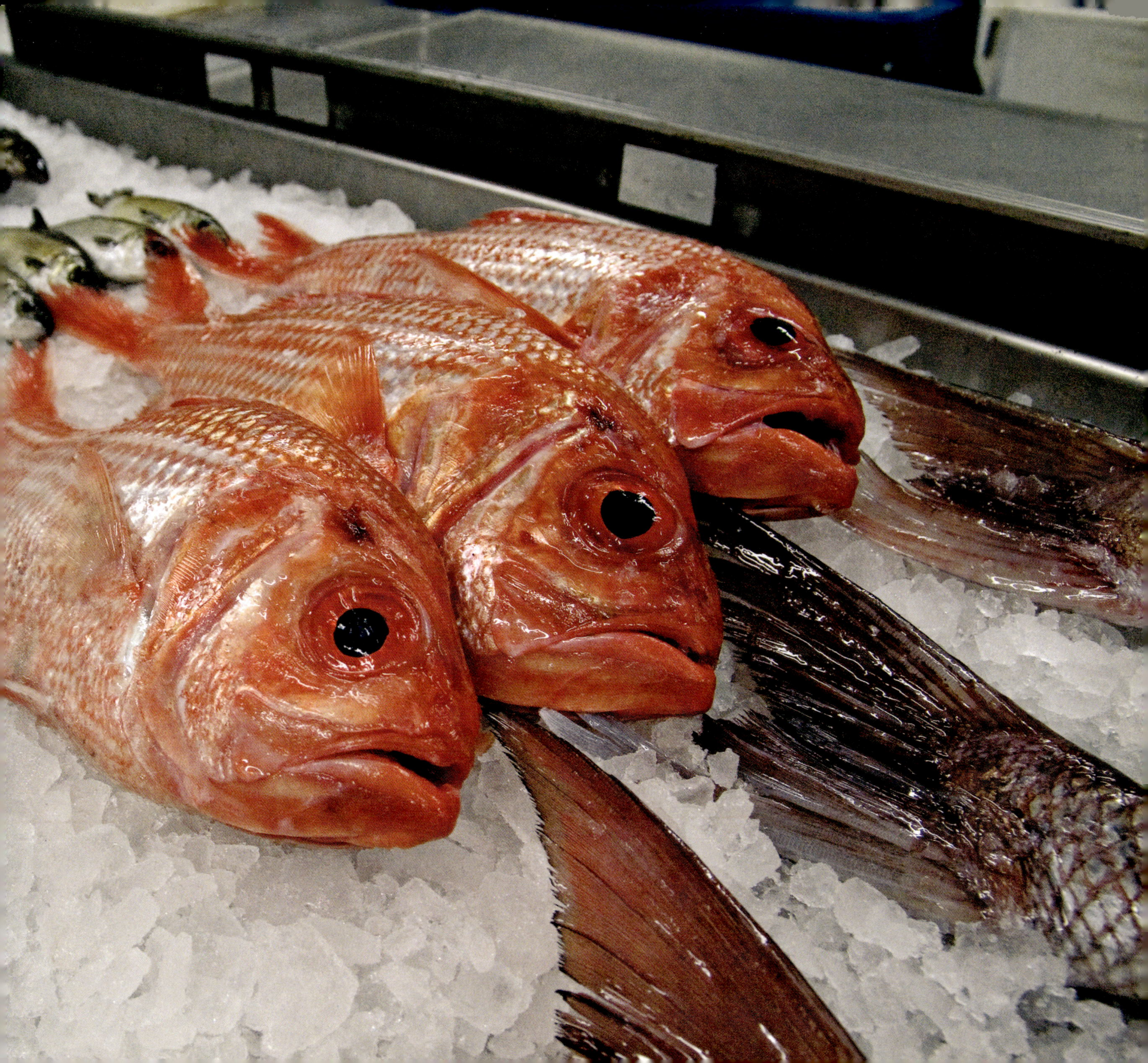

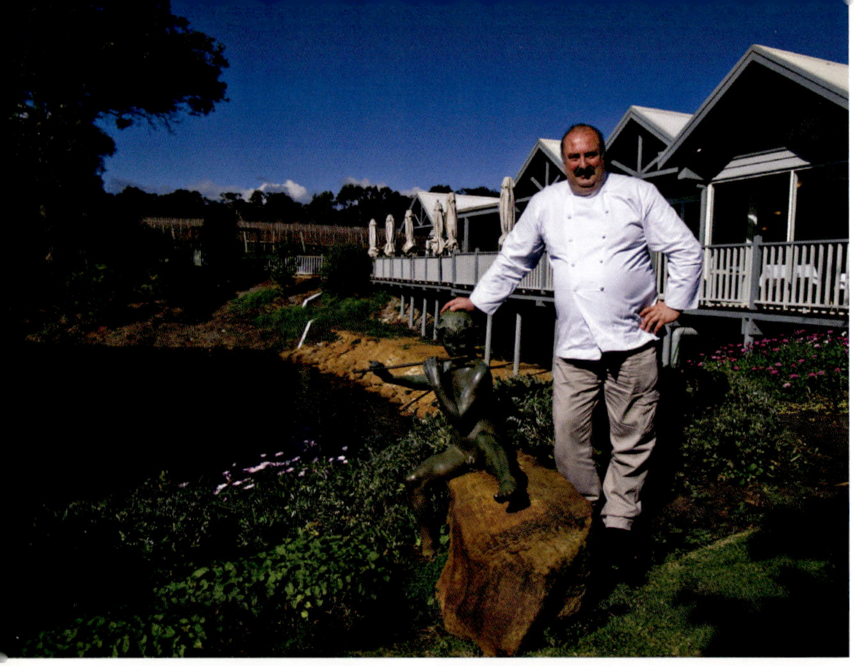
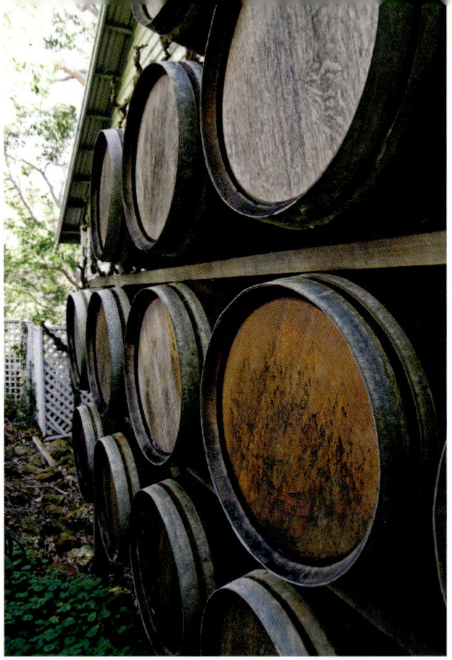
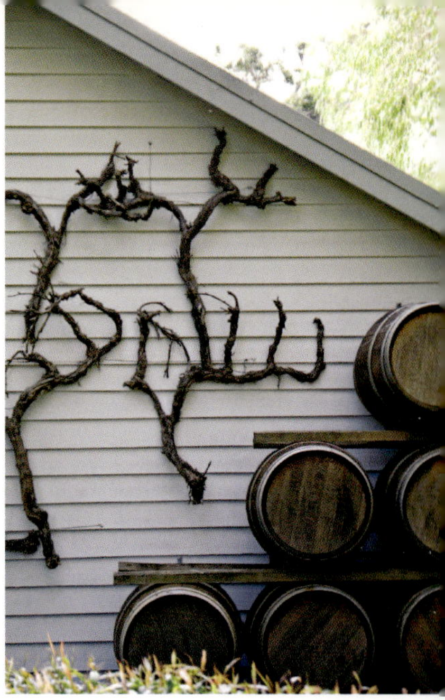
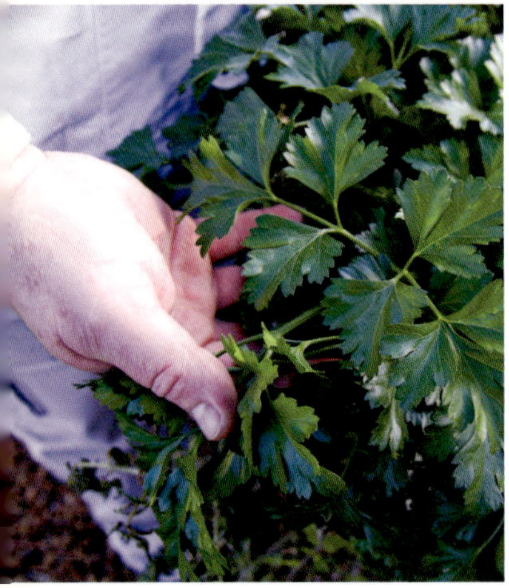
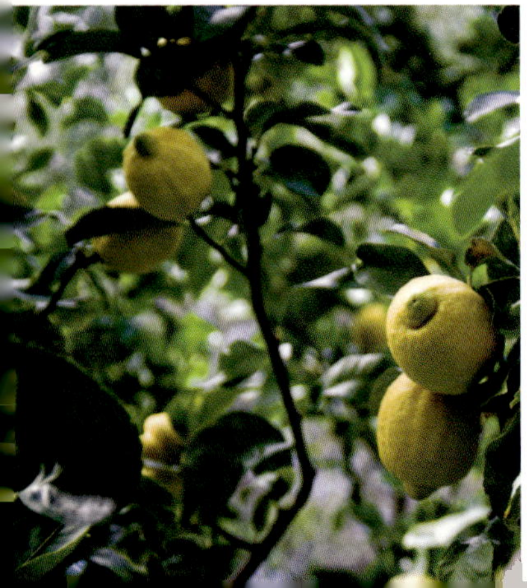
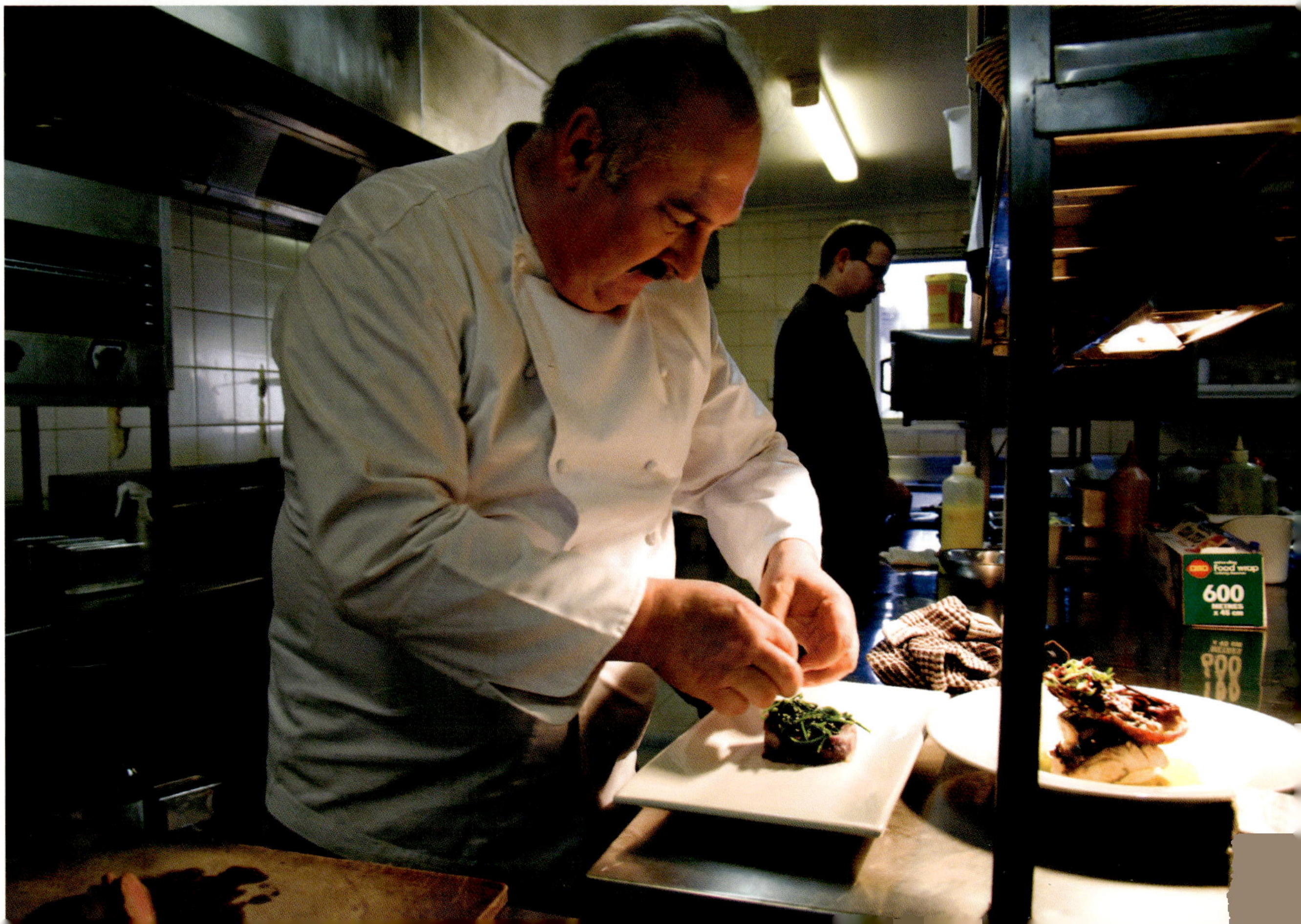
food wrap
600

Francois Morvan

FLUTES AT BROOKLAND VALLEY, WILYABRUP

Claiming he was "brought here by the wind," Francois Morvan arrived at Flutes Restaurant within the Brookland Valley Vineyard in 2001, boasting a curious background in French cooking and time spent running a successful restaurant in tropical Broome.

Starting his cooking apprenticeship in Brittany, Francois moved to Paris in the late 1970s. After a stint in Thailand in the early 1980s, he then continued on to the Gold Coast before moving to Western Australia to work on the launch of Observation City hotel at Scarborough Beach, back in the heyday of the America's Cup. He then spent time overseeing a new Queensland resort before settling in Broome and running the restaurant at the Cable Beach Club resort.

It was in Broome that a friend mentioned the magic words 'Margaret River' and Francois found himself going with the wind to his next sea change. He is passionate about what he does and doesn't consider it work. "This is a lifestyle, not a job. Cooking is too hard if you don't like it. There is so much pressure".

His philosophy is simple. "You don't serve it if it's not good enough, so make sure you get it right. You're only as good as your last dish".

Francois' signature style of classic, unpretentious fare has seen Flutes become a firm favourite on the Margaret River dining scene. The restaurant itself is in a beautiful spot, overlooking Wilyabrup Brook and landscaped gardens set against a backdrop of hill, forest and pasture.

When it comes to cooking, Francois likes to keep things simple. "I find by planning a lot of variation in your food, it can lose a lot of flavour".

"When you've got a good piece of fish, chicken or meat, the most important thing is the seasoning. Not too much and not too little. Just the right amount at the right time".

Pan-fried duck and roasted whole quail

WITH PURPLE CONGO POTATO CRUSH, WILTED SPINACH AND SHIRAZ JUS

SERVES 4

POTATO CRUSH
- 600 g Purple Congo potatoes, peeled and cut into 2cm dice
- 20 g softened butter

SHIRAZ JUS
- 10 g butter
- 200 g finely chopped brown onion
- 300 ml shiraz
- 500 ml beef stock*
- Salt and pepper

*Beef stock recipe - see page 142

WILTED SPINACH
- 5 g butter
- 100 g baby English spinach
- Salt and pepper

QUAIL
- 10 g melted butter
- 4 large quail
- 20 seedless white grapes
- Salt and pepper

DUCK MAGRET
- 4 x 160 g duck magrets (or breasts)
- Salt and pepper

METHOD

POTATO CRUSH
Season the potatoes with salt and pepper and steam until tender. Drain and crush roughly in a mixing bowl. Adjust seasoning to taste. Keep warm until needed

SHIRAZ JUS
Melt butter in a heavy-based saucepan, add chopped onions and sauté until translucent and light brown. Add the shiraz, bring to boil then reduce the heat. Simmer until reduced by ⅔. Add beef stock, bring to boil, then reduce heat and keep simmering until reduced by ⅔. Season to taste and pass the jus through a fine mesh strainer into a clean saucepan. Keep warm until needed.

WILTED SPINACH
Melt butter in a wok. Add spinach, toss it in the butter, season to taste and cook until wilted. Keep warm until needed.

QUAIL
Pre-heat the oven to 200°C. Fill each quail cavity with five of the grapes.
Brush the birds with melted butter and season with salt and pepper. Bake for two minutes. Turn the oven down to 180°C and cook for another 8-12 minutes or until cooked. (To test if the quail is cooked, insert a skewer into the thickest part of the bird, between the body and thigh. If there's blood, it needs more cooking. If the juices are clear, it's cooked). Put to one side to rest and keep warm until needed.

DUCK MAGRET (BREASTS)
Pre-heat the oven to 180°C. Score the skin with a knife at 5 mm intervals. Season with salt and pepper. Heat a heavy-based frying pan and fry duck skin-side down for three minutes or until golden brown. Turn and cook for another three minutes. Transfer to the oven and cook for 5-8 minutes. The duck should be served pink.

TO SERVE
In the centre of plate, press ¼ of the potato into a round form approximately 9 cm in diameter. Remove the form slowly (the potato should hold together) and repeat on each plate. Top each mound of potato with ¼ of the wilted spinach and place a quail on top. Slice each duck magret into six pieces. Fan three of the slices and place on one side of the potato pyramid. Repeat on the other side. To finish, drizzle 20 ml of the shiraz jus over each duck fan. Serve the remaining jus in a sauce dish. Enjoy…

*Wine Match:
Brookland Valley
Pinot Noir*

Pan-fried duck and roasted whole quail

WITH PURPLE
CONGO POTATO
CRUSH,
WILTED SPINACH
AND SHIRAZ JUS

FRANCOIS MORVAN
FLUTES RESTAURANT
RECIPE - SEE PAGE 102

Braised pork belly

IN SOY, GINGER, CHILLI AND STAR ANISE WITH SEARED CARNARVON SCALLOPS AND STEAMED BOK CHOY

STEPHEN REAGAN
NEWTOWN HOUSE
RECIPE - SEE PAGE 108

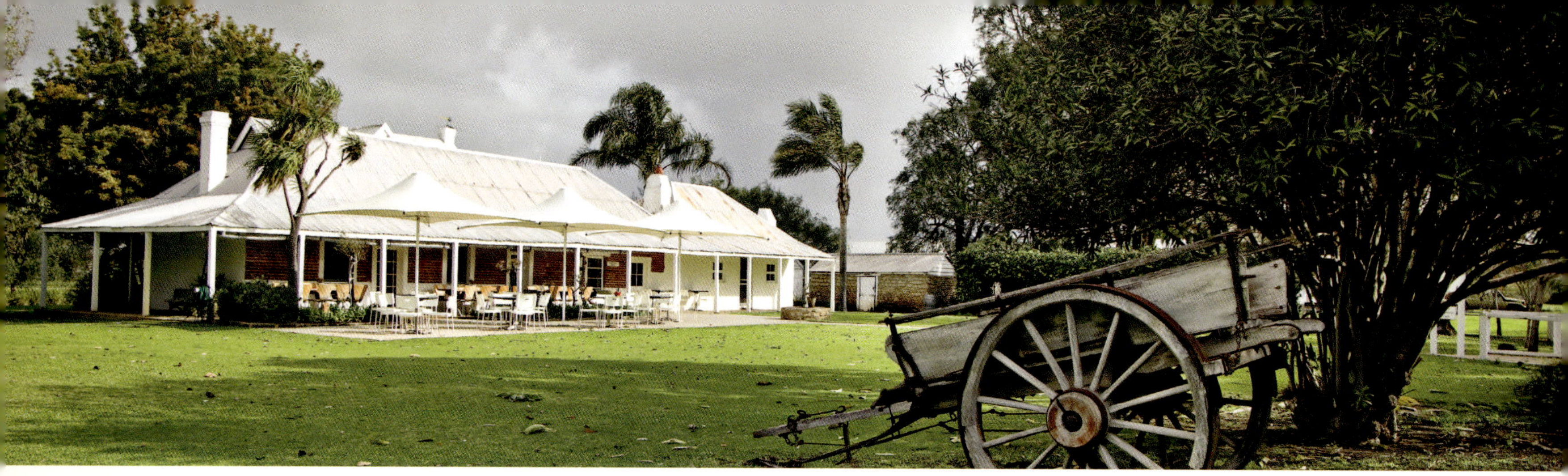

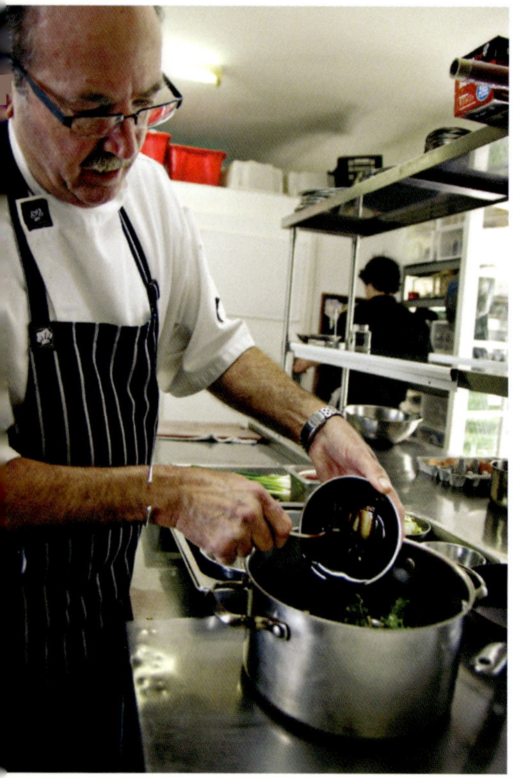

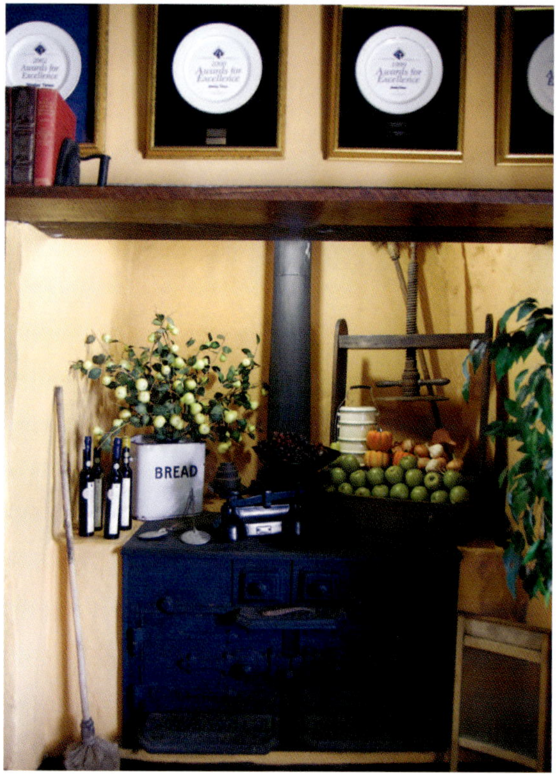
Awards for Excellence
BREAD

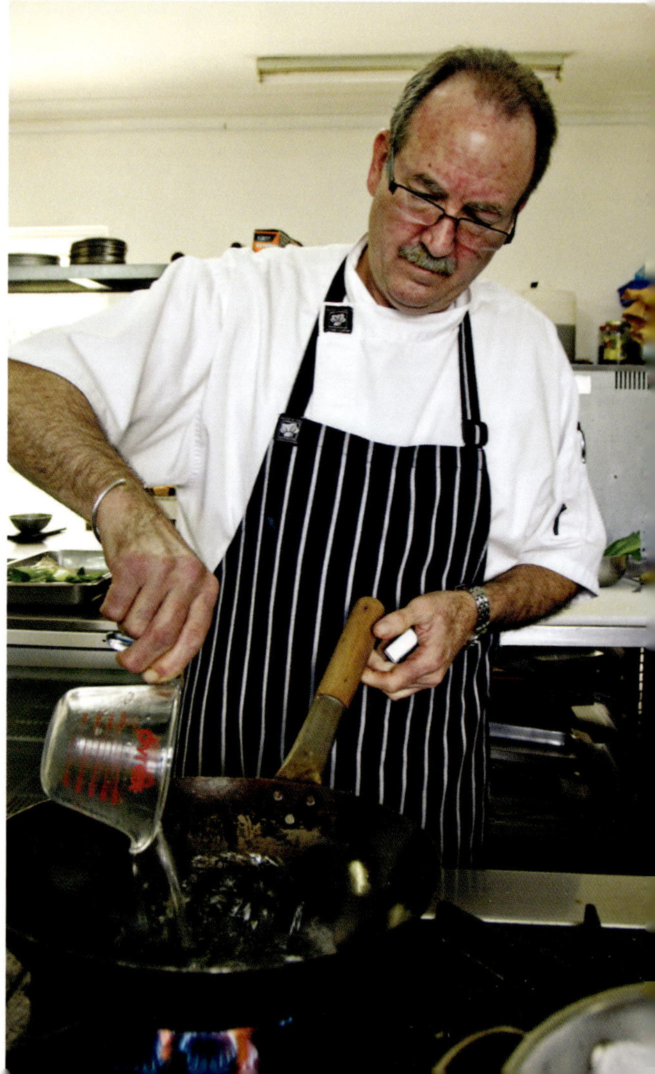

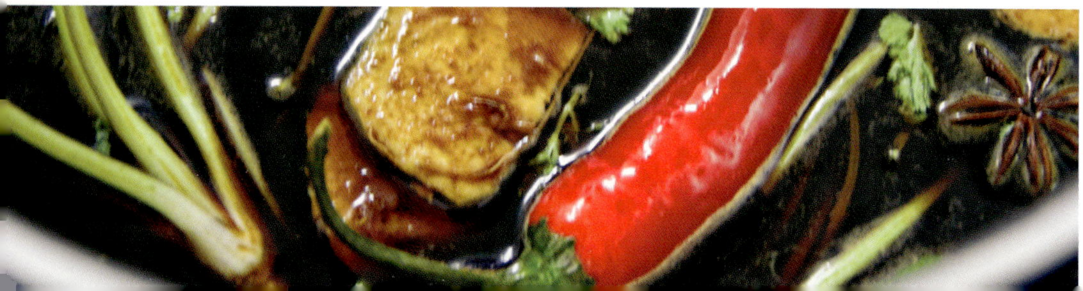

Stephen Reagan

NEWTOWN HOUSE, BUSSELTON

For the past 20 years, Stephen has owned and cooked at Newtown House, an original settlement homestead built in 1851. Over two decades, he has built a reputation as one of the Margaret River region's most respected and consistent chefs.

For five years back in the 1980s, Stephen cooked at Leeuwin Estate and saw the very beginning of Margaret River's quality dining take shape.

"Things were really different when I first arrived here," he recalls. "The area was very new and offered little in the way of dining out. There was Leeuwin and the odd place where you could get a ploughman's lunch, but that was about it".

Shortly afterwards, in a role with the Department of Trade and Commerce, Stephen began championing the promotion of local wineries and Western Australian produce to Asian and European markets.

Today, Stephen says Australia is a melting pot of cultures that have moulded people's tastes in food and contributed to the country's hybrid food culture.

"I see it as a good thing that Australia's relatively young culture gleans from all sorts of places. You only have to go to Northbridge to see the transition from 30 years ago. Back then it was little Italy and now it's little Chinatown or little Vietnam. It's changing all the time".

Stephen is a big fan of slow roasting, "Things cooked this way are really nice and if you do it with duck leg it's also absolutely awesome. You need a bone or some fat to hold it up and you need to cook it slowly so it doesn't toughen up and dry out".

Stephen likes to offset the richness of meats like pork belly and duck with a layering of flavours. "Fresh and crunchy, sweet and sour, salty and bland. Good food is about creating balance," he says.

Whether cooking for himself or others, the chef maintains it's always important to cook what you like. "Otherwise you'll stop cooking," he says. "It's got to be something that turns you on".

Braised pork belly

IN SOY, GINGER, CHILLI AND STAR ANISE WITH SEARED CARNARVON SCALLOPS AND STEAMED BOK CHOY

SERVES 6

PORK
- 750 g pork belly, trimmed and cut into 12 even pieces

BRAISING LIQUOR
- 300 ml salt-reduced soy
- 300 ml kecap manis
- 100 ml sweet sake
- 100 ml dry sherry or Chinese wine
- 300 ml vegetable stock*
- 1 red chilli, left whole
- 5 cm piece of ginger, sliced
- 2 garlic cloves
- 6 star anise
- 1 pandanus leaf
- 1 small bunch of coriander leaves and roots

*Vegetable stock recipe - see page 143

GARNISH
- 1 spring onion
- 1 handful of bean shoots
- 1 fresh red chilli, sliced finely

TO SERVE
- 3 heads of bok choy
- 12 Carnarvon scallops
- 2 tbsp cornflour

Wine Match: Edwards Chardonnay

METHOD

PORK
Place all braising liquor ingredients except cornflour into a medium-sized heavy-based saucepan and bring to the boil. Reduce to a simmer and add pork belly pieces. Cover braising liquor and pork with a cartouche and cook over low heat until pork belly becomes soft and unctuous – approximately three hours. Remove pork belly and set aside. Strain liquor to remove chilli, star anise and other spices. Take half of the strained liquor and thicken with cornflour. The rest of the liquor can be kept for use another time to braise or marinate chicken thighs, wings, drumsticks and duck, or as a marinade for pork ribs.

GARNISH
Julienne the spring onion, beanshoots and red chilli. Place on ice.

TO SERVE
Sear the scallops in a hot pan with a little vegetable oil for approximately 30 seconds per side or until the scallops are evenly caramelized. Steam the bok choy until tender. Reheat pork belly in thickened liquor. Place steamed bok choy on plate. Arrange two pieces of pork belly alongside and pour over a little of the sauce. Top with two scallops and garnish with the julienned spring onion, beanshoots and red chilli.

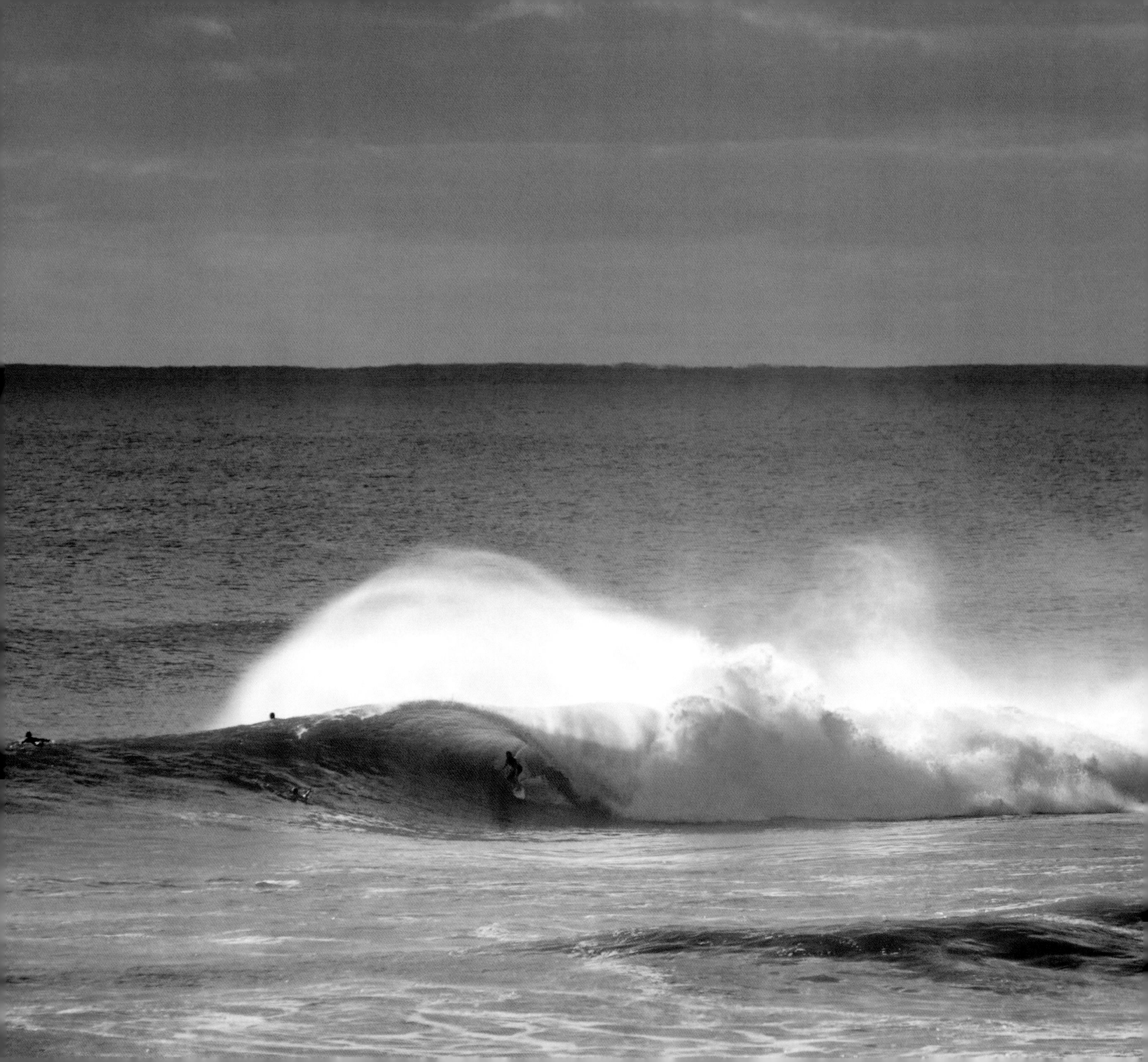

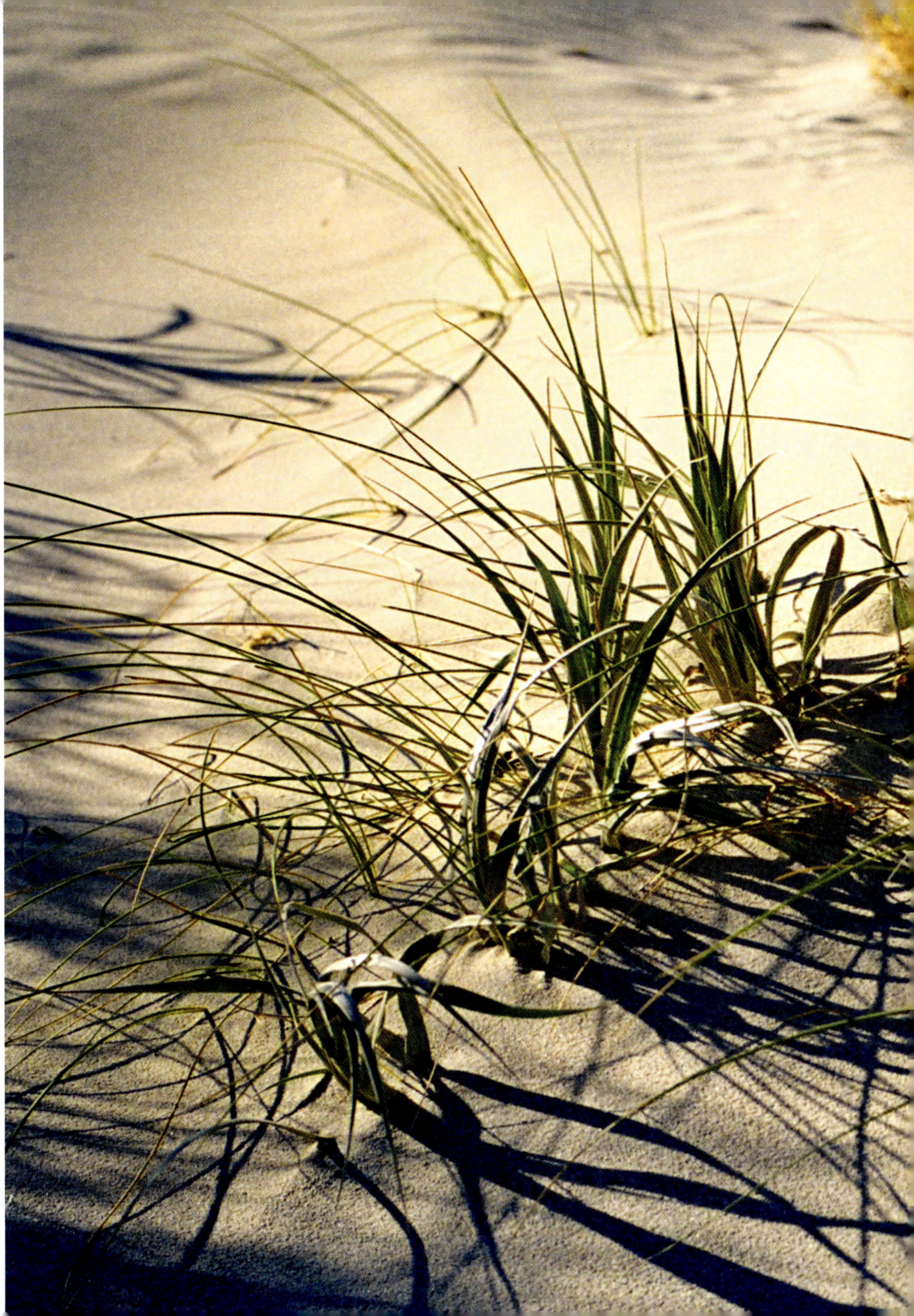

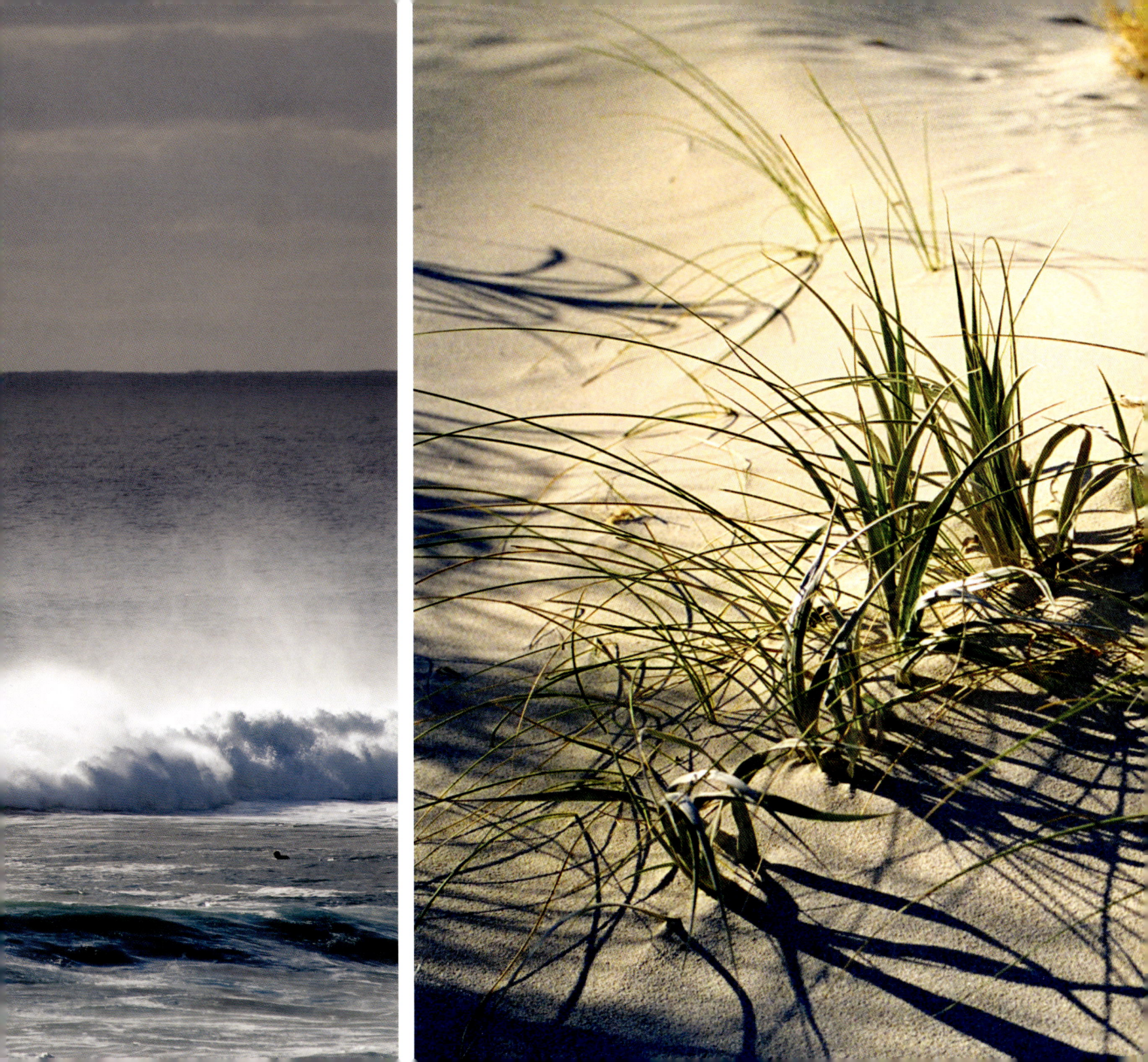

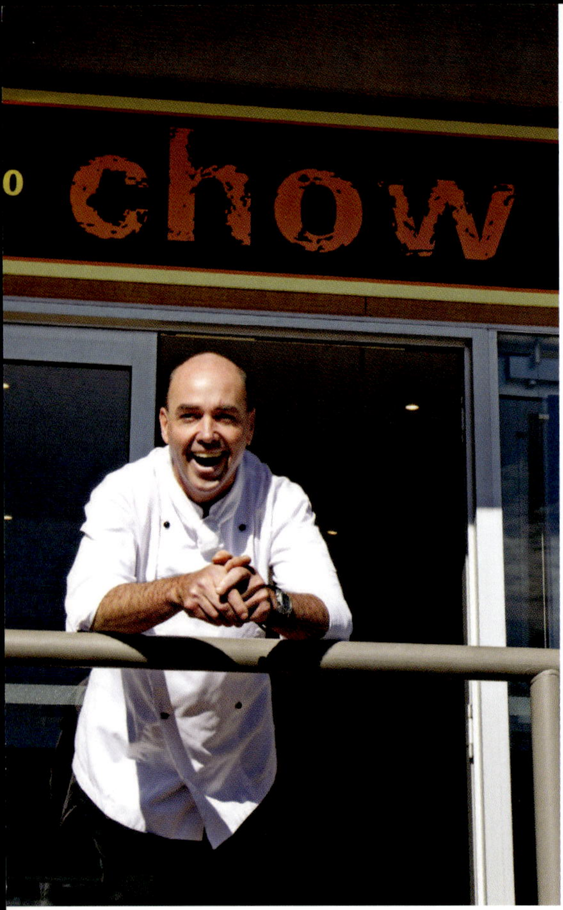
chow

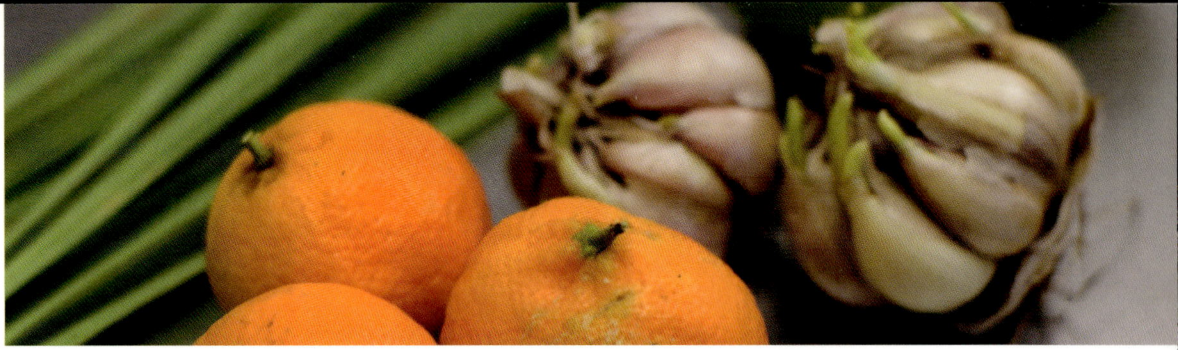

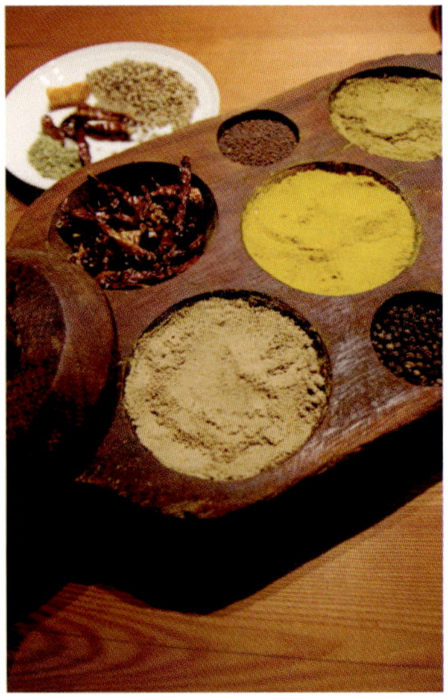

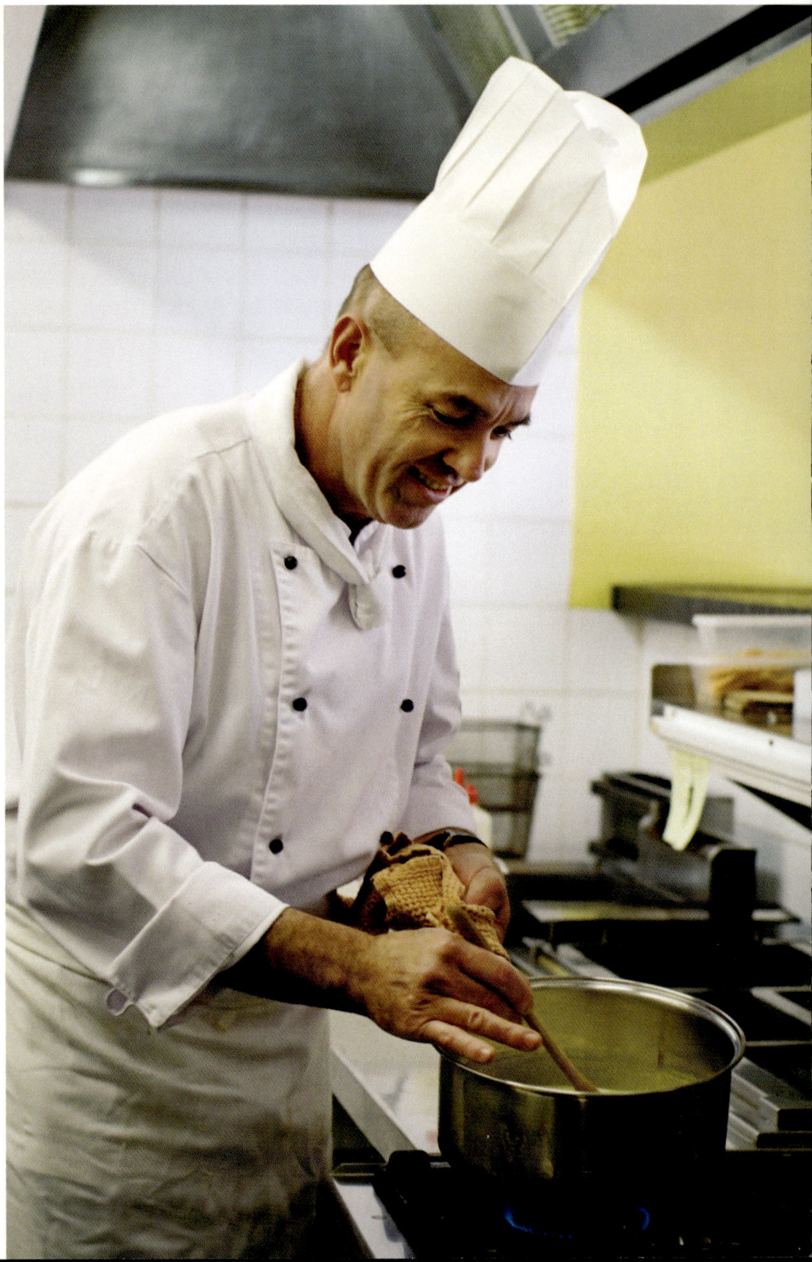

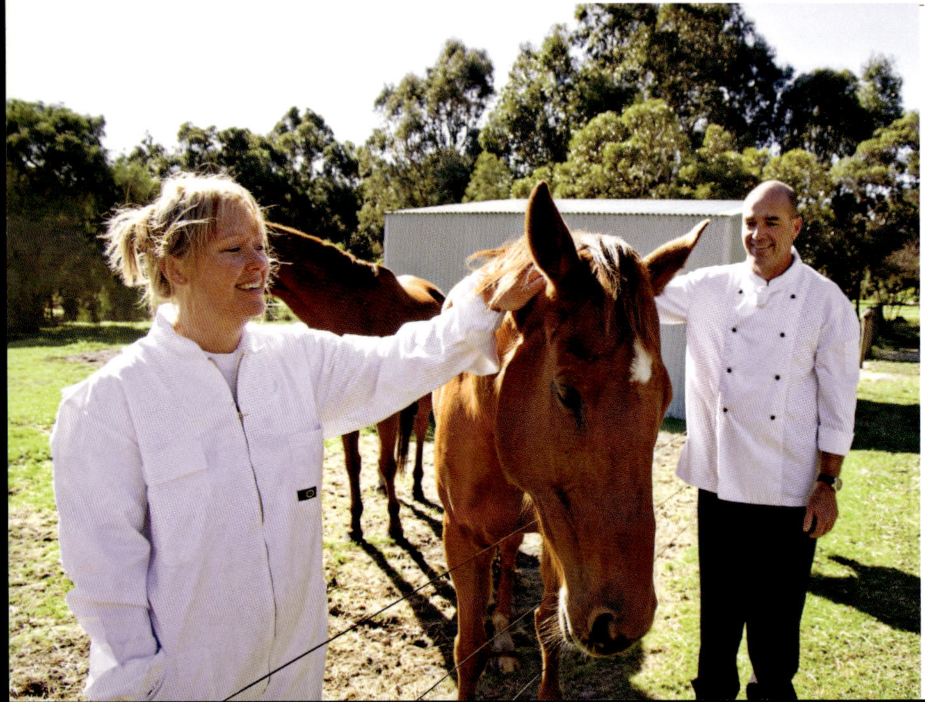

Simon and Ronnie Winter

CHOW CUISINE TO GO, MARGARET RIVER

Many foodies from the close-knit town of Margaret River will remember Simon and Ronnie from their days at the popular Valley Cafe in the mid 1990s.

With a combined cooking experience of over 40 years, Simon and Ronnie are Margaret River food legends, ready to cook up a storm of flavours from around the world at their unique gourmet take-away food outlet. This includes a range of generous desserts, designed for two people or two nights.

Simon says the feedback from satisfied customers makes for satisfied chefs. "When you're out in the surf and some guy next to you says, 'Gee Simon, that great meal you cooked at Chow last night is why I'm surfing so well," it makes you feel a million bucks".

The couple's philosophy is simple. "You should be able to look your customers in the eye, knowing you're serving up food that you're satisfied with," says Simon. "If it's not, we simply don't serve it up".

The couple like to emphasise this point to their apprentices. "We tell them to keep trying until they get it right," says Simon. "No matter how long it takes, it's got to taste good".

Growing up in City Beach, Simon met Ronnie while both worked at the Sheraton Hotel in Perth. For the past eight years, the duo have enjoyed working alongside each other at Chow. Three golden retrievers and two ex-racehorses complete the couple's rural lifestyle. "Ronnie is the brains and ideas while I'm the engine," says Simon.

As well as teaching Simon to ride, Ronnie maintains a thriving vegetable garden. Her garlic crop supplies the Chow kitchen, while her latest foray into beekeeping is not only a hobby but looks set to yield 200 litres of honey each year.

"It's so relaxing on a summer's afternoon, hanging out with the bees as you attend to them," she says. "You can't rush anything otherwise you end up upsetting them".

The obliging couple declare a similar satisfaction with looking after their customers. Ronnie says some dishes are even named after a few of their favourites.

"There's the Gillian, for instance, a glass noodle salad with chicken and prawns," says Simon.

"People ring up and say, 'three Gillians thanks'!".

Yellow Wagyu beef curry

WITH HOT 'N' SOUR SALAD

SERVES 6 AS A MAIN COURSE

BEEF
- 1.5 kg boneless Wagyu beef shin

SPICE MIX
- 1 brown onion roughly sliced
- 50 g finely diced fresh garlic
- 40 g diced fresh ginger
- 10 g coriander seeds
- 3 g cumin seeds
- 3 g fennel seeds
- 5 dried red chillis, soaked in hot water for ½ an hour
- 5 g grated fresh tumeric root
- 4 tbsp coriander root
- 400 ml coconut cream
- 400 ml coconut milk
- 6 tsp brown sugar
- 40 ml fish sauce

MASTERSTOCK
- 6 L water
- 3 cloves garlic, sliced
- 3 cm knob ginger, sliced
- 1 small handful of green spring onion ends
- 1 stick cassia bark or cinnamon
- 2 star anise
- 375 ml light soy sauce
- 375 ml shao hsing wine
- 75 g rock, palm or other brown sugar

RICE
- Steamed rice for serving

Wine Match: Happs Three Hills Nebbiolo

METHOD

MASTERSTOCK
Bring all ingredients to the boil and simmer for 30 minutes. Reserve until required.

BEEF
Braise the beef in 2 L masterstock for three hours or until tender. Drain the beef then wrap tightly in plastic film and refrigerate overnight. Reserve the masterstock for a rainy day.

YELLOW CURRY SAUCE
Dry sauté onions, garlic and ginger on low heat until caramelized, they will turn a golden brown. Roast coriander, cumin and fennel seeds. Grind to a fine powder. In a food processor, blend chilli, onion mix, turmeric and coriander root to a paste, then add ground spices. Keep coriander leaves for salad.

Slice meat thinly. Bring coconut milk and coconut cream to a simmer. Add the paste and meat, seasoning first with sugar and then with the fish sauce and tasting as you go. The idea is to add as much as needed to achieve a balanced flavour. Continue to simmer until beef has warmed through.

HOT 'N' SOUR SALAD
To help give an Asian influence to your salad, include ingredients such as ginger, coriander, lime juice, green papaya, fresh red chillies, peanuts and beanshoots.

TO SERVE
Put a scoop of steam rice on a plate. Pour beef curry over the rice. Serve Asian salad on the side.

Note : Masterstock is used extensively in Asian cooking for adding flavour to poached meats. Many chefs make their own, boiling it after each use and re-using it again and again.

Yellow Wagyu beef curry

WITH HOT 'N' SOUR SALAD

SIMON AND RONNIE
WINTER
CHOW CUISINE TO GO
RECIPE - SEE PAGE 114

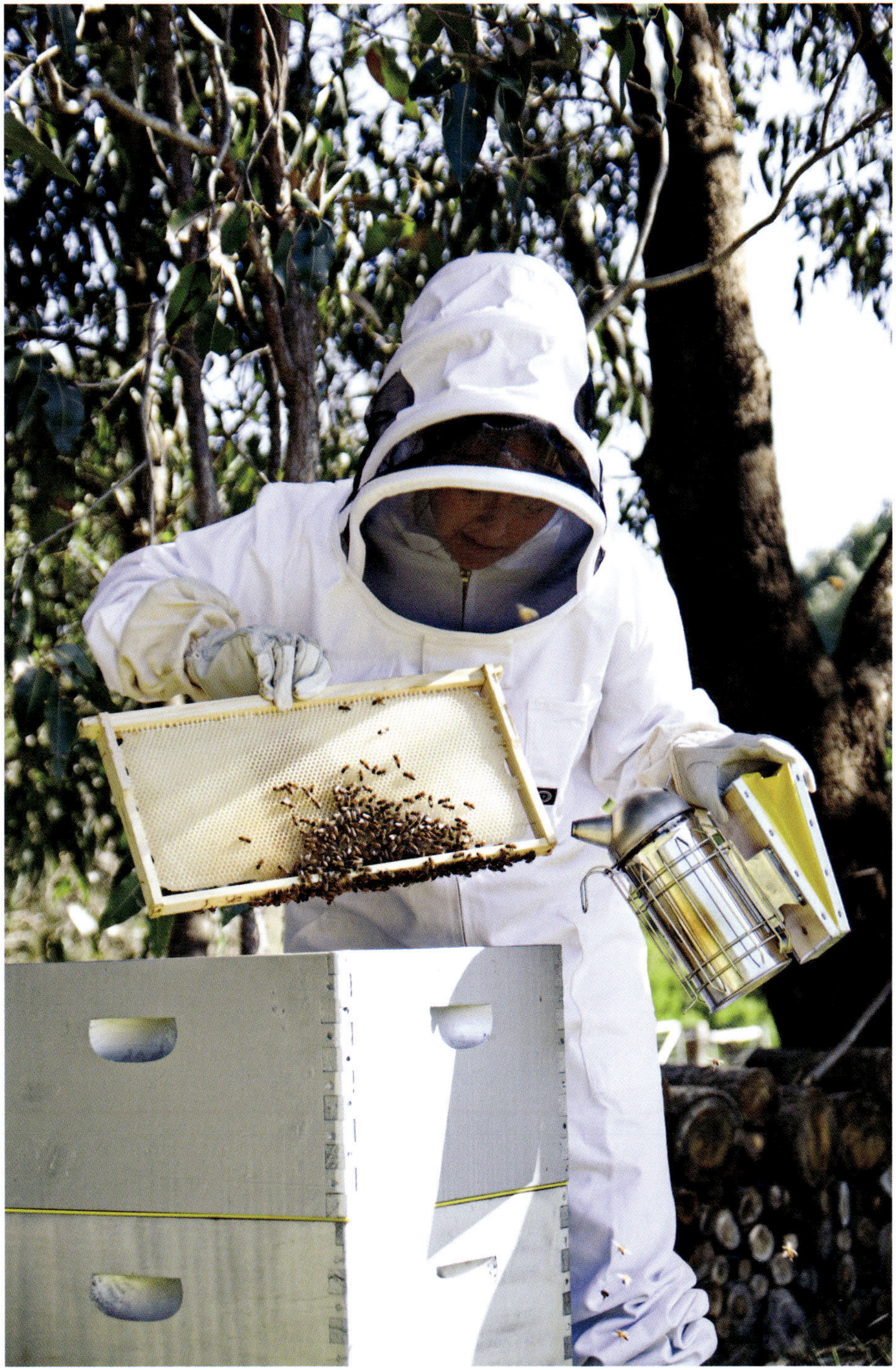

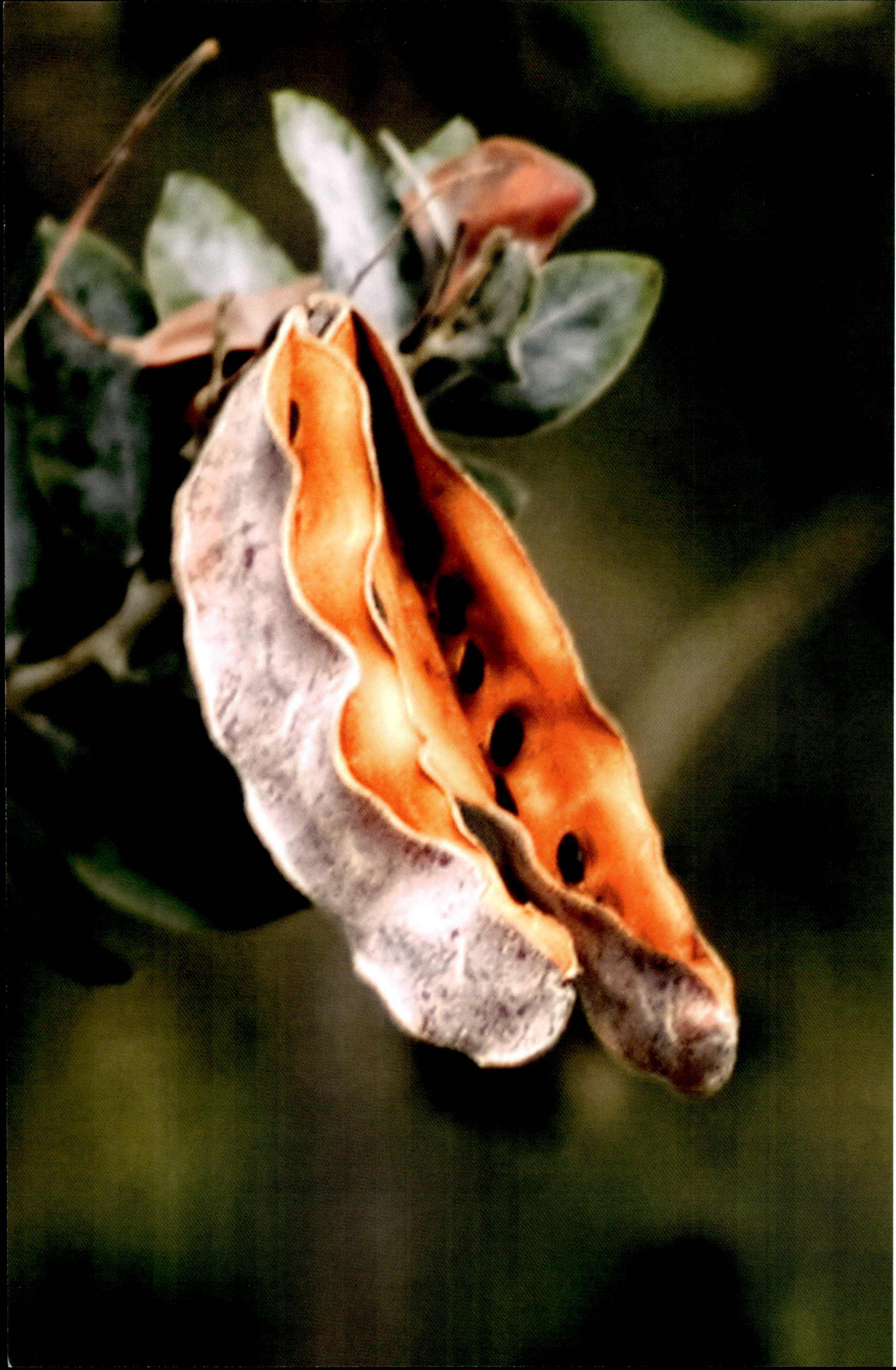
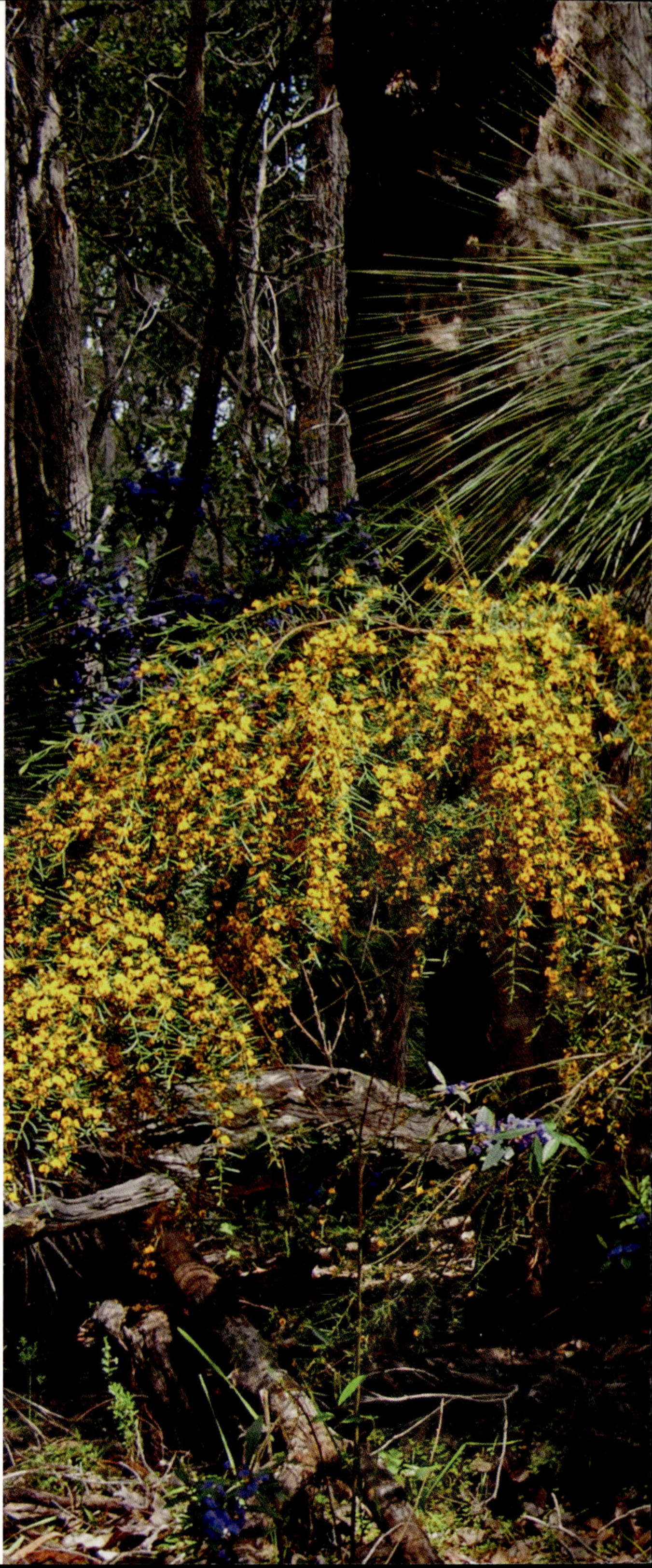

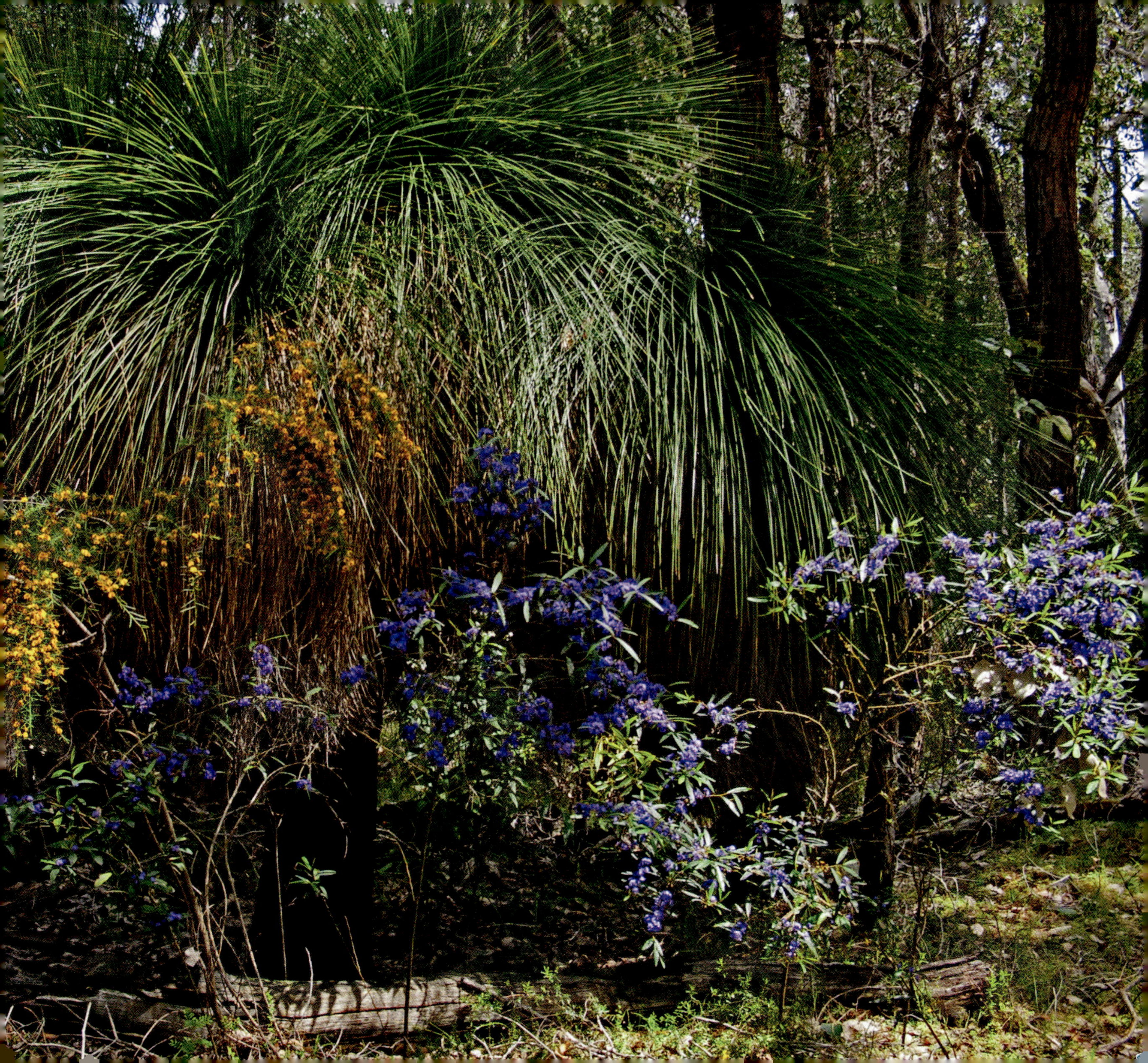

desserts

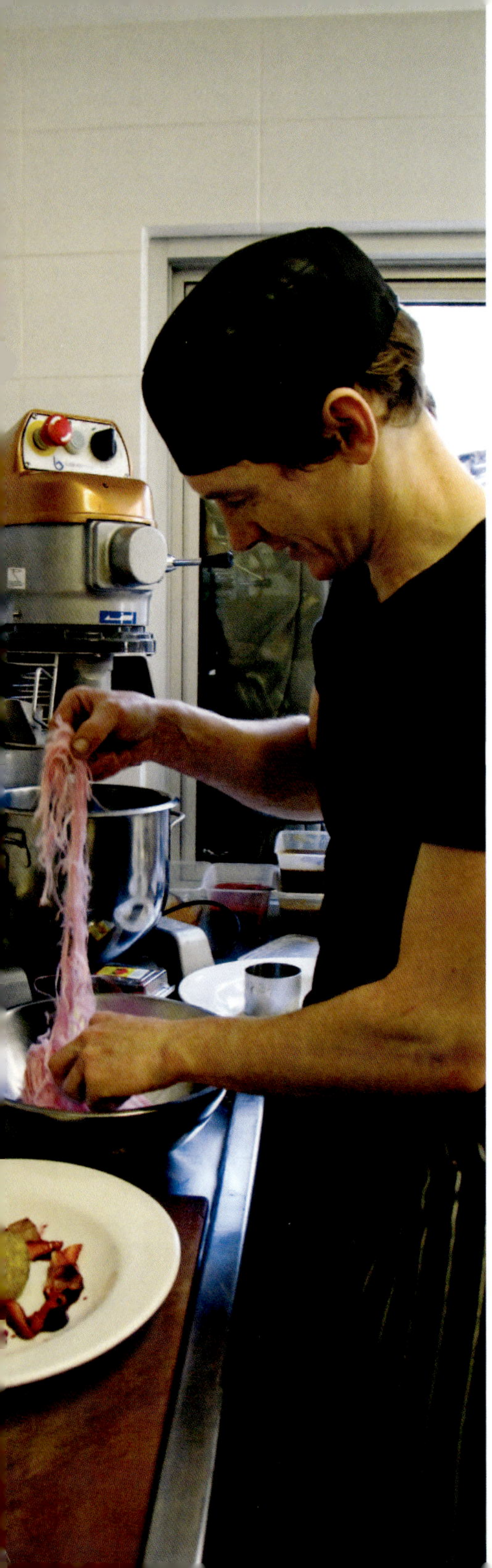
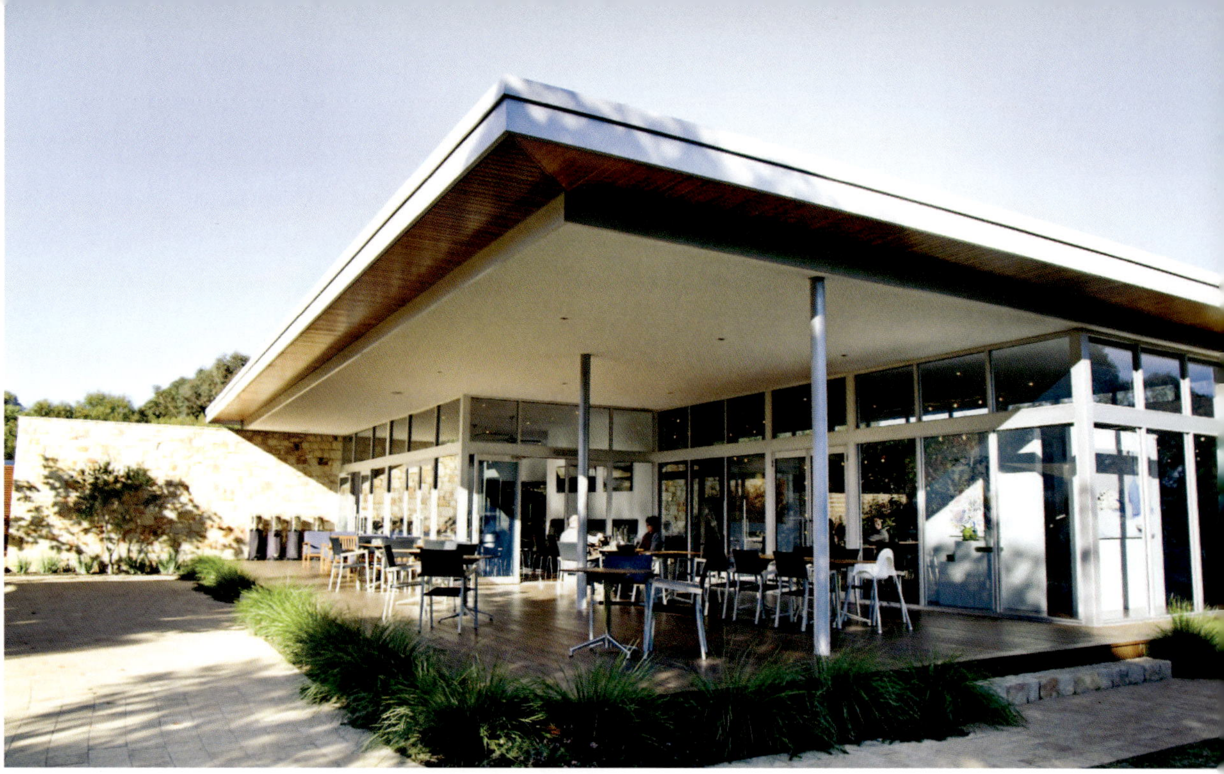
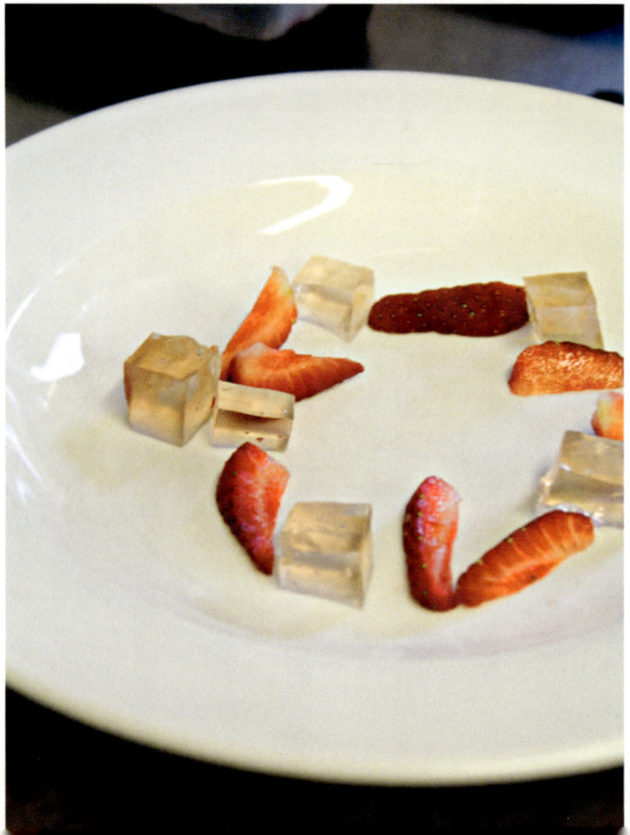
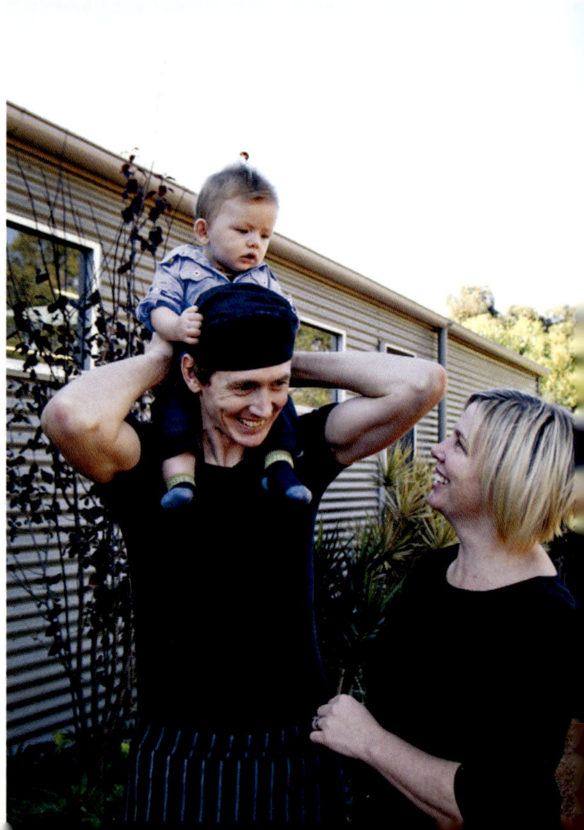

Blair Allen

THE STUDIO BISTRO, YALLINGUP

Blair's rural upbringing in the Wheatbelt town of Merredin, in central Western Australia, has instilled in him a deep connection to the land as well as a great respect for what it produces. It also helped him gravitate towards a career in cooking.

He recalls how, at the age of 10, his dad took him to help slaughter three sheep. "It was brutal and honest and made me appreciate the food on my dinner table all the more".

Blair's mother also played a pivotal role in his career choice. "Living in a small town like Merredin, patisseries were rare and mum was always making wedding cakes for friends. Luckily some of her pastry skills rubbed off onto me".

At an early age, Blair looked after the family vegetable patch and has fond memories of going out to pick mushrooms after the first rains. "I believe strongly in paying respect to where food comes from and will be giving my son the same lessons when he's old enough to understand".

After completing his qualifications, Blair cooked at Alto's in Subiaco. Here he fell in love with the simple pleasures of the modern Italian kitchen as well as his future wife Renee, Alto's restaurant manager.

Blair and Renee moved to the South West seven years ago. "I immediately felt more connected to the community and environment," says Blair. "And although the work was challenging, at least there was plenty of it".

Blair initially worked at the Quay West Resort, Bunker Bay. He then spent three years as a sous chef at Voyager Estate before being promoted to head chef.

When Nigel and Sue Smith asked him to come aboard at The Studio Bistro, he couldn't resist. The bistro opened in late 2010 and sits in beautifully-landscaped native gardens adjacent to a national park.

Blair and his team design their menu to offer innovative and sensational taste experiences, using seasonal local ingredients wherever possible. Meat and dairy products are sourced locally, and Blair likes to catch his own Blue Swimmer crabs, King George whiting and local squid.

"As long as it's fresh, local and sustainable it's good enough for me," he says.

Chocolate and vanilla bombe,

PRALINE, ROSE JELLY, BERRIES AND FAIRY FLOSS

SERVES 6-8

CHOCOLATE GANACHE
- 250 g dark chocolate
- 150 ml cream
- 25 g glucose syrup

BOMBE BASE
- 250 g sugar
- 100 g water
- 4 egg whites
- Seeds scraped from 1 vanilla pod
- 400 ml cream

ROSE JELLY
- 250 ml water
- 150 g sugar
- 1 tsp rosewater
- 1½ gelatin leaves
- 5 g organic dried rose petals

PRALINE
- 125 g sugar
- 25 ml water
- 25 g hazelnuts, toasted and brown husks removed
- 25 g blanched almonds, toasted and brown husks removed
- 25 g pistachios, toasted

BERRIES
- 50 g frozen raspberries
- 50 g frozen blueberries
- 50 g sugar
- Juice and zest of half a lemon
- 50 g fresh strawberries

TO SERVE
- Rose-flavored Pashmak fairy floss

Wine match: Carpe Diem 'Pasitto Dolce' Sauvignon Blanc, Margaret River — or, if you're feeling a little frisky, a Studio Bistro Espresso Martini!

METHOD

CHOCOLATE GANACHE
Heat the cream and glucose in a saucepan and stir to combine, bringing almost to the boil. Immediately pour this over the chocolate. Allow to sit in a warm place for a few minutes, then stir until smooth. Allow to cool to room temperature.

BOMBE BASE
Place the sugar, water and vanilla seeds in a saucepan and bring gently to the boil. Heat this syrup to softball stage or about 120°C on a sugar thermometer. Whisk the egg whites until soft peaks form. With the mixer running, gradually pour in the hot sugar syrup and continue to whisk until the mixture cools to room temperature. Whisk the cream until soft peaks form and fold, a third at a time, into the meringue. Lightly fold in the chocolate ganache to form a brown ripple through the creamy mixture. Transfer to a container and freeze for at least six hours.

ROSE JELLY
Heat the water, rosewater and sugar to a simmer. Taste and add more rosewater as needed. Meanwhile soak the gelatin leaves in cold water for about five minutes or until soft. Drain and squeeze out the excess water. Stir the soaked gelatin and flower petals into the warm syrup and stir until gelatin has dissolved. Pour the mixture into a dish lined with cling film. Allow to set for at least six hours. Turn the jelly out and cut roughly into chunky squares or pieces. Reserve for later use.

PRALINE
Place the sugar and water in a pan and bring to the boil over moderate heat. Simmer until the syrup turns a light golden colour. Stir in the nuts then turn out onto silicone paper. Allow to cool completely. Blend the praline in a food processor until it reaches the consistency of raw sugar granules. Reserve for later use.

BERRIES
Place all ingredients except the strawberries into a saucepan and bring to a simmer. Stir and remove from the heat. Allow to cool, chop the strawberries and stir these into the mixture.

TO SERVE
Scoop some of the bombe mixture, form into balls and roll in the praline to completely coat the outside. Place one bombe in the centre of each bowl or plate and position some jelly around it. Drizzle with the berries and top with a little fairy floss garnish with extra rose petals if desired. Serve immediately.

Chocolate and vanilla bombe,

PRALINE, ROSE JELLY, BERRIES AND FAIRY FLOSS

BLAIR ALLEN
THE STUDIO GALLERY
AND BISTRO
RECIPE - SEE PAGE 124

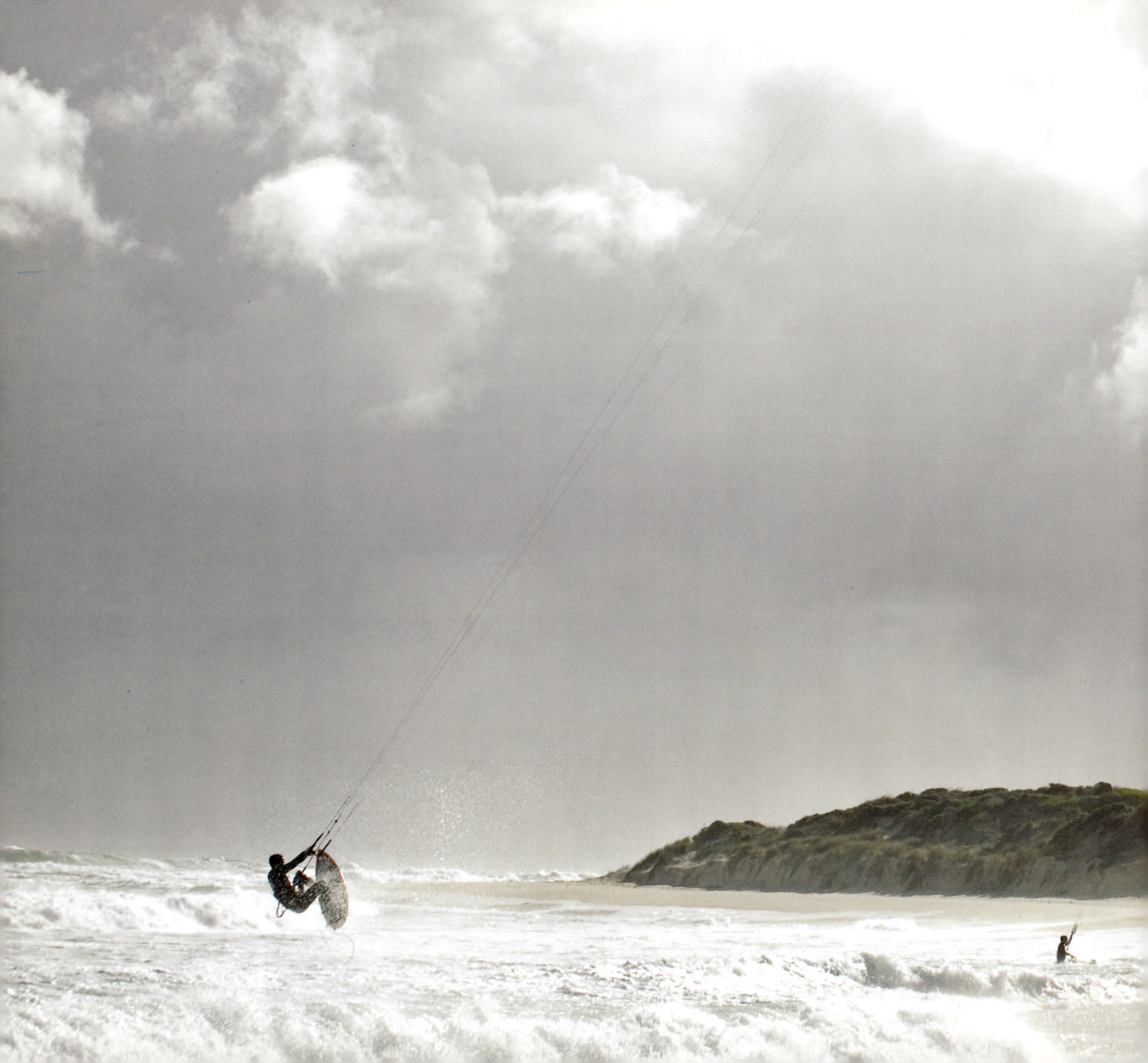

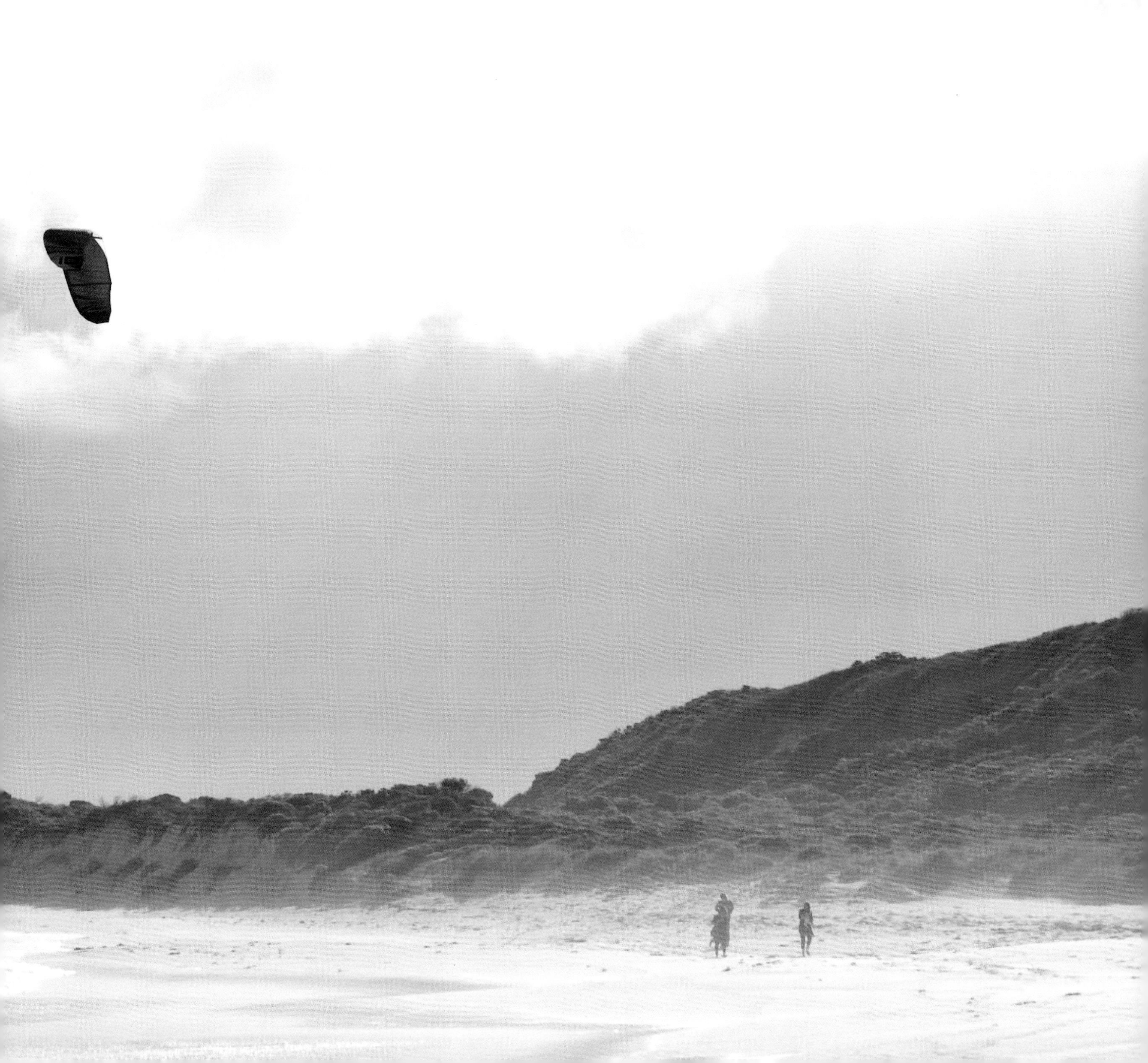

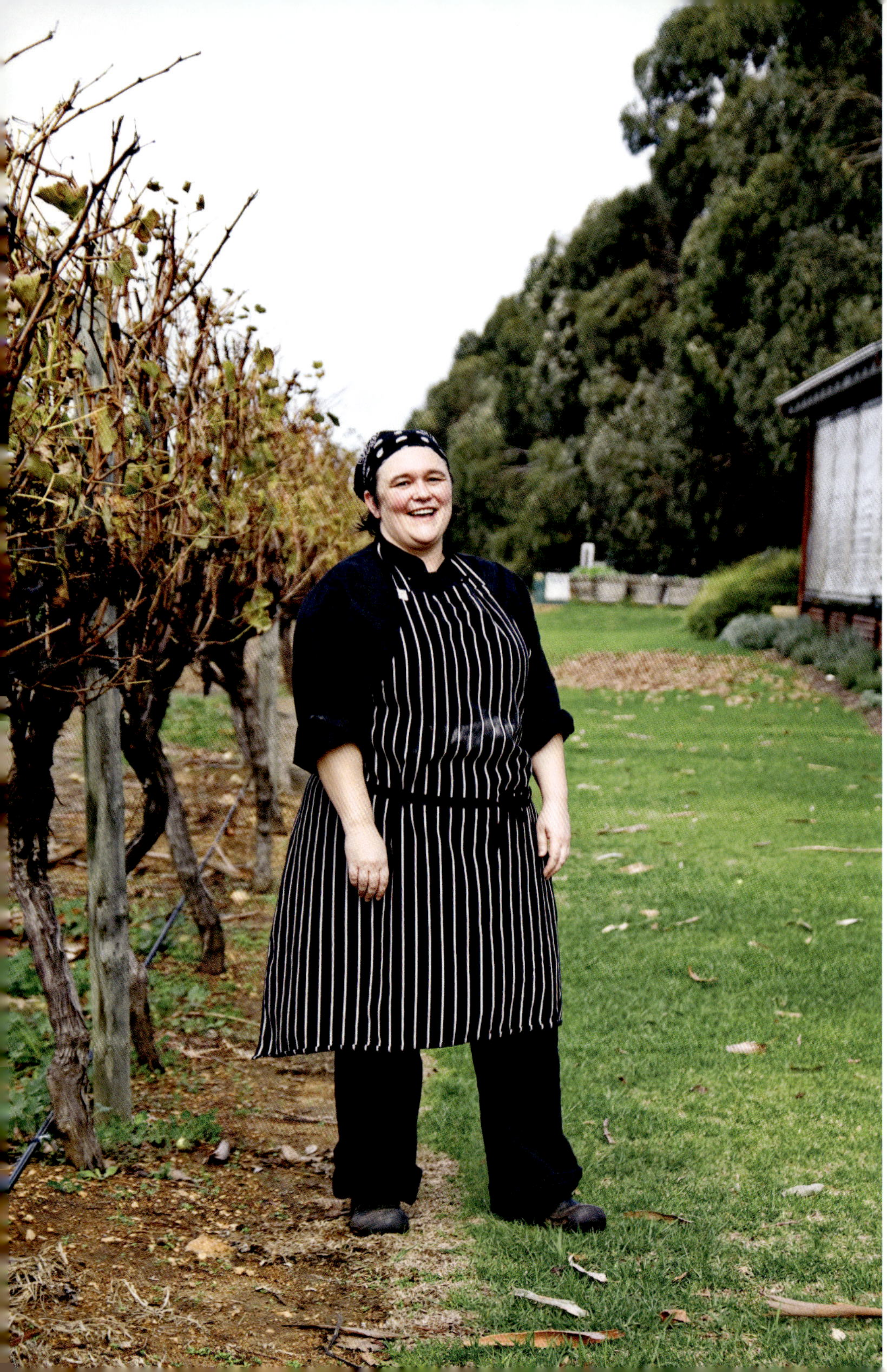

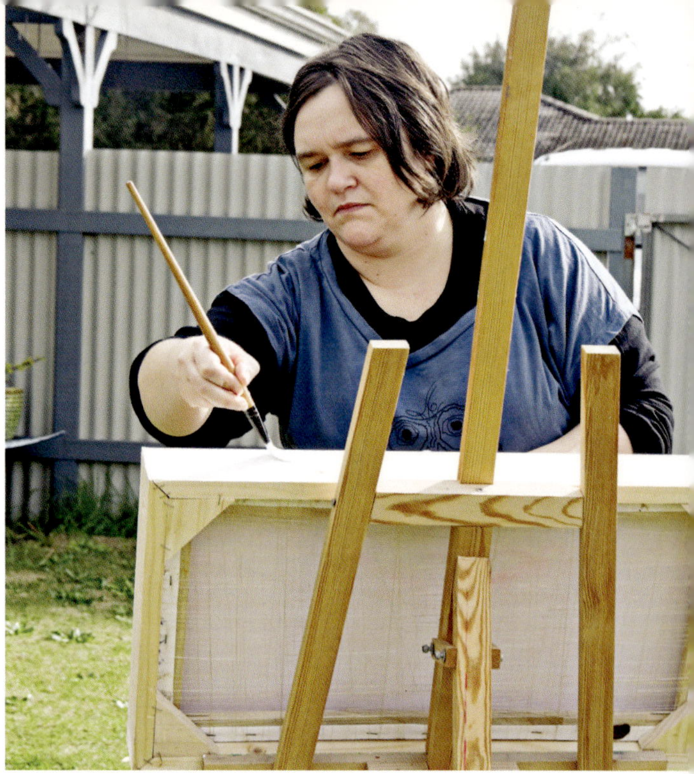

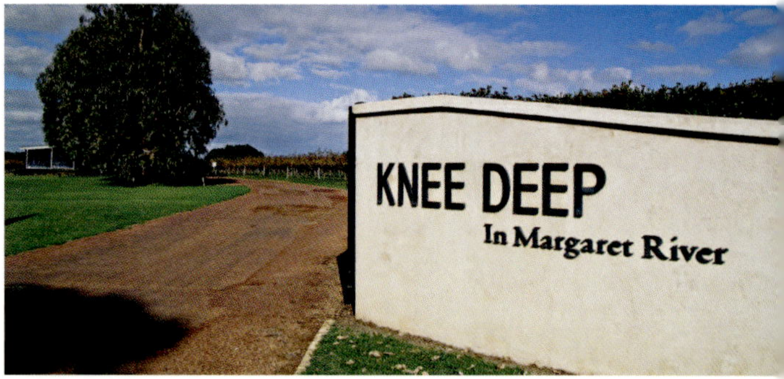
KNEE DEEP
In Margaret River

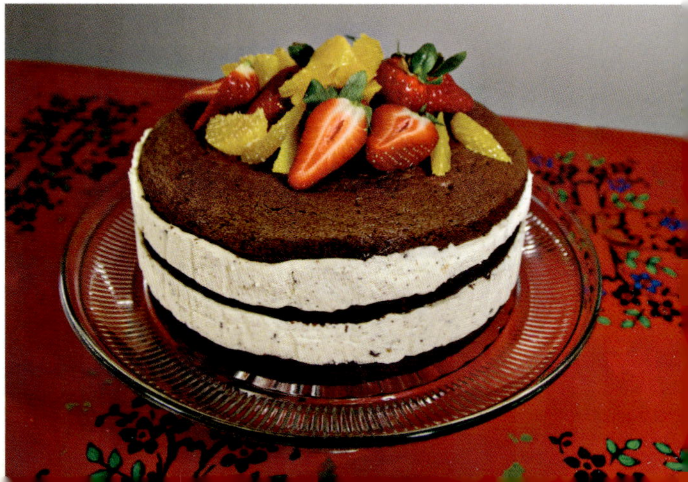

Michelle Babb

KNEE DEEP WINES, WILYABRUP

Michelle grew up in rural Busselton surrounded by home-grown food. Influenced by a family of talented cooks, Michelle's passion for baking grew from an early age. "The kitchen was the hub of the household growing up. We ate mostly home-grown produce as Mum always had a vegetable garden and a few chickens. Even now I often drop by mum's place to raid the garden for fresh herbs and vegetables".

While studying for her fine arts degree, Michelle worked as a short order cook. "I learned to put aesthetically pleasing things together on the plate. It's always important to remember that we eat with our eyes as well as our mouths".

Michelle's cooking style has been influenced by the people she has worked with during a diverse career. "I did a stint at Peppers Hotel and Resort Group in the east before returning to the wineries of Margaret River," she says.

Since joining the kitchen brigade at the award-winning Knee Deep restaurant, Michelle has incorporated a love of eye-catching artistry into her work as a chef and particularly enjoys making desserts. "There's a lot of skill involved in presentation. I get to play a lot with colour and texture".

Michelle's flair for the visual also sees her moonlighting as a painter of quirky hand drawings on custom-made canvas handbags and canvas oil paintings sealed with resin. Her work can be seen in local galleries and is also sold internationally.

Her strong sense of home, freshness and beauty is a trademark of Knee Deep. "The dishes and flavours we serve are based around seasonal produce, strongly influenced by our eclectic kitchen team. We also try to support local producers and businesses when constructing our menu".

When not cooking some of the region's finest contemporary Australian cuisine or at work in her art studio, Michelle says she prefers to dine at a wide variety of restaurants to help her gain an insight into current trends.

"I like to travel and have spent time living overseas and in the eastern states. But I'm always drawn back to my home town".

Cookies and cream parfait

WITH ORANGE BUTTERSCOTCH SAUCE

MAKES ONE CAKE WHICH SERVES 16

CHOCOLATE SPONGE
- 1 tbsp butter
- ½ cup cocoa
- ½ cup water
- 4 eggs, separated
- 1 cup sugar
- 1 cup self-raising flour

COOKIES AND CREAM PARFAIT
- 300 g white chocolate
- 5 egg yolks
- 500 ml cream
- 2 tbsp dark chocolate, crushed with a rolling pin
- 2 tbsp crushed shortbread biscuits (or any non-cream biscuit of your choice)

ORANGE BUTTERSCOTCH SAUCE
- 2 ½ cups sugar
- 1 ½ cups water
- 1 cup orange juice
- 75 g butter
- ½ tsp salt
- Zest of one orange

Wine Match: Knee Deep Sweet Chardonnay

METHOD

CHOCOLATE SPONGE

Pre-heat oven to 180°C. Line and grease a 20 cm cake tin. Place butter, cocoa and water in saucepan and heat until butter has melted and mixture is smooth. Beat egg whites until stiff. Gradually add yolks then sugar, beating until all the sugar is dissolved. Fold in chocolate mix and sifted flour. Bake in the oven until skewer comes out clean when inserted into cake. Allow to cool completely before cutting into three horizontal layers.

COOKIES AND CREAM PARFAIT

Melt white chocolate in a bowl over a pot of simmering water, being careful not to let the bowl touch the water. In a separate bowl, whip cream until soft peaks form. Put the egg yolks in a bowl over a pot of simmering water and whisk until they are thick and foamy. Stir through the melted white chocolate. Allow mixture to cool slightly, then gradually fold in the whipped cream, finely crushed dark chocolate and crushed shortbread. Refrigerate until ready to assemble cake.

ORANGE BUTTERSCOTCH SAUCE

Combine sugar and water and boil until you have a deep, amber-coloured toffee. Pour in orange juice and stir to combine. Whisk in butter, orange zest and salt. Keep whisking occasionally until sauce has cooled.

TO ASSEMBLE

Line a 20 cm cake tin with baking paper. Put one disc of cake into bottom of tin and top with ½ of the parfait mix. Top with another layer of cake then add the remaining parfait mix. Add the final cake disc. Freeze for at least four hours.

TO SERVE

Michelle recommends removing the finished cake from the freezer and allowing it to soften a little before portioning into 16 wedges. Serve with orange butterscotch sauce and garnish with fresh seasonal fruit.

Cookies and cream parfait

WITH ORANGE
BUTTERSCOTCH SAUCE

MICHELLE BABB
KNEE DEEP WINES
RECIPE - SEE PAGE 132

Eaton Mess

ANTHONY JANSSEN
GNARABAR AND WHITE
ELEPHANT CAFE
RECIPE - SEE PAGE 138

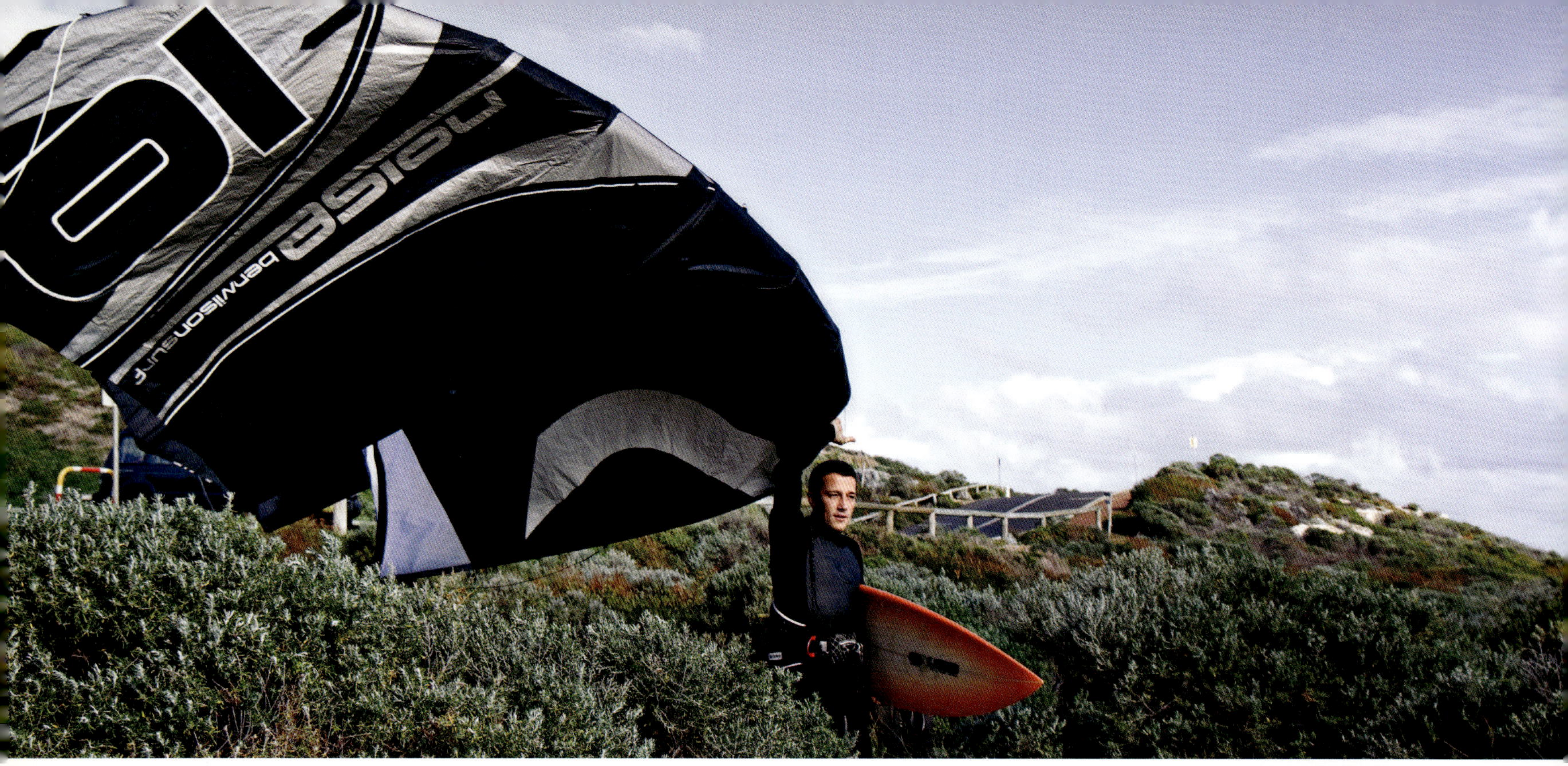

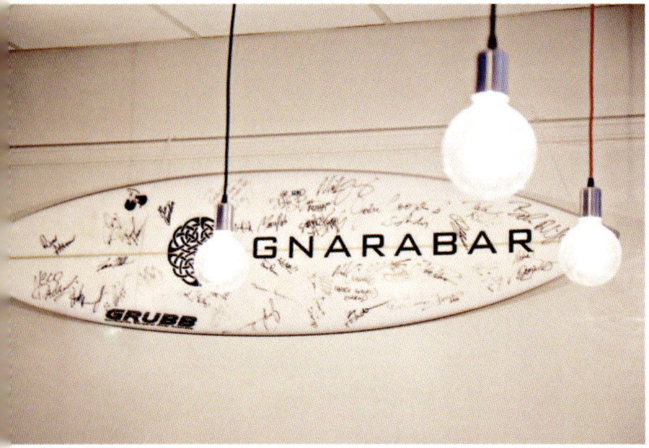
GNARABAR
GRUBB

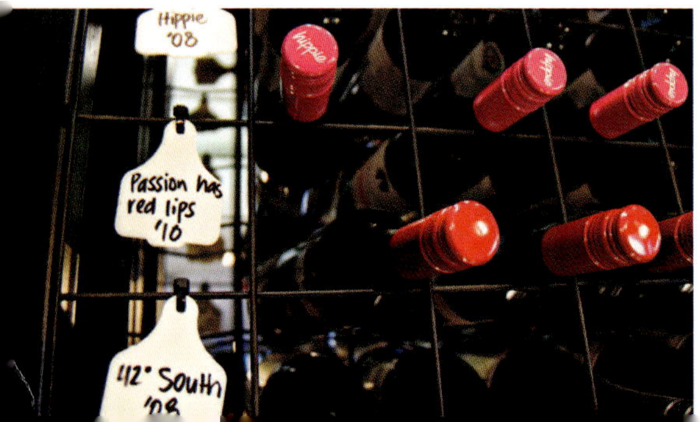
Hippie '08
Passion has red lips '10

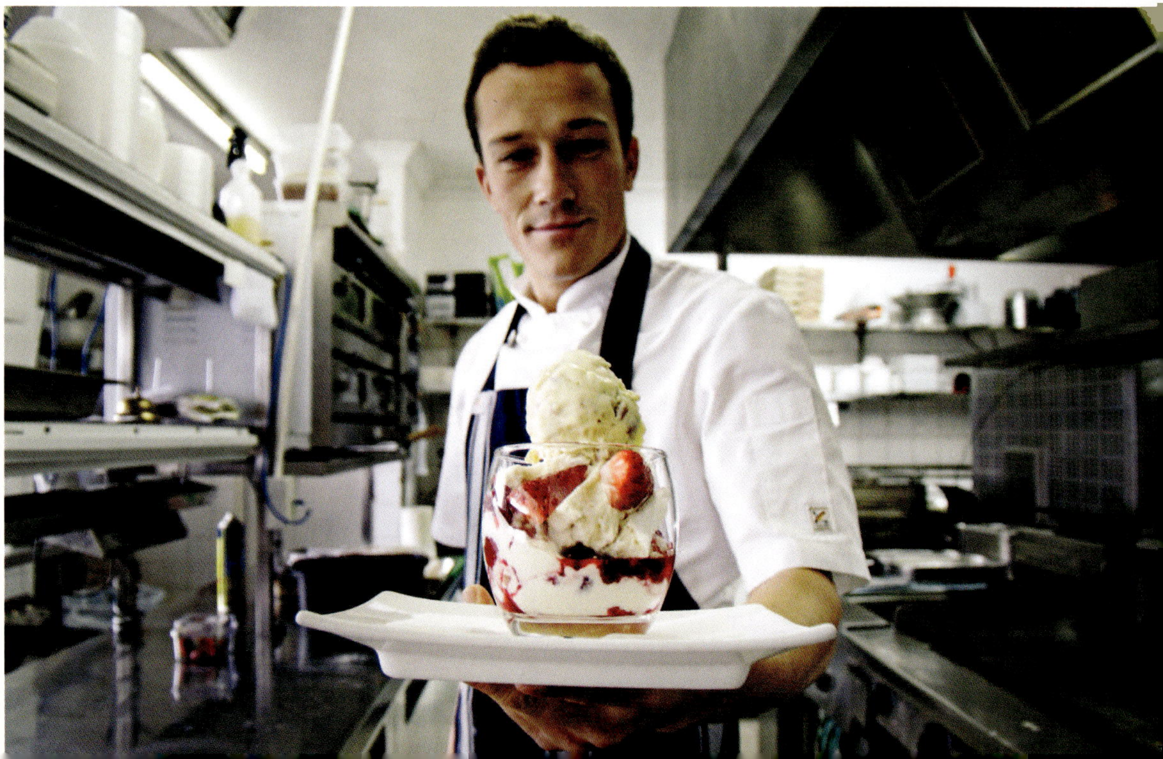

Anthony Janssen

GNARABAR AND WHITE ELEPHANT CAFE, GNARABUP

Anthony, or AJ as he's known locally, owns Gnarabar and its close neighbour, the White Elephant Beach Cafe.

Winner of the 2011 Telstra Small Business Award, Gnarabar restaurant and bar exude a casual and sophisticated beach-side vibrancy. The 60-seater opened in 2006 and remains true to AJ's vision — "a restaurant that offers good food, good service and keeps the customers coming back".

AJ left school in Year 10 and received his early training as a cook in the regional Victorian town of Bendigo. He then moved to the Whitsunday Islands, where he cooked at Palm Bay Hideaway, in the heart of the World Heritage-listed Great Barrier Reef. He also trained at the luxury resort Raes on Wategos Byron Bay, where he learned to cook traditional and modern Thai cuisine.

AJ moved to Margaret River because of the ocean. Under his ownership, Gnarabar was an instant success with locals and visitors, but running one restaurant wasn't challenging enough for AJ. So he set himself another challenge — renovating an old beach kiosk at Gnarabup and opening the White Elephant Beach Cafe. Here AJ continues the Gnarabar tradition of great food, coupled with one of the most magical beach views in the country.

On his days off the entrepreneur likes to head down to Surfers Point, one of Margaret River's most popular surfing beaches. Here, the rolling swells and sea breezes provide ideal conditions for AJ and his mates to indulge in their favourite adventure sport of kite surfing. (See AJ in action on page 128)

"Working for yourself never feels like work," he says. "It's your own project so you're more innovative. And if you do it right, you've got the time to enjoy life".

AJ says the secrets to his successes are consistency and a young crew of dedicated professionals. "Our crew are the heart and soul of the business and without the team we couldn't operate. And they continue to be our focus going forward".

As for patrons, "we cater to the surfer in bare feet and boardies and to the the people in luxury properties over the hill," says AJ. The son might want a burger but dad wants something more fancy. Here they can have both".

Eaton Mess

SERVES 6

MERINGUE
- 3 egg whites
- 150 g castor sugar
- 1 pinch salt
- 5 tsp lemon Juice

RHUBARB MIX
- 300 g rhubarb, peeled, washed and chopped into 1cm pieces
- 150 g Granny Smith apples, peeled, washed and chopped into 1cm cubes
- 8 tbsp castor sugar
- 4 tbsp water
- 2 tbsp lemon juice
- 2 whole star anise

RHUBARB CREAM
- 300 ml whipping cream
- 8 tbsp rhubarb mix

TO SERVE
- 12 strawberries, quartered
- 6 scoops of good quality vanilla ice-cream

"Our best selling dessert is an old English classic, reinvented here by my business partner Benjamin Bishop," says Gnarabar's Anthony Janssen. "The secret is to make sure the meringue is really crisp and white. The tartness of the rhubarb balances it perfectly"

METHOD

MERINGUE
Pre-heat oven to 140°C. Line a 40 cm oven tray with greaseproof paper. Whisk egg whites until soft peaks form. Gradually add sugar one third at a time, whisking well in between each addition. Continue whisking until all sugar is incorporated and meringue is stiff and really shiny. Spread meringue on tray and bake for one hour or until crisp. Allow to cool.

RHUBARB MIX
Place all ingredients except lemon juice in a heavy-based saucepan and cook over low heat until the rhubarb is stewed and the apple soft. Remove from the heat and add the lemon juice. Remove the star anise. Allow to cool.

RHUBARB CREAM
Whisk cream until firm peaks form. Fold through four tablespoons of the rhubarb mix.

TO SERVE
Break meringue into small, uneven pieces. Layer in six glasses or bowls with remaining apple and rhubarb mix, fresh strawberries and rhubarb cream. Place a scoop of vanilla ice cream on top.

Gutshofer
Ziegenkaese
Holland-Coat
8.50/100gm

Corazon Quince
Paste

MARGARET RIVER
ORGANIC CREAMERIES
HAVARTI
5.50 / 100 gm

Queso de Manchego
La Mancha, Spain
Ewes milk
1050 /100

STOCKS AND OTHER RECIPES

Fish Stock
MAKES ABOUT 750 ML

- 1 tbsp butter
- 1 onion, roughly chopped
- 1 carrot
- 1 stick of celery
- 750 g fish bones and heads
- 1 cup white wine
- 1 L cold water
- 10 peppercorns
- 2 bay leaves
- Handful of fresh parsley stalks

METHOD

Heat butter in stockpot or large saucepan. Add onion and saute until soft. Add remaining ingredients and simmer for 20 minutes only, skimming occasionally. Strain and cool. Refrigerate and use within two days, or freeze for up to two months.

Beef Stock
MAKES ABOUT 1.5 L

- 2 L cold water
- 750 g beef bones
- 1 onion
- 2 carrots
- 2 celery sticks
- 2 bay leaves
- 10 peppercorns
- 2 sprigs thyme

METHOD

Pre-heat oven to 220°C. Bake bones for 30 minutes. Add vegetables. Continue cooking until bones are browned and vegetables have some colour on them. Turn off oven and allow to cool a little. Add bones, vegetables and all remaining ingredients to a stockpot or large saucepan. Bring to the boil and simmer for at least 90 minutes, skimming occasionally. Strain and cool. Refrigerate and use within two to three days, or freeze for up to three months.

Vegetable Stock
MAKES ABOUT 800 ML

- 1 L cold water
- 2 courgettes
- 3 onions
- 2 cloves of garlic
- 30 g butter
- 2 leeks
- 2 carrots
- 2 celery stalks
- 1 bulb of fennel
- Half a cup of roughly chopped mixed herbs: basil, chervil, parsley, thyme, coriander or whatever other flavours you like.

METHOD
Roughly chop the vegetables. Melt butter in a stockpot or large saucepan and sauté the vegetables, garlic and peppercorns until brown. Cover with water and bring to the boil. Skim and simmer for 15 minutes. Add fresh herbs and simmer for another two minutes. Strain straight away and cool. Refrigerate and use within five days, or freeze for up to four months.

Chicken Stock
MAKES ABOUT 700 ML

- 1 L cold water
- 400 g chicken wings*
- 1 carrot
- 1 stick of celery
- 1 onion
- Half a leek (well peeled to reveal the deeper, softer leaves)
- 2 bay leaves
- 5 peppercorns
- 2 sprigs of thyme
- 1 fresh parsley stalk

METHOD
Bring chicken wings to the boil in the water and skim. Add all other ingredients and simmer for one hour. Strain and cool. Refrigerate and use within two days, or freeze for up to three months.

*If a brown chicken stock is required, simply bake the wings in a medium oven for 30 minutes before adding water.

Grilled Polenta Cake

HERE IS A SIMPLE RECIPE FOR POLENTA.
TRY IT WITH DENNIS MIFSUD'S MALTESE RABBIT STEW.
SERVES 6 AS A SIDE DISH

- 6 cups water or chicken stock.
- 1 ¼ cups polenta
- 20 g butter
- ½ cup finely grated parmesan
- Olive oil for greasing the baking tray

METHOD

Grease a 16 x 26 cm baking tray. Place water or stock in a large saucepan and bring to the boil. Add the polenta in a steady stream, stirring until combined. Reduce heat to medium and cook, stirring regularly, until soft and smooth. Add butter and parmesan, pour into the greased pan and smooth over. Once cool, cover and place in the fridge for a minimum of four hours, or overnight. To serve, cut into portions, brush with oil and place under grill on high heat until slightly brown.

Note: This recipe is for traditional polenta grain, which will required approximately 40 minutes' cooking. If you're time poor, one-minute polenta is a perfectly adequate alternative but the consistency will not be quite as good.

Creamed Leek

SERVES 6 AS A SIDE DISH
TRY THIS WITH TONY HOWELL'S BUTTER-POACHED MARRON

- 2 leeks
- 6 tbsp double cream or crème fraiche
- 1 tbsp butter
- Salt and pepper to taste

METHOD

Finely slice and wash the leeks, being careful to remove all grit. Melt butter in frying pan on a medium heat. Add leeks and soften without colouring. Add the cream or crème fraiche and cook for a couple of minutes until sauce has thickened. Add salt and pepper to taste.

mchenry hohnen
WINE TASTING ⬇
Try our new vintage

2009 ROLLING STONE
— BORDEAUX STYLE

2010 CALGARDUP BROOK
CHARDONNAY

2010 ROCKY ROAD
CHARDONNAY

LOCAL SUPPLIERS
spices, condiments and general supplies

Many of these outlets are closed on Christmas Day, New Year's Day, Boxing Day and Good Friday.

COWARAMUP

COWARAMUP COUNTRY STORE

24 Bussell Highway
Cowaramup WA 6284
Telephone: +61 8 9755 5217

Janine and Edward Pitala stock a full range of gourmet products from local and national producers, fresh produce and everything you might need for breakfast, lunch and dinner.

MARGARET RIVIERA

4 Bottrill Street
Cowaramup WA 6284
Telephone: +61 8 9755 9333

Romano and Alison Rotelli own the Fine Food of Margaret River and Margaret River Jam Co labels and sell an extensive range of their own and locally-produced olive oils, cheeses, jams and pickles.

DUNSBOROUGH

MEAL UP

Shop 3, Bay View Centro
Dunn Bay Road
Dunsborough WA 6281
Telephone: +61 8 9755 3411
Email: food@mealup.com.au
www.mealup.com.au

Sells pantry essentials including exotic spices, herbs, gluten-free foods, cheeses and organic products. Available are Bannister Downs milk, local olive oils, free-range eggs, jams and venison.

MARGARET RIVER

BLUE GINGER

31 Station Road
Margaret River WA 6285
Telephone: +61 8 9758 7619
www.bluegingerfinefoods.com

A fine food store selling a great range of condiments for Asian, Middle Eastern and Mediterranean cooking. Dried fruit, flour, pulses and rice are sold in bulk. Also available are local products, including Margaret River lupin tempeh and locally-baked bread.

RIVIVE HEALTH FOOD

Unit 1, 120 Bussell Highway
Margaret River WA 6285
Telephone : +61 8 9757 2059

Sells both organic and non-organic pulses, rice, flour, grains and spices in bulk. Also has a full range of health food products and health supplements, including Margaret River tempeh.

THE LARDER

Shop 2/99 Bussell Highway
Margaret River WA 6285
Telephone: +61 8 9758 8990
Email: sales@larder.biz
www.larder.biz/

A gourmet deli selling a wide range of regional produce including Yallingup Wood-Fired bread, Margaret River organic cheeses, spices, organic grains and rice, as well as aged vinegars and handmade pastas.

WILYABRUP

HAYSHED HILL

511 Harmans Mill Road
Wilyabrup WA 6280
Telephone: +61 8 9755 6046
Email: info@hayshedhill.com.au
www.hayshedhill.com.au

Hay Shed Deli Cafe provides an impressive array of in-house, local and international gourmet products. The deli cabinet is full of cured meats plus local and international cheeses, all available for takeaway.

PROVIDORE

448 Tom Cullity Drive
Wilyabrup WA 6280
Telephone: +61 8 9755 6355
Email :cafe@providore.com.au
www.providore.com.au

Sells the most amazing range of fruit vinegars, verjuices, jams, tapenades, dessert sauces, infused olive oils and spice mixes, all made on the premises.

LOCAL SUPPLIERS
meat and fish supplies

CARBUNUP

MORANGUP PARK MEATS

Carbunup River Store
Lot 8 Bussell Highway (cnr Wildwood Rd)
Carbunup WA 6280
Telephone: +61 8 9755 1444
www.morangupparkmeats.com.au

This family-run business not only supplies a vast range of free-range and hormone growth enhancer free beef, lamb, pork and chicken, but also sells cheese and authentic traditional smallgoods. The 'Platinum' beef range is Meat Standards Australia (MSA) inspected and aged. The shop also carries a large range of Australian seafood, as well as Aussie native meats. All products are vacuum-sealed for convenience.

MARGARET RIVER

BURNSIDE ORGANIC FARM

287 Burnside Rd
Margaret River 6285
Telephone: + 61 8 9757 2139
Email: info@burnsidebungalows.com.au
Website: www.burnsidebungalows.com.au

Owners Lara & Jamie McCall have put fifteen years of passion into their intensive certified biodynamic farm. A remarkably productive 15 hectares with olives, avocados, vines, capers, macadamias, fruit orchards, vegetable gardens, cows, sheep, pigs, geese and chickens. This is a very small working farm and whilst Lara and Jamie are happy to sell to the public appointments via phone MUST be made.

KOONAC GOAT FARM

Rosa Brook
(please look at the website for directions)
Margaret River WA 6285
Telephone: +61 8 9757 4180
Email: info@koonac.com.au
www.koonac.com.au/index.html

The farm is run by Sonja Gammeter and Andreas Frutiger, who sell goat meat, hand-raised orphaned (goat) kid and a range of does and bucks. Their goat meat is sold to butchers in the region, restaurants and private customers.

PLEASE NOTE: Koonac is a farm not a tourist place, but is nonetheless open to visitors. It is strongly recommended you make an appointment before visiting.

MARGARET RIVER GOURMET MEATS

Shop 2, 120 Bussell Highway
Margaret River WA 6285
Telephone: +61 8 9757 2313

Sells locally-sourced meats, free-range chicken and turkey, homemade sausages and local fresh fish, along with frozen seafood.

MARGARET RIVER VENISON FARM SHOP

5103 Caves Road
Margaret River WA 6285
Telephone: +61 8 97555 028
Email: mrv@mrvenison.com
www.mrvenison.com

Run by Graham & Cynthia Morrison and their daughter Kylie Kennaugh, the farm produces venison free of hormones and growth promotants. On sale are biltong, sausages, roasts, steaks, mince, fillets, kebabs and medallions. The shop also sources meats from other parts of Australia including crocodile, spatchcock, rabbit, emu and kangaroo.

MCHENRY'S FARM SHOP

5962 Caves Road
Margaret River WA 6285
Telephone: +61 8 9757 7600.
Email : freya@mchv.com.au
www.mchv.com.au

This family-owned cellar door, deli and butchery is located a five-minute drive from the township of Margaret River. It stocks preserves, pickles, olive oils, ice cream and jams, much of it made in-house. The free-range Jarrahdene pork and Arkady Wiltshire lamb are truly regional products, grown on the family farms and butchered on site. Here, too, are genuine house-cured and smoked products including ham, bacon and chorizo, along with beautifully-aged grass-fed beef and, of course, McHenry Hohnen wines.

34 DEGREES BLUE

164 Kinsella Road
Margaret River WA 6285
Telephone: +61 8 9758 8900

Brodie and Jarrad Craven stock West Australian fish and fly in salmon from Tasmania twice a week. Prawns, squid tubes and scallops are from Exmouth and Shark Bay. Premium fish such as dhufish, pink snapper, and hapuka are locally line caught from Augusta/Hamlyn Bay and Windy Harbour.

LOCAL SUPPLIERS
fruit, vegetables and dairy

MARGARET RIVER

MARGARET RIVER FARMERS MARKET

The Old Hospital, Community Resource Centre
Cnr Tunbridge & Farrelly Streets
Margaret River WA 6285
When: 2nd and 4th Sat of each month
8am to 12pm.
Email: margaretriverfarmersmarket.com.au

The Margaret River Farmers' Market is a vibrant and bustling community event that offers a huge range of fresh seasonal produce, dairy products, meat, gourmet deli items and wine.

STATION ROAD GREENGROCERS

31 Station Road,
Margaret River WA 6285
Telephone: +61 8 9757 9998

Sourcing from local producers as much as possible, this outlet stocks certified organic fruit and vegetables, herbs and biodynamic diary products.

THE GARDEN BASKET

Unit 2, Lot 158 Boodjidup Rd
Margaret River WA 6285
Telephone: +61 8 9758 8184

The Garden Basket stocks a wide range of biodynamic diary products, local seasonal produce and organic produce. It also imports out-of-season produce to keep customers happy.

METRICUP/COWARAMUP

THE MARGARET RIVER DAIRY COMPANY RETAIL SHOP 1

Bussell Highway, Metricup WA 6282

THE MARGARET RIVER DAIRY COMPANY RETAIL SHOP 2

Bussell Highway, Cowaramup, WA 6284
Telephone: +61 8 9755 7588
Email: mriver@manassen.com.au
www.mrdc.com.au

These two outlets supply locally-produced brie, camembert, club cheddars, feta and baked ricotta

VASSE

VASSE MARKETS

Vasse Community Hall
Phone: +61 8 9753 2188
When: 1st and 3rd Sat of each month
7.30am to12pm

Located mid-way between Margaret River and Yallingup, Vasse conveniently holds a market on alternate Saturdays to the one in Margaret River. It is a haven for food lovers and discerning cooks who will relish the choice of fresh produce sold direct by producers.

PANTRY STOCK

We recommend you stock your pantry with the following products so you're prepared for the recipes in this book. We have included only those items that have a long shelf life.

BAKING

Baking paper (not greaseproof)
Citric acid
Cocoa
Dark cooking chocolate
Gelatin leaves
Pectin
Rosewater
Vanilla pod

FLOUR

00 Flour
Cornflour
Plain flour
Self-raising flour

OILS

Extra virgin olive oil
Sesame oil

SALTS

Pink salt
Rock salt
Sea salt

SAUCES

Chinese rice wine
Coconut cream
Coconut milk
Fish sauce
Kecap manis (sweet dark soya sauce)
Light soy sauce
Pomegranate molasses
Salt-reduced soya sauce
Sweet sake

SEEDS

Poppy seeds
Pumpkin seeds
Sesame seeds

SPICES/CONDIMENTS

Bay leaves
Black peppercorns
Cassia bark
Chilli jam
Cinnamon quill
Cloves
Coriander seeds
Cumin seeds
Dried red chillies
Fennel Seeds
Garlic powder
Smoked paprika
Star anise
Tomato paste
Turmeric powder
Vanilla pods
White peppercorns

SUGARS

Caster sugar
Dark brown sugar
Glucose syrup
Light brown sugar
Palm sugar
Rock sugar

TEAS

Jasmine tea
Green tea

VINEGARS

Balsamic vinegar
Chardonnay vinegar
Chinese rice vinegar
Sherry vinegar

WINES

Shao hsing (Chinese) wine
Sherry

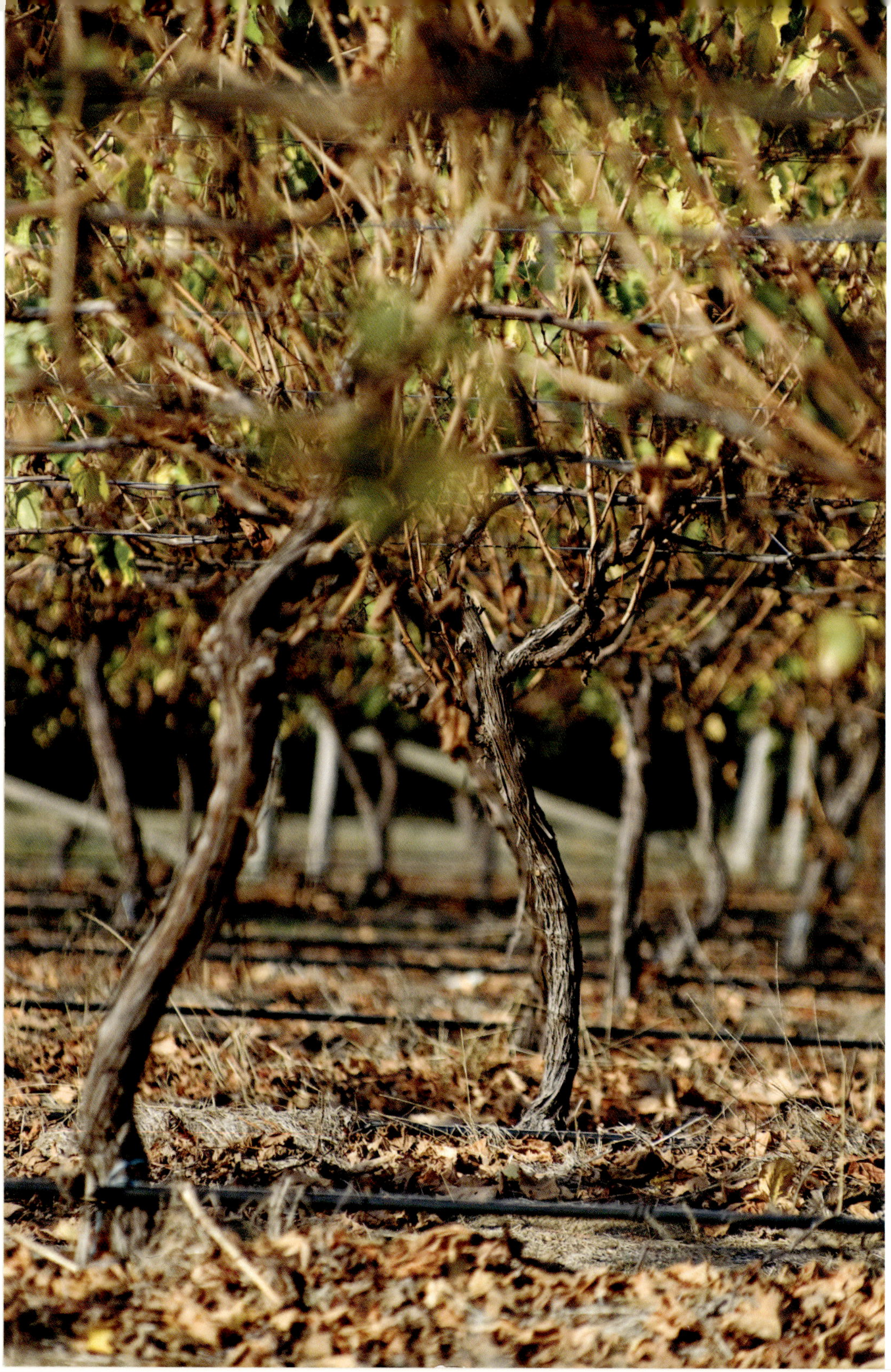
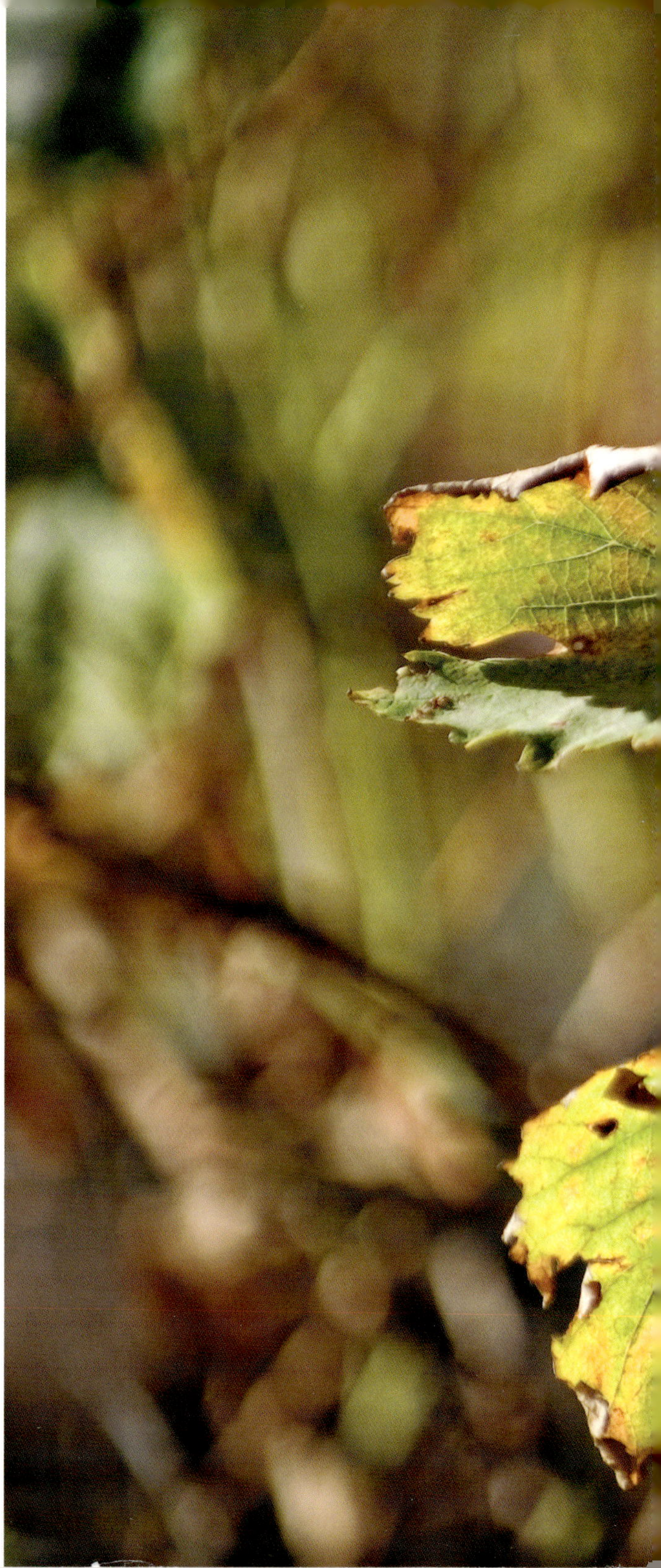

Sue-Lyn Aldrian-Moyle

THE PHOTOGRAPHER AND CO-AUTHOR

As a photojournalist, Sue-Lyn's work has taken her to Hong Kong, Cambodia and throughout Europe, eventually leading her back to WA and down to Margaret River where, like so many of us, she has fallen in love with the community and the region's picturesque landscapes. An interest in exploring different societies has seen Sue-Lyn go off-road solo through the outback of Western Australia to produce the photo-essay "Women of the West: Rural Women of Western Australia," and cling on to the back of a dirt bike through isolated jungle villages and trek across burning landfill in Cambodia as a newswriter and exhibitor. She is also an arts grant recipient for the body of work titled "In Transition: China's Hong Kong", which focuses on the impact of the former colony's return to communist China. Sue-Lyn loves coming back to the relative quiet of Margaret River. Her biggest travel success? Persuading her husband to move from the big cities of Europe to find his own favourite fishing spot at Redgate beach.

Lisa Hanley
THE AUTHOR

Lisa is a qualified chef who has been in the food and wine industry for 25 years. She spent six years on Rottnest Island, where she undertook an apprenticeship and pursued her passion for surfing. She has lived a varied life, from running her own restaurants to appearing on cooking shows to teaching cooking classes and representing Western Australia in major surfing competitions in the nineties.

Lisa holds a Diploma in Hospitality and was the owner and chef of her second restaurant by the time she was 30. Both her restaurants were on the Lonely Planet magazine recommended list during her nine years of ownership.

Her love of surf, vineyards, great food and a close community saw her spend three years as the Restaurant and Function Manager of Watershed Premium Wines, which culminated in the award for Best Maître'd' and Manager at the 2010 South West Regional Awards for Excellence. Margaret River has a special place in Lisa's heart, for it is here she met her husband Simon and developed deep and lasting friendships. Lisa, Simon and their one-year-old son moved to Sydney in late 2010, where Lisa continues to be heavily involved in the hospitality industry and is passionate about training the hospitality workers of tomorrow.